PRAISE FOR *HEALING COLLECTIVE TRAUMA*

"Brilliant, compassionate, and practical support for collective healing in a traumatized world."

JACK KORNFIELD, PHD
author of *A Path with Heart*

"Our world is waiting for us to develop into a new way of being on this precious planet we share with one another and with all of nature. Thomas Hübl's wise and thought-provoking book invites us into the important step of becoming systems-sensing beings, opening our awareness to the profound interconnections that often are beneath what is visible to the eye. Mystics are sometimes defined as those who believe in the reality of the invisible; in this mind-opening sense, a scientific view inherently is concerned, too, with that which cannot be perceived with our eyes. As a mystic, our experienced guide offers his own experience with feeling into collective trauma and how our cross-generational experiences of overwhelming events can be profoundly impairing our personal and our shared ways of living in the subjective and objective worlds. Drawing on his own extensive, international experiences of helping heal systems trauma, the witnessing of the collective healing process by participants in his innovative workshops, and the insights of many luminaries in the field, Hübl has woven a poetic and profound journey for the reader to consider new ways of both understanding and healing our collectively waiting world to support the cultivation of a new, compassionate, and connected life for us all."

DANIEL J. SIEGEL, MD
New York Times bestselling author of *Aware, Mind, Brainstorm, Mindsight,* and *The Developing Mind;* executive director, Mindsight Institute; clinical professor, UCLA School of Medicine

"In *Healing Collective Trauma*, Thomas Hübl identifies the most pressing challenge to humanity. In contrast to the contemporary focus on external sources of challenge such as climate change and famine, we become reacquainted with our history as a self-traumatized species. This history highlights that the greatest challenges to humanity are the products of how we treat each other. Rather than emphasizing the embedded feelings of intergenerational wounds as motivators to achieve, to dominate, and at times to justify retribution, the real task confronting humanity is to successfully resolve these self-perpetuating and self-inflicted injuries. If we can heal these wounds, we will have the opportunity to experience the benefits of becoming a truly connected species and sharing the generative and expansive products of feeling safe and trusting others."

STEPHEN W. PORGES, PHD
author of *The Polyvagal Theory*

"We tend to believe in free will. That it is *we* who ultimately determine our destinies; that we are the captains of our own ships. However, in experiencing depth therapy and honest reflection, we soon realize that this is an illusion. We discover, rather, that our seemingly independent choices are built upon a shaky foundation. Unbeknownst to us, we may be profoundly influenced by events, not only from families and life events but by circumstances that our ancestors (and their ancestors in turn) have experienced during lifetimes long past. And yet their impact persists outside the realm of our conscious awareness. These lingering 'ghosts' have powerful influences on our emotions, reactions, behaviors, and choices. Some of these ancestral influences have had negative (even traumatic) effects on us, while others are life supporting and life affirming. Addressing ancestral influences may also be a key in transforming hate to compassion and understanding between previously warring factions. These essential factors are often neglected in peacemaking efforts. In this comprehensive book, Thomas Hübl brings in a spiritual and 'mystical' dimension to greatly increase our understanding of these powerful hidden influences and how to heal them. This book is a gift to all those (professional and laypersons) wanting to enrich their lives and find greater freedom in this life."

PETER A. LEVINE, PHD
author of *Waking the Tiger, Healing Trauma*, and *Trauma and Memory*

"Modern mystic Thomas Hübl offers a work so rich it encompasses three domains, any one of which alone would have been fresh and important: He raises the issue of collective trauma from the latest psychological perspectives. He moves seamlessly to explore what he terms 'subtle' processes—energetic, intuitive. He integrates both perspectives, weaving between a precise description of the nervous system and processes of the soul, and he offers specific tools and techniques for healing at both levels. A much-needed, brilliant addition to the literature on trauma."

TERRY REAL
author of *I Don't Want to Talk About It* and
founder of Relational Life Institute

"This is a very important book. Many years ago, my clients taught me that parts of them carried what I came to call 'legacy burdens,' which are powerful beliefs and emotions that they absorbed from ancestors or from the culture. I learned how to unburden individuals and wondered if it was possible to do that with large groups. I was thrilled when I learned that Thomas Hübl had been doing so with what he called 'collective trauma.' I believe his work has tremendous potential for bringing harmony and healing to the many polarizations in societies that are unconsciously driven by past traumas. While we have increasingly come to understand the profound impact traumas have on individual lives, we have yet to fully appreciate the impact of historic violence or catastrophe on the paths that groups or societies take. By intuiting, studying, and describing the effects of collective trauma,

Hübl clarifies the roots of war and of the disintegration of countries or ethnic groups. He offers a clear method for releasing the burdens of collective trauma en masse, which he has used with large groups in different countries around the world. I am so grateful for this work."

RICHARD C. SCHWARTZ, PHD
creator of the Internal Family Systems model of psychotherapy and
adjunct faculty, Department of Psychiatry, Harvard Medical School

"Thomas Hübl offers a wise and textured understanding of the tapestry of collective trauma and how attending to cultural and historical threads heals the very foundation of humanity."

RUTH KING
author of *Mindful of Race* and
founder of the Mindful of Race Institute

HEALING COLLECTIVE TRAUMA

A PROCESS FOR INTEGRATING OUR INTERGENERATIONAL & CULTURAL WOUNDS

THOMAS HÜBL

WITH JULIE JORDAN AVRITT

sounds true

BOULDER, COLORADO

Sounds True
Boulder, CO 80306

This book is not intended as a substitute for the medical recommendations of physicians, mental health professionals, or other health-care providers. Rather, it is intended to offer information to help the reader cooperate with physicians, mental health professionals, and health providers in a mutual quest for optimum well-being. We advise readers to carefully review and understand the ideas presented and to seek the advice of a qualified professional before attempting to use them.

Published 2020, 2023

Cover design by Jennifer Miles
Book design by Meredith March
Illustrations © 2020 Meredith March

Cover image © 2019 Yehudit Sasportas
Cad-Ot no. 1, 2019
Archival pigment print, 70x50 cm
Chapter no. 7
Liquid Desert Project

Printed in the United States of America

BK06618

ISBN: 978-1-64963-054-4

The Library of Congress has cataloged the hardcover edition as follows:

Names: Hübl, Thomas, author.
Title: Healing collective trauma : a process for integrating our intergenerational
   and cultural wounds / Thomas Hübl ; with Julie Jordan Avritt.
Description: Boulder, CO : Sounds True, 2020. | Includes bibliographical
   references and index.
Identifiers: LCCN 2020010322 (print) | LCCN 2020010323 (ebook)
   | ISBN 9781683647379 (hardback) | ISBN 9781683647386 (ebook)
Subjects: LCSH: Psychic trauma–Social aspects. | Social psychology.
   | Intergenerational relations. | Post-traumatic stress disorder.
Classification: LCC BF175.5.P75 H84 2020 (print) | LCC BF175.5.P75
   (ebook) | DDC 155.9/3–dc23
LC record available at https://lccn.loc.gov/2020010322
LC ebook record available at https://lccn.loc.gov/2020010323

10 9 8 7 6 5 4 3 2 1

FSC
www.fsc.org
MIX
Paper | Supporting
responsible forestry
FSC® C103098

Bowing down to the revelation of our emerging Future,
which is calling us . . .

CONTENTS

FOREWORD

I t is a great pleasure to commend to you this insightful, wise, and critically important book on healing collective trauma, written by my friend and colleague Thomas Hübl.

For the last forty years, I have had the chance to witness the deep impacts of collective trauma while serving as a third party and negotiation adviser in conflicts and wars around the world, most recently in the Colombian civil war, the Korean nuclear crisis, and the Middle East conflict. I have experienced just how difficult, frustrating, and elusive it can be to bring bloodshed to an end.

The big question I have often asked myself is: Why is peace so challenging when it brings so much benefit, especially given that war inevitably brings great loss to all parties and their societies?

There are many reasons, but surely one of the most central is the underlying collective trauma that remains unaddressed. During the Korean War, millions of people died and millions more were displaced. More than two hundred thousand people were killed in the Colombian civil war and more than seven million were displaced. Even when a semblance of normality returns, the underlying scars remain. With unhealed wounds, there appears to be a drive to keep repeating the same patterns of conflict. Truces or peace agreements are often difficult to sustain.

One of the great historic innovations of the Colombian peace process was the involvement in the negotiations of members of the civilian population, the victims of that civil war. Numerous delegations of war victims were invited to come to Havana to testify to the negotiators on both sides about their experiences and to be heard by the media and Colombian society. These individuals were selected carefully by the UN and national universities to reflect the diversity on all sides of the conflict. Many, perhaps most, were women. To the surprise of many observers who feared the experiment would stir up old wounds and obstruct the peace process, the great majority of the victims did not call for punishment, but rather appealed to end this vicious conflict and offered the prospect of forgiveness and reconciliation with their enemies.

Giving voice to the war's victims, offering empathetic listening, and bringing positive societal attention to the trauma not only reminded the negotiators of what was at stake, but helped Colombian society begin the slow process of healing old wounds.

If we are to bring about peace and, more generally, well-being in our world, it is essential that we learn more about collective trauma and how we can heal it. That is why this pioneering book by Thomas Hübl is so valuable. It helps us see the dimensions of the collective trauma underlying the world's ills and highlights the opportunities we have to heal our communities and ourselves.

As a complex phenomenon, not easy to grasp, collective trauma benefits from the wide-ranging perspectives that Thomas brings. In this work you will find an unusual blend of the material and the mystical. Thomas combines a keen psychological and scientific curiosity with a deep spiritual understanding. The result is greater insight from which we can all benefit.

One valuable lesson I have learned from Thomas is the wisdom of our responses to trauma. Rather than stigmatizing our tendency to freeze in reaction to overwhelming stress, Thomas compassionately underscores the intelligence that the freeze response reflects. It is this same intelligence that we need to harness if we are to heal our wounds.

Perhaps most importantly, while Thomas delves into the inner collective darkness, he never loses hope for humanity. Even as he seeks conceptual clarity and deep understanding, he keeps his focus on what is practical and useful to the great task at hand. He shows us a way to open our minds, open our hearts, and thus open our individual and collective will to peace. Since each of us, in our own way, experiences collective trauma of some kind, each of us can benefit greatly from understanding how to heal.

I am grateful for all that I have learned from Thomas about collective trauma. My sincere hope is that you, the reader, will benefit from his work in the same way. Our world needs it.

WILLIAM URY
Boulder, Colorado

ACKNOWLEDGMENTS

The wisdom at the heart of this book centers on a group presencing process for healing and integrating our collective trauma, and it could never have emerged without each of the tens of thousands of courageous and inspiring people who have attended my workshops and retreats through the years. To each of you, and to the living memory of your ancestors throughout time, I offer my heartfelt gratitude. Thank you for teaching me. And thank you for trusting me to foster a safe container for your experiences, so that you could presence, acknowledge, heal, and integrate them with others.

The creative collaboration and sheer hard work required to bring this book into form would not have been possible without the support of many. I wish to thank Julie Jordan Avritt for her beautiful work, poetry, and intellectual refinement. Her relentless engagement to dive deeply into such a complex and widespread topic made our collaboration possible. I also wish to thank the team at Sounds True, most notably Jennifer Yvette Brown, for her belief in and devotion to the project and for her ever-present guidance and support, and Gretel Hakanson, for her keen eye and editorial care.

The participatory wisdom of several notable experts—on trauma, therapy, human development, international peacebuilding, collective presencing, and integral philosophy—have made these pages, and my own life and work, profoundly richer. Thank you to Christina Bethell, Patrick Dougherty, Gabor Maté, Scilla Elworthy, Otto Scharmer, and my dear friend Ken Wilber. Ken's life and work inspired my path deeply from the time I was a medical student.

I wish to express my undying appreciation to Terry Patten, whose friendship, encouragement, and tactical support helped bring my work to the United States. And for William Ury, whose friendship and deeply shared path are continually inspiring and whose foreword elevates the book from its first pages. My deepest thanks also to Gregor Steinmaurer, Laura Calderón de la Barca, and Markus Hirzig—my core team members and Collective Trauma Integration Process assistants—for the unique contribution of their time, words, and wisdom. Thank you also to Claire Lanyado, Stacey Marvel, Ute Kostanjevec, Heike Barra, Anne Vollborn, Bar Edri, and everyone working with me at Inner Science, LLC, and Sharing the Presence, GmbH. Your skills and dedication are invaluable. A very deep thank you to the members of the Pocket Project, for your ongoing courage, commitment, and contribution to the research and understanding of collective trauma and to its healing in all parts of the world.

A special word of thanks for David Ifergan, my dear friend and steadfast spiritual mentor, who has gifted me through the example of his living devotion to the ancient roots of the deeply mystical.

I owe my deepest gratitude, of course, to my brilliant and beautiful wife, Yehudit Sasportas. Thank you for introducing me to the profound depths of art and artists and for reconnecting me to the mystical dimensions of Judaism and the richness of the Jewish community. Most of all, thank you for the sacred gift of your love. And to our daughter, Eliya, whose very spirit is the richest blessing! Thank you for the gift that it is to be your father and for the mysterious yet magically mundane truths you teach me every day about growth, development, relation, and love.

Finally, thank you, God, for each of these. And for the downward streaming of evolutionary Light in the process of divine unfolding/enfolding.

PROLOGUE

And God said, "Let there be light," and there was light.

Genesis 1:3 (New International Version)

The medicine is already within the pain and suffering. You just have to look deeply and quietly. Then you realize it has been there the whole time.

Saying from the Native American oral tradition

Forty years ago, Helen Epstein, a young journalism professor at New York University, published a groundbreaking book that altered the course of Western psychological research in trauma and validated many things that aboriginal peoples and Eastern thinkers had known for centuries. The book, titled *Children of the Holocaust*, was part ethnography, part oral history, and part memoir and was the first published work outside academia to explore the subject of the second generation (2G)—the sons and daughters—of Holocaust survivors. Her work inspired startling new questions: Had the unspoken horrors of Nazi Germany been in some way passed down to the descendants of those who had lived through them? If so, what might this traumatic inheritance mean for other traumatized groups and their progeny?

Epstein's book was a noble exploration of the intergenerational transmission of trauma, kicking off decades of often difficult, and sometimes illuminating, research in Israel, the United States, Switzerland, and beyond. While more research must be done on the subject, there is much to learn from what has emerged.

In 1981, the Jewish scholar and theologian Arthur A. Cohen described 2G this way: "It is the generation that bears the scar without the wound, sustaining memory without direct experience."[1] In his 2006 text, *Healing the Soul Wound*, clinical psychologist and researcher Eduardo Duran assessed that in the overall body of research on the subject of historical trauma and its transmission, there is evidence to suggest that "not only is the trauma passed on intergenerationally, but it is cumulative." Duran further contends that "when trauma is not dealt with in previous generations, it has to be dealt with in subsequent generations." Moreover, when unresolved trauma is passed on, it may become "more severe" in successive generations.[2]

Early in his career, Duran's work with Native American populations in California uncovered a critical cultural difference in how the indigenous community perceived and spoke about the effects, consequences, or *symptoms* of historical trauma that they directly experienced, such as poverty, illness, alcoholism, family separation, mental and emotional health conditions, and more. The Western world had become dominated by clinical, pathological descriptions and labels for all manner of emotional and interpersonal distress, but these communities didn't use such terms. Instead, they referred to the suffering that had blighted their people during European colonization and had been passed down through the generations since as "spiritual injury, soul sickness, soul wounding, and ancestral hurt."[3]

My work has shown me that trauma is never purely an individual problem. And no matter how private or personal, trauma cannot belong solely to a family, or even to that family's intricate ancestral tree. The consequences of trauma—indeed, the cumulative effects of personal, familial, and historical traumas—seep across communities, regions, lands, and nations. The burden borne by a single person, family, or community invariably and inevitably reaches its larger society, touching even those who share little in the way of common identity or custom. The impact of human-created suffering extends beyond the original subject or subjugated group; trauma's legacy weaves and wires our very world, informing how we live in it, how we see it, and how we see and understand one another.

Many of us are aware of the manifest ways that unhealed trauma can create long-term personal pain and developmental problems for individuals. What is perhaps less well understood is how unhealed *collective* trauma may place similar burdens on the health of human cultures and societies, even placing our planetary home at risk. The symptoms of collective trauma appear to reveal themselves in the condition of collective bodies of all kinds—our communities, schools, organizations, institutions, governments, and environments—revealing where we are injured, fractured, or imbalanced. Indeed, it is my belief that unresolved systemic, multigenerational traumas delay the development of the human family, harm the natural world, and inhibit the higher evolution of our species.

I vividly remember sitting with my grandfather, *Opa* in German, as a young boy, listening attentively as he shared stories from his experiences of the Second World War. He had been a private in the Austrian *Bundesheer*, or "Federal Army," and was serving when Austria was annexed by Nazi Germany. Sadly, this meant that he and his fellow soldiers were conscripted into service for the German Third Reich.

Opa's stories of the war included being met in the open by enemy soldiers, where both sides chose simply to turn around and walk back, rather than engage in lethal combat. He often spoke of the good-heartedness and heroism of ordinary men, many of whom had been forced to fight, even though their hearts weren't in the cause. A young man at that time, my grandfather was badly injured by an exploding bomb. Sustaining severe injuries to his leg, he was sent home, no longer able to serve.

Before the war, my grandfather had been a passionate soccer player, full of vigor and athleticism. Afterward, both his passion and agility were reduced. Though he kept much of the evidence buried throughout his life, he had been changed by unrelenting heartbreak, wrought by the trauma of his experiences in the war. For the rest of his life, Opa was weighed down by the stygian gloom of the past, which was ever present in the room. At times, a distant, disconnected quality colored his benevolent eyes.

Though I could very much *feel* these things as a boy, I couldn't yet understand them. I was very close to my grandfather, and as I grew, I began to feel even more things. Some of these I couldn't name; they stemmed from hidden emotional layers, the consequences of the scars of war. Others were more tangible. The relationship between Opa and my grandmother, *Oma*, for instance, was often eruptive. (Oma had lost her mother when she was only fourteen, forcing her to fight her way through life.) Deep trauma haunted my grandparents' lives, as it had everyone who'd been touched by the war. Quietly, this quality of hidden personal and cultural suffering—present everywhere in Austria as I was growing up—began shaping my life and my future. I became compelled to learn all that I could about it.

While still in high school, I became passionate about emergency medicine and determined to become a paramedic, volunteering for the Red Cross. After a long period of training, I reached my goal and threw myself into work I cared deeply about. When I wasn't working or studying medicine, I served as a teacher for new paramedics. I loved the fast-paced, deeply present work. It required quick thinking, sound judgment, and fast action, as well as a grounded stance toward human suffering. Being called to assist at one crisis after another taught me how to see more deeply into human lives, all walks of them. I attended to both the rich and the poor in their most intimate moments of fear and pain and observed those of all ages and creeds as they struggled to survive the most traumatizing situations of their lives.

Many times, I was present in the final moments of a person's life.

Over time, I observed how the experiences of our patients weren't held in isolation, solely impacting the injured or dying and their loved ones. As emergency responders, we were exposed to that cascade of human suffering, and it affected us. Paramedics at that time received no guidance about how to deal with the psychological repercussions of trauma, neither for our patients nor ourselves. Even so, my desire to understand suffering so that I might better serve in a healing capacity only continued to grow. I decided to become an emergency physician.

At nineteen years old, I had begun my own regular meditation practice. And, in parallel to my coursework and medical studies, I began investigating many of the world's wisdom traditions. I took these habits with me when I entered medical school in Vienna, where I spent my days working shifts and my nights deep in study. It was an amazing time, and I loved it—I felt I was in service to life itself. It was there that I first sensed something going on *beneath the surface* in my country. Whenever I traveled outside Austria, which I loved, I felt a strange sense of liberation, as though I could breathe more easily somehow. But each time I returned, a sense of resistance and constriction came back. This quality mystified me and began to feel like a call toward some deeper or higher understanding. I continued working and studying, until at twenty-six, I felt a powerful pull to leave it all behind and embarked on a period of silence and meditation.

People close to me were concerned. Why was I choosing to give up everything to just "sit around"? But I knew I had to do it; I had to enter deeply into the roots of the *I am* in order to learn the answers to the questions I sought.

I started my quest in India, then with my former wife, Lenka, I traveled to the Czech countryside where I spent many hours per day in meditation, driven to explore deeper levels of consciousness. I'd been inspired by inveterate sages and philosophers like Sri Aurobindo, Ramana Maharshi, and the writings of American philosopher Ken Wilber since I was twenty years old. I longed to experience what they were pointing to, to deepen my awareness and investigate the vast terrain of the interior world. That experience lasted four intense years and not only altered the course of my life, but profoundly grew and changed me.

I never went back to medical school.

When I returned to Vienna, I brought greater awareness and personal insight to my life and work. But I also brought home a more refined perception of my country's collective psyche and the subtle, yet powerful, energetic layers of history that it holds.

A year later, a friend took me to meet a teacher who was traveling through Europe—a wise, white-haired man who seemed to share my own profound drive for exploring the deeper nature of human consciousness. The instant we met, he keenly and accurately described parts of my experience that no ordinary stranger could have identified. I felt powerfully seen and this soothed my soul. Soon, this encounter opened teaching doors for me. People began inviting me to all kinds of places to teach and run workshops myself.

My life had radically changed: I'd spent four years predominantly in silence and now I was traveling between countries to speak and teach. Soon, I was running workshops and retreats for thousands of people and learning so much more about human consciousness. All that had been shown to me during my four-year retreat came to life. When I went to Berlin for the first time, I was aware of a heavy energy, present as a result of a collective wound. Though its scabs were invisible, it nevertheless itched the people there. The injury itself had occurred as a result of one of the largest human atrocities in history, and more than a half-century later it continued to fester. While the Holocaust Memorial honors those who were persecuted and killed, and open dialogue is fostered throughout Germany, I could sense that many things remained hidden, buried deep in the collective shadows. My time there was a revelation. It allowed me to see that a similar psychic wound existed in the people of my native Austria, a massive lesion that hadn't yet healed.

In this way, each group that I taught throughout Germany was in fact instructing *me*. I began to witness a profoundly recursive pattern, emerging again and again in groups of all types and sizes. The central locus of the pattern was an often-powerful eruption of energetic material related to the Holocaust and the Second World War. After three or four days facilitating a group, this material surfaced as waves of emotion, physical sensation, and memory, including the phenomenon of *mass memory*, often experienced by large portions of the group during any given session. As this happened, scores of participants would begin to cry all at once, collectively experiencing images of the war as though they were personal memories. It would then take another one or two days for us to carefully process and integrate all that came up.

Amazed by the consistency of this pattern and the profound shifts that were possible within a dynamic group-change process, I was inspired to explore the collective shadow more deeply.

In cities all over Germany, with very different groups of participants, the same process arose. I recognized that it only happened after participants had achieved a certain level of connection and safety with each other and with me, and after a strong enough quality of group presence and coherence had been reached. What it delivered was often profoundly healing. Life had been pointing me toward a process for integrating collective trauma, and I knew this needed to be studied closely. I became devoted to learning all that I could. As I worked with the process, I grew better able to guide participants through its incredible waves of mass energy, assisting each group toward deeper regulation.

My period of contemplation and exploration of consciousness had brought me to my true calling—a purpose and mission that I've been passionate about ever since.

It was during those years teaching in Germany that I met my beautiful wife, Yehudit Sasportas, an Israeli-born, international artist—and my life changed again. Her work, like my own, dealt directly with themes of individual and collective trauma.

After I had traveled nonstop for years, we took up residence together in a Berlin flat. Yehudit introduced me to an astonishing world of art, previously unknown to me. My wife's deeply inspiring approach to trauma through art, and the study of Judaism, brought another lens to my own research into collective trauma. And she introduced me to

Israel, where we later relocated so that she could continue her teaching commitment as an extraordinary professor in the fine arts department at the Bezalel Academy of Arts and Design. Israel quickly became my new teacher, bringing me further into my investigation into the impact that exposure to war and continuing conflict—long-standing historical, cultural, and ancestral traumas—have on a nation of people.

Out of this work evolved a clear process for the integration of collective trauma, which I refer to as the Collective Trauma Integration Process (CTIP). I continue to facilitate CTIP events in both Germany and Israel and many other parts of the world and recently completed one for 150 people from thirty-nine countries. The CTIP can be done successfully in groups of all sizes, even those of up to 1,000 participants.

Today, we continue building on the lessons of this work through the efforts of the Pocket Project, an international nonprofit organization that Yehudit and I cofounded. At the Pocket Project, we work in unison with many brilliant researchers and collaborators all over the world with the shared mission of *contributing to the healing of collective and intergenerational trauma and reducing its disruptive effects on our global culture.*

There are many current crisis zones in our world today, places where the reality of war is imminent and ongoing. Yet, even where peace appears to exist on the surface, the ravages of the not-so-distant past can be felt. Every region has its own distinct trauma signature. It's as if a massive elephant sits in the human living room; few may see or acknowledge it, but we are all impacted by its presence. Everything about our societies—from geopolitics to business, climate, technology, health care, entertainment and celebrity, and much more—is dominated by the existence of this elephant, by the residue of our collective trauma. And as long as we fail to acknowledge or adequately care for it, the elephant will grow larger.

This book is offered as a step toward recognizing and attending to the growing crisis of collective trauma. It provides an exploration of the symptoms, habits, and unconscious social agreements that collective trauma creates. Growing like mold spores in the dark and fragmented underground of the human psyche, trauma's seeds are evidenced all around us: widespread isolation, endemic depression, violent divisions, systemic injustice, and countless other destructive forms, including our burgeoning climate crisis. But, though it is urgent, this book is not apocalyptic. Its pages offer possibilities for how we might shed light on the dark and come together in revolutionary ways to directly address our generational and cultural traumas in order to heal ourselves and our world.

As a contemporary mystic and a prior medical student, I'm interested in bridging the wisdom gap between our world's ancient spiritual traditions and the current understanding afforded by science. I believe that we now find ourselves at the precipice of a new era; one that asks for a marriage between science and spirit, between soul and scholarship. Evolution itself seems to be extending the invitation.

The collective psyche is holographic: We are both one and many, unique and unified, individual and whole. We are each responsible to each other, to our ancestors, and to our descendants, as well as to the Earth, which is our home. Together, I believe we can and must heal the "soul wound" that marks us all. In so doing, we will awaken to the luminous possibility and profound potential of our true and mutual nature as humankind, a collective race of beings within the greater Cosmic order.

Integrated and unified, may we soon step together into the Light of a thriving future, better equipped to cocreate worlds.

INTRODUCTION TO THE
PAPERBACK EDITION

*Now, just at a time in history when it appears to be crucial for us
to work together, we see evidence of a shared consciousness
beginning to appear on a global scale.*

– Roger D. Nelson, *Connected*

My friend and colleague William Ury made a poignant statement to me about the social dilemma on everyone's minds in 2020. "COVID-19 is an immediate report card on society," he said. "It's giving us feedback on everything: economic inequality, social injustice, the quality of leadership and culture, the state of political polarization. You can try to spin it, but COVID-19 isn't listening; it's impersonal. The virus simply wants to expand itself and likes our habitat for the purpose. The virus *likes* polarization."

It's true. Intense polarization has made it difficult for us to come together to meet the crises of our time, and COVID-19 is just one among many large-scale challenges humanity now faces or soon will. Yet, the coronavirus pandemic is connected in some way to many other enduring social problems: from institutional racism and police brutality to the accelerating climate crisis. As of this writing, unprecedented wildfires blaze across the American West and beyond, incinerating millions of acres, destroying thousands of homes and businesses, and injuring or killing humans and animals alike. A record number of tropical cyclones have churned out of the oceans already this year, creating incomprehensible damage and historic flooding. In their soggy aftermath, a dense blanket of mosquitoes now swarms across certain land regions, killing wild and livestock animals where they stand and posing new risks to human health.

In 2020 (a year that once sounded utterly futuristic and full of promise), powerful nations spar over resources, oil rights, water rights, and missile technologies, as existential nuclear threat looms once again. Mass civil protest has exploded across the United States, Canada, the United Kingdom, Israel, Lebanon, Russia, Belarus, Brazil, Chile, Philippines, Hong Kong, and beyond. While the vast majority of political and civil protests have been nonviolent, others erupt into chaos, as tribalized constituents, culture warriors, and ordinary citizens clash in fury and outrage. Online and in real time, masses defy pandemic lockdown orders, while elsewhere, armed civilians lay siege to government itself. In multiple countries, people pour into the streets to protest police brutality, and in others, to demonstrate against societal disregard of women and girls. In all corners, vulnerable democracies weather ongoing assault via new or revived methods of digital, social, and political attack, threatened by authoritarian powers from within and without.

Many live in fear for their lives and for their futures.

All of this and more is clear and indisputable evidence: the collective body-mind—that part of us that is vastly and mystifyingly connected—is traumatized and therefore greatly fragmented, disconnected, polarized, and separated. Why? From a mystical perspective, every systemic and seemingly intractable social problem, regardless of where it plays out in the world, springs from the same source: the deep, compounding, unhealed morass of humanity's unresolved past. The events of 2020 highlight and amplify this truth and came about due to the unresolved social, historical, and generational layers of trauma already within us that need to be accessed, acknowledged, felt, processed, and integrated.

Like the dark matter of the social fabric, collective trauma cannot be observed directly; we can only observe its effects (i.e., its symptoms), for which we need use of more than our eyes. Trauma, particularly sustained or repeated trauma, splinters us. It damages our internal and external coherence. It distorts perception and disrupts the flow of life force through a living system, whether a person's or a planet's. Trauma injures the capacity to relate to and with one another, which is to say, trauma produces the illusion of separation.

For evidence of incoherence and fragmentation, we need only consider the degree to which either *hyper*-arousal (e.g., social anxiety, intensity, distrust, agitation, fear, aggression) or *hypo*-arousal (e.g., numbing, apathy, lethargy, disconnection, ennui, pessimism) is present. We might think of these phenomena like the "check engine" light of culture. Wherever there is fragmentation, there is disrelation; the capacity for sustained human connection breaks down. In this way, a negative feedback loop is established in which fragmentation yields disrelation yields polarization yields disorder yields chaos.

The frozen, unresolved past actually slows down or inhibits our ability to meet the challenges of the present. Amid the turmoil, ambient anxiety, distrust, and disconnection feel suddenly more intense than at any other time in recent memory. Even so, all of the painful symptoms we experience—whether as individuals or as a collective—are actually arrows pointing our attention to the need to begin the work of making ourselves and our societies more whole.

Consider something: evolution designed the immune system to handily disarm most invading pathogens and many kinds of toxins. When overwhelmed, however, the natural immune response can accelerate into hyperdrive, prompting in-built defenses to turn and attack the body itself (prolonged hyperarousal), or may even shut down, creating greater vulnerability to invaders (prolonged hypoarousal). The existing degree of health, wellness, and resilience within the system is what turns the tides.

There is no question that experiencing a traumatic event can make a person (or a community) more vulnerable to the harmful effects of future stress and adversity. It is also true that some adversity is necessary to aid a person (or a community) in developing hardiness and greater resistance to future stress and trauma. In this way, a positive feedback loop is established: where sufficient resilience exists in the system, the neural pathways that mediate stress and affirm resilience are further reinforced.

Many external factors aid in resilience-building, of course, such as access to safe housing and health care, economic stability, and the presence of familial or communal supports (e.g., connection, communication, empathy, and attunement). In the absence of these and other markers, people and societies experience greater stress and vulnerability to breakdown in the face of hardship, further deteriorating health and wholeness and limiting the capacity to flourish and thrive.

Still, even amid COVID-19, global uprisings, economic instability, and climate chaos, there are many ways we can come together to consciously activate and enhance our resilience, and new methods are being discovered all the time. The heart of this book centers on one such practice, the knowledge of which I acquired over many years facilitating group process work in multiple countries, and the results of which have been profound. It is evidence that, while we each carry in our bodies many thousands of years of ancestral trauma and the attendant pain and suffering experienced by preceding generations, if we are alive today, it is because every single one of our genetic forebears stretching back through time survived long enough (through countless periods of volatility, chaos, and change) to reproduce a resilient child. And that child went on to do the same.

We exist at all because of human resilience, which is our birthright. Everything our progenitors survived in order to bring us forward lives in us today—not just their struggle and suffering, but also their skill, talent, tenacity, perseverance, and genius. Like the vast root network of a great redwood tree, the energy and information of innumerable generations run through our modern bones, tissues, nervous systems, and brains. What's more, millennia after millennia, humans have learned and developed countless means and methods through which to mend, heal, and restore ourselves and one another—and all of that wisdom is also here, present in our very cells.

The question is: In the face of mounting social dilemmas, will we continue to react without thinking (or numb ourselves) against whatever disturbs our personal sensibilities or challenges our various tribal perspectives of the world? Or will we instead choose to listen more deeply to one another, make more space within and without to host other persons and perspectives, and, along the way, learn to behave more responsively, rather than reactively, to the circumstances of our lives?

Trauma fragments our human light, burying it away in shadow. But just as a committed person is able to pursue healing and liberate themselves from the consequences of past trauma, so can families, organizations, communities, and even societies. My work has proven this awesome truth to me again and again: when we engage this kind of healing work together, we release great stores of frozen, disconnected, separated, and buried energy, freeing vast quantities of life force and intelligence that had previously been blocked and hidden from view. Once liberated, these vast reserves of energy become available in the field within and around us and can be used, not just for further healing but for brilliant innovation and responsive change. For new growth! This is perhaps the greatest untapped natural resource on our planet.

The climate crisis, an existential crisis we ourselves created and from which no one is exempt, exists because of our unhealed, unmet past. After all, trauma is karma is destiny. Yet, as the ecological emergency forces our attention, we can engage in acts of collective healing. We can unlock the great reserves of untapped energy and potential hidden inside us and thereby activate better possible futures. Even in the middle of worldwide disruption, we can enhance individual and societal resilience to meet the challenges of our time. We can choose to honor our shared uncertainty, anxiety, and fear as much as our innate strength, determination, and capacity to transform.

We are equipped to awaken the evolutionary resilience inherited from ancestors long since passed and able to open ourselves to connection with all future descendants. We can learn to hold in presence the unresolved past so as to better meet our future unfolding. In mutual support and collaboration, we can raise individual and group awareness, tap new levels of collective intelligence, and enact a fresh vision for our world. By leaning in and listening together, we open doors to emergent capacities, higher insights, and richer frames of correlation and connection. We engage higher reaches of the human spirit and more fully embody our true potential.

It turns out that you and I are like T cells in humankind's collective immune system; both the problem and the remedy is *us*. We have everything we need within us to heal ourselves, our societies, and our planet. And we must, for there is no time to waste.

I

MYSTICAL PRINCIPLES
OF HEALING

We have not even to risk the adventure alone, for the heroes of all time
have gone before us. The labyrinth is thoroughly known. We have only
to follow the thread of the hero path, and where we had thought to find
an abomination, we shall find a god. And where we had thought to slay
another, we shall slay ourselves. Where we had thought to travel outward,
we will come to the center of our own existence. And where we had thought
to be alone, we will be with all the world.

Joseph Campbell
The Hero with a Thousand Faces

The late American mythologist Joseph Campbell explored two types of deeds that any hero or heroine might resolve along the archetypal quest. The first fulfills a material objective, the performance of some tangible and ultimately courageous act, however difficult or seemingly impossible. The second deed is less clear because it is spiritual in nature. It involves a journey along which the hero uncovers hidden mystical knowledge about human existence, often returning with a sacred message or some life-giving elixir.[1]

As Campbell discovered, whether the deed at the center of a quest is physical or spiritual, the path of any hero, in any story—from humanity's earliest myths to its modern-day movie scripts—follows a common trajectory. And whether we encounter dragons or demons, sirens or

1

saints, an illusory city of celestial musicians or merely the mundane trials and temptations of an "ordinary" life, we are each the hero of our own stories.

Every hero's journey is one of ultimate transformation. The story of the fool is to become wise. The story of the cynic is to break open in vulnerability and authenticity—to become real. The story of the despairing is to find hope, faith, and renewal. The story of the fearful or weak is to awaken into the nobility of one's own true strength. These are fundamental journeys of the spirit, the narrative arc of souls. Of course, before we embark, we must respond to *the call*, a clarion invitation that is always sounding but can only be heard in the heart of great longing.

At this time in human history, there is a new calling, a powerful invitation rising from a sense of deep collective longing. It calls us toward a *shared* quest—one that will entail both practical and spiritual action. At its core, it is a journey of collective healing. To succeed, we must begin to make whole the rift between the worlds of science and spirit, to create a sacred marriage between vital, yet formerly contradictory, domains. Its fulfillment brings unity in place of division, integration rather than separation. As with all great heroic journeys, our very survival depends on it.

This book is an effort to amplify the urgency of the call and to inspire the hero/ine in all of us.

THE PRINCIPLE OF ENSŌ

Mystical wisdom arises from a direct and unmediated experience of the numinous that is both personal and universal. This experience reveals a glimpse into the great and unfathomable mystery at the center of All That Is, leaving seekers with a sense of heightened awareness—a clearer perspective of self and other, human and cosmos. When doctrine, dogma, sectarian politics, and power structures are lifted from the religious or spiritual lens, timeless principles for how to live a healthy, harmonious, and fulfilled existence flow in. Whatever the culture, religion, or epoch, the principles that are at the core of the great Wisdom Traditions reveal perennial truths about the human condition, the nature of reality, and for some, that which is called the Divine.

Mystical theory is never simply about knowledge. It is about resonance, coherence, re-membering, and fulfillment. It is about creating deeper clarity of perception. The ancient *ensō* symbol found in the Zen school of Buddhism, sometimes called the "circle of enlightenment" or the "infinity circle," is frequently depicted in Japanese calligraphy as a perfectly imperfect open circle. The ensō is often used to represent *satori*. The words *satori* and its relative, *kenshō*—which translates as "seeing into one's true nature"—are commonly translated as "enlightenment." The sacred symbol of the ensō represents vast space, that which lacks nothing and yet holds nothing. It simultaneously depicts cycles of beginnings and endings and the greater infinity that contains them. It symbolizes both completion and the space of opening in renewal.

Ensō symbol

The ensō reveals the path of energy as it seeks transformation through substance, in order that it may return into peace more fully developed. Our lives reflect this principle.

When a part of my life energy, or *chi*, becomes arrested, unable to fulfill its natural developmental path, it fragments from the whole and lands in the unconscious. As a result, I am unaware of this split but nevertheless carry it with me in the form of additional psychic baggage. We could say that this process is similar to computer fragmentation: when a cycle can't complete itself, the system becomes hampered by fragmented files or disintegration.

Let's say that I find myself in a difficult conversation with a colleague at midday and become irritated and defensive or anxious. For the rest of the day, I find myself thinking back on the conversation, replaying it in my mind. Each time I do this, I reexperience the irritation and anxiety I felt when the conversation first occurred so that these feelings persist, even after I've stopped thinking of my colleague. That evening, I meet a friend for dinner. If I still haven't resolved the day's experience, I may as well set an extra place at the table for my energetic baggage. Even if I don't explain how I'm feeling or why, my friend will likely feel its residual presence. And should something come up over dinner that touches further irritation inside me, I will leave carrying still more baggage or fragmentation.

The unresolved energy that I carry weighs me down and colors my experiences, preventing me from showing up fully in the present moment. This baggage or fragmentation is karmic; it is the energy of the unmet past. Because it hinders precise alignment to the present moment, it creates a distortion not only in my perspective but also in my experience of space-time itself.

In the mystical traditions, fragmentation, stagnation, and isolation are observed as areas of weakness, illness, or disease. When organs, structures, systems, or people become shut down, closed off, isolated, or unfulfilled, their internal and external ability to communicate and receive information has been stunted or lost, and the health of the organism may be at risk. Healing is the work of opening or returning connection. It is the fulfillment of the ensō.

When we do healing work, we safely unpack the unconscious luggage we carry. We "defrag" in an effort to bring about greater integration. Healing permits us to travel lighter and brighter, to be more fully and deeply present to the moment, as less of the past splits our energy and attention and weighs us down. We begin to feel a sense of deeper presence, of "here-ness," and to see and sense our world with greater clarity and precision. Like it does for Dorothy in *The Wizard of Oz*, our world goes technicolor.

With the fulfillment of the ensō, there is a return to peace. The openness of the circle permits divine intelligence to pour in. Here, what had been the ordinary world becomes nonordinary, and previously isolated, stagnated sectors suddenly breathe open and awaken with energy and vitality. Newly flowing and interpenetrating systems exchange intelligence and dance with life.

In the chapters ahead, as we consider more mainstream and contemporary psychological, neurological, epigenetic,[2] and sociocultural findings related to the subject of trauma, we will return always to ancient mystical principles related to being human and to healing. In this way, we are binding the hands of science and spirit in a sacred handfasting, weaving a double helix between ancient wisdom and contemporary understanding.

DESTINY OF THE UNHEALED HERO

From a mystic's (or Jungian's) perspective, every experience or emotion from the past that remains unacknowledged, unprocessed, or denied is stored in the realm of the unconscious, or shadow. These experiences have not been integrated by the psyche or spirit, and so they will—indeed, they must—surface again and again in new but familiar forms. *What we think of as destiny is in fact the unintegrated past.* And the fragmented, unintegrated past appears always as a false future of repetition, a preprogrammed path along which every individual and every culture sets out until the contents of that past have been brought into the light of consciousness, reconciled and healed. This mystical wisdom reveals itself in the study of history and psychology, and undergirds philosopher George Santayana's words, "Those who cannot remember the past are condemned to repeat it."[3]

We may choose to understand these repetitions of shadow content as *karma*, a Sanskrit word originally meaning "effect" or "fate" (i.e., destiny). Or we may recognize them in light of our contemporary understanding as trauma—specifically as *retraumatization*, the unconscious act of repeating the conditions of earlier traumas upon self and others.

Everything that resides in my unconscious inevitably flows into and blends with yours and everyone else's. All together, this forms the collective shadow, which may be visualized as a series of dark subterranean lakes, flowing deep beneath our everyday awareness. The dark water of the collective shadow becomes a way station for the energetic residue of unresolved conflicts, multigenerational suffering, and all manner of unhealed trauma. It harbors the unacknowledged hatred of one nation for another, the suppressed terror echoing within a racial group or gender, and the unexpressed outrage felt by a tribe or religious faction.

Psychic energy that is held in the shadow remains out of sight until it becomes activated by external conditions and an accumulation of energetic momentum within the social field. Once activated, the dark contents of the shadow surface like a Loch Ness monster, cresting in the form of patterns of human behavior and consequence, from recurring toxic relationship patterns to poisonous social histories. These repetitions are the silent summoning of our unhealed injuries and unexamined failures. Freud termed the tendency to repeat the painful past *Wiederholungszwang*, or "repetition compulsion," theorizing that unconscious retraumatization is an attempt to find conscious resolution to the original trauma.[4] Whether surfacing as histories of poverty, family violence, or addiction, or on the social scale as ethnic hatreds, war, or social collapse, repetition compulsion is an ancient undercurrent in human affairs—one that can be healed.

While our will is our own, our choices are inevitably bound and restricted by karma, by trauma, by what we conceive of as "the past"—all that we have denied, disowned, dissociated, and suppressed. The unconscious denial of any experience freezes some portion of our available energy in shadow, thereby restricting our freedom and movement. With every denial or suppression of the past, we create our destiny, which is the repetition of suffering.

Still, as the great spiritual myths reveal, the hero discovers that by acknowledging and repairing the folly of his past, by integrating all he has been, he may become truly free—and more of what he truly *is*.

THE FUTURE CAN REWRITE THE PAST

In both philosophy and quantum physics there is a theory referred to as *retrocausality*, which posits that certain, perhaps very special, effects may in fact precede their causes. While retrocausality remains hotly debated in both fields, new support continues to emerge. In 2017, the esteemed Royal Society published a paper by physicists Matthew S. Leifer and Matthew F. Pusey titled "Is a Time Symmetric Interpretation of Quantum Theory Possible without Retrocausality?" which presents theoretical support for retrocausality.[5]

If proven, the theory of retrocausality could mean that influences from the present or future are able to act on, and thereby *change*, the past. From the mystical perspective, this is an essential principle of grace and is always true. The future indeed has the power to rewrite the past. In fact, when we integrate shadow or trauma, we're utilizing this principle because healing past energy creates a forward ripple effect. This releases light and energy that was previously held in shadow, offering greater movement and freedom of will in the present.

The retrocausality principle is at the heart of the work I facilitate around trauma healing for both individuals and groups, whether they're the members of a family, organization, or community of practice anywhere in the world. A deeper examination of retrocausal healing will be explored later in this book.

There is still some essence of truth in German zoologist and evolutionist Ernst Haeckel's words, "Ontogeny recapitulates phylogeny." Put very simply, the origin and developmental stages of a single organism across its life span (ontogeny) looks a lot like the changes that occurred in its ancestors as a whole throughout time (phylogeny). We are meant to develop, to evolve, as all life develops and evolves, and along a similar trajectory—fundamentally, consciously, systemically, *mutually*. As we awaken in consciousness, we create room for the light of inspiration and innovation to fill and pour through us. This activates flow states, unimpeded currents of pure evolutionary energy. This emergent, creative, and spontaneous stream of light and information is the essence of the authentic future, that which is original and nonrepeating.

As our karmic past is cleared, as trauma is healed and integrated, the genuine future can arrive to meet us. When we greet it from a place of presence and attunement, the world catches fire. Suddenly everything changes, yet nothing is lost. Like Paul on the road to Damascus, where before we were blind, now we see. We recognize new vistas.

We tend to see our world in three dimensions, but physicists tell us there are many more. To attempt to "see" multidimensionally, imagine a hologram. A holographic image is a photographic recording of a light field, appearing visually as a 3D object. While a photograph itself is merely a 2D representation, it can be projected in such a way that it is experienced as a higher dimension (i.e., 3D). Now imagine that you are a being who resides somewhere in, say, the fifth or sixth dimension, so that you are able to see and observe your own dimension, as well as every lower plane that it incorporates—just as we can see and recognize the first through the third dimensions. From your new point of view, you'd likely have a very different perspective on time, which is the fourth dimension. Time appears quite linear to us from our vantage down in 3D, where we commonly assume the past is always behind us, and the future is always before us (and never the twain shall meet). But from a higher dimensional perspective, we might recognize how it is that effects can precede their causes, and thus, how the future can change the past.

PERCEPTION DISTORTION
IS SPACE-TIME DISTORTION

When we become burdened by the stories we tell ourselves about the past, we cannot show up fully in the present; we can't bring our most essential energy into our work or relationships. Whether we move through a day replaying content from a difficult romantic exchange or a frustrating business meeting, an active percentage of who we are is occupied in the past and therefore absent in the present and not available to the here and now.

Imagine that everything you perceive and remember, intuit and feel, see and experience is a projection on a kind of internal movie screen. Your experience of the room you sit in, the book or device you're holding, the words you're reading right now, and your own bodily sensations and feelings is merely perception projected onto this inner screen. Now, imagine that when you are fully available to the present moment, your movie screen is clear and crisp, and the surround sound has perfect clarity. But when you become occupied with thoughts or feelings about the karmic past, your screen becomes wrinkled and puckered. And when traumatic experiences happen to you, this screen becomes warped, and the sound is made tinny and staticky. Now, imagine that as you attempt to watch, advertisements or someone else's movie entirely becomes superimposed over your own! Any of this would make it difficult to clearly interpret what you're sensing and experiencing.

Everything we perceive about our world becomes distorted to the degree that we are fragmented by trauma and bound by the unresolved past. Perception of self and other desynchronizes. Cultural perceptions twist and distort. Since that unresolved content *is* the past, space-time itself warps.

Mythologically, such distortions are treated as illusions. Their purpose is to test the insight and spiritual fortitude of the hero. Whether these distortions appear in ourselves or others, in our families or societies, it's important to recognize the power they possess to destabilize and further fragment.

LOCATING TRAUMA'S COSMIC ADDRESS

We might think of the human body as a hologram, nonlinear and multidimensional. All parts of a hologram contain the image of the whole, just as the cells of the body—whether skin cells, heart cells, brain cells, and so on—contain the genetic blueprint for the entire body.

The energy flowing vertically along the spinal column represents what is happening *now*, but because the body is a multidimensional space-time template, it simultaneously reveals a full energetic record of its own past. The nervous system is the body's intelligent central core, and it contains a detailed *akasha*[6] of an individual's entire developmental history.

With healing practice, we can learn to zoom in and feel deeply into or align with any of the holographic coordinates of the energetic nervous system, in both ourselves and others. By developing this skill, we can learn to use our own nervous systems to attune in relation to that of another. This allows us to access impressions or emotional sensations relating to experiences that occurred at specific points in space and time. This subtle competency grows in clarity as we learn to connect through the receiver of our own nervous system, establishing a data connection through deeper precision. By attuning to another person in this way, always with permission, we can simply feel, within our own system, the approximate age or stage in life at which a painful experience or trauma occurred. This is its "cosmic address."

Unhealed trauma damages our capacities for presence and embodiment and harms our ability to relate and connect with others in a healthy way. When we can host our experiences within, we can more functionally relate without. As stressful and disconcerting as our world appears, if we can host it, we can respond to it.

THE DIVINE HUMAN MATRIX

We are each a pulsing fiber optic cable alive in a matrix of light. The source of this light, whatever we call it—source energy, life's seed, the Divine—touches us from the *authentic* future. It is an evolutionary intelligence that seeks to download itself into and through us. From this conscious, ever-emergent wellspring, we are offered the full accumulated treasure of human life. It exists within us as an electricity that rushes upward vertically along every familial thread and arcs out horizontally along the fibers of our nervous systems, connecting each to the other and animating the full current of humanity in vibrating unison. The divine human matrix carries the encoded story of our race, back to its very genesis. All those alive today have been entrusted to hold this living record and chosen by evolution to update and renew it into a new tomorrow.

When a human incarnates, a stream of light enters into and travels upward along millennia of spiraling DNA and accumulated genetic histories. Pushing through thousands of years of karmic substrate, a single human soul emerges into a world weighed down by ancient, modern, and postmodern bands of tribal pain and cultural trauma. Its light surfaces, finally, at the conception and crown of a single bawling infant. Each child is new and innocent and perfect but has entered an incomprehensible story, one requiring great strength of spirit.

Shadow is created by arrested energy and is bound to vertices in the living matrix. But the fullness and beauty of what we are as an organic web of light, vibrating with information and potential, isn't diminished by these places of contraction, disunity, and devolution. As our collective story has unfolded, humans have descended again and again into real and mythological underworlds.

We carry the record of our darkest experiences in our bones and skin and teeth, in our families, communities, and societies. As we explore the subject of the human shadow and its longing for integration and release, we will look to medicine and mysticism, sages and scientists. The points of pain that we feel in our individual and collective bodies were left by accumulating traumas, but the call so many of us hear is an invitation toward collective healing, the ultimate hero's journey.

If we accept the call, we are likely to encounter the dark. But if we survive the dark, our eyes will have opened and we will be infinitely and indescribably changed.

2

THE MATERIAL SCIENCE
OF TRAUMA

I appreciated that all animals have some form of mental life
that reflects the architecture of their nervous system.

Oliver Sacks
The River of Consciousness

The mind is its own place, and in itself
Can make a Heaven of Hell, a Hell of Heaven.

John Milton
Paradise Lost

Our earliest ancestors are believed to have emerged some six million years ago, with modern humans arriving roughly 200,000 years back.[1] Having populated the entire planet in so relatively short a span, we might say that our species is both prolific and resilient. For as long as humans have existed, we have survived countless natural and human-made catastrophes: earthquakes, tsunamis, droughts, floods, plagues, wars, genocides, and rivers of unspeakable violence. Throughout all of these, our species has continued to prosper and flourish, regardless of how fragile a single human life, or psyche, may be. Yet, despite our evident resilience, we are not immune to suffering—we have caused and borne much misery—and this twin legacy of trauma and resilience bears out in every human's ancestral DNA and in every culture's psychic inheritance.

To live in the modern world is to be familiar, however unconsciously, with the effects of trauma. From soldiers living with the debilitating effects of posttraumatic stress and high suicide mortality to societies plagued by nameless anxieties, phobias and fears, obsessions and compulsions, addictions and fatigue—we are saturated with real-world examples of the impacts of human suffering, from East to West and across the developing and developed world.

For many there is a palpable sense that, in our time, both human-made and natural disasters are somehow increasing in number and escalating in speed. With an exponential increase in human population, as well as an explosion in the technologies that allow us to connect and communicate around the world, our impact—as much as our *awareness* of our impact—has been powerfully enhanced over a relatively brief period. Since the time of the First World War, armed conflicts have gone unabated, and since the close of the Second World War, racial, ethnic, and religious pogroms and persecutions continue unchecked in many parts of the world. These dilemmas have roots in ancient human behaviors, yet their powers for ill are amplified by modern weapons and the technology of social media to spread harmful ideas and hateful propaganda.

And yet, these are not doomsday prophesies; our world is hardly so bleak. After all, the fact that we can now address questions regarding psychological trauma or its healing is an evolutionary capacity. Humankind as a whole appears to develop and evolve in much the same way that individual people do, though the path can be impeded by blocks, regressions, suppressions, unintegrated shadows, and unhealed trauma.

The ultimate question regarding the darkness we see outside us is not whether it will consume our world but instead whether we can *reframe* our understanding of that darkness. How can we come to recognize the dark as a part of ourselves so we may integrate its lessons and through them be transformed? And how would such healing, on a collective scale, advance the care of the planet that is our home?

Before we can address these existential and fundamentally mystical questions, we may wish to investigate practical concerns such as defining trauma and determining how its effects are addressed by scientific and public health communities around the world. Focusing through the lens of science, this chapter is an examination of these questions and an introduction to the contemporary scientific view of human trauma.

EFFECTS OF TRAUMA ON INDIVIDUALS

Bessel van der Kolk, MD, medical director and founder of the Trauma Center at Justice Resource Institute, professor of psychiatry at Boston University School of Medicine, and author of the *New York Times* bestseller, *The Body Keeps the Score: Brain, Mind, and Body in the Healing of Trauma*, describes trauma as any event or ongoing experience with a significant impact on the survival, or animal, part of the brain. When trauma occurs, our "automatic danger signals are disturbed, and we become hyper- or hypoactive: aroused or numbed out."[2] As a result, we may regress into primal states of fear or aggression (i.e., resorting to our survival instincts of flight and fight), or we may become paralyzed (i.e., survival instinct to freeze), unable to rationally gauge the level of threat or use reason to defend ourselves against future persecution.

Inevitably, as van der Kolk and other researchers have demonstrated, trauma has the power to change the central nervous system. It alters the way we assimilate memory and leaves us highly reactive to any stimuli that mirrors, however unconsciously, the original experience.[3]

When a family or community fails to validate a traumatized person's experiences or to establish a sense of caring and safety after the fact, the trauma is less likely to be metabolized with resilience and more likely to express itself in symptoms of post-traumatic stress.

POST-TRAUMATIC STRESS

Catastrophic stressors commonly produce post-traumatic effects in survivor communities. These can include suffering life-threatening experiences in war zones, regions of intense tribal conflict, or areas of ongoing gang violence; surviving a terrorist attack; bearing witness to mass violence (e.g., mass shootings, suicide bombings, etc.); surviving a natural disaster; experiencing a major accident or life-threatening injury; or suffering sexual assault, intimate partner violence, or other domestic violence, including child abuse.

The consequences of post-traumatic stress can be severe enough to disrupt mood, behavior, cognition, sleep, interpersonal relationships, and a sense of well-being, leaving countless individuals with a condition today referred to as post-traumatic stress disorder, or PTSD. Common symptoms of PTSD—ranging between hyper- and hypoarousal—are severe anxiety, agitation, irritability, and/or depression; hostility, distrust, fear, and/or aggression; hypervigilance or numbness; poor impulse control, including self-destructive behaviors (e.g., hypersexuality or risk-seeking); loss of interest in pleasurable activities or usual routines; and emotional detachment, avoidance, and social isolation. Other common identifying symptoms of PTSD include flashbacks, as well as nightmares and patterns of disturbed sleep.[4]

In 1980, when PTSD first appeared as a diagnosable mental health condition, the types of events meeting the criteria for the condition were classified solely as those perceived as life-threatening or as a genuine risk of violence or injury to self or others.[5] In the decades since, trauma researchers around the world have learned how certain repetitive and pervasive traumatic stressors, even when they may not directly pose a risk to life, can nonetheless present a genuine risk of injury to spirit, psyche, and body—and in particular, to a child's chances for healthy development.

COMPLEX TRAUMA

Judith Lewis Herman, MD, professor of clinical psychiatry at Harvard University Medical School and Director of Training at the Victims of Violence Program at the Cambridge Health Alliance, is the author of *Trauma and Recovery: The Aftermath of Violence—From Domestic Abuse to Political Terror*, now considered a classic in the study of PTSD and a defining contribution toward the understanding of trauma on sufferers.

In her work, Herman delineates between two classes: Type 1 traumas, which designate single-incident traumas or one-time events of significant impact with core and observable effects, and Type 2 traumas, which describe incidents of ongoing and repetitive trauma and may include occurrences such as a chronic, long-term experience of childhood abuse and neglect or a protracted history of domestic violence. Herman called Type 2 trauma and its effects "complex trauma," and in *Trauma and Recovery*, she proposed its diagnostic classification as "complex post-traumatic stress disorder," or C-PTSD, outlining the ways that long-term consequences of complex trauma are both similar to and different from those experienced by sufferers of PTSD.[6]

Herman wrote:

> *Repeated trauma in childhood forms and deforms the personality. The child trapped in an abusive environment is faced with formidable tasks of adaptation. She must find a way to preserve a sense of trust in people who are untrustworthy, safety in a situation that is unsafe, control in a situation that is terrifyingly unpredictable, power in a situation of helplessness. Unable to care for or protect herself, she must compensate for the failures of adult care and protection with the only means at her disposal, an immature system of psychological defenses.*[7]

More than two and a half decades later, draft proposals of diagnostic criteria for C-PTSD are being presented for inclusion into the World Health Organization's eleventh revision of its diagnostic manual, *The International Classification of Diseases* (ICD-11).[8]

DEVELOPMENTAL TRAUMA

Complex trauma can be experienced by anyone, at any age, but its study sheds significant light on the experiences of children with histories of abuse and neglect. Working with other experts and researchers and adding to the insights of complex trauma, Dr. Bessel van der Kolk has presented a new category of trauma that he calls developmental trauma, as well as a corresponding list of criteria for consideration as a formal diagnosis: developmental trauma disorder, or DTD. Repetitive traumas that occur in the developmental years bear deleterious impacts on the psychological and relational health of a growing human, including, in particular, risk for comorbid mental illness and physical disorders or disease.[9]

Like complex trauma, developmental trauma encompasses many forms of suffering but most often points to a child's repeated exposure to interpersonal violence, maltreatment, or neglect, as well as to the subjective experiences of shame, humiliation, betrayal, and guilt a child may carry over afterward. Developmental traumas may include psychological abuse, repeated separation from caregivers, traumatic loss, and exposure to inappropriate sexual behavior.

Exposure to chronic traumatic stress in the developmental years may impair healthy functioning in the following seven critical areas:

1. *Attachment*: As an infant develops, the earliest bond with his primary caregivers becomes the template for his sense of self and sense of other. When a child's relationship with his primary caregivers is traumatic, his capacity to connect and bond with others is injured, and his ability to regulate emotions and tolerate stress may become compromised.

2. *Biology*: Growing children who experience complex trauma often fail to develop neurologically in line with their peers and, as a result, may struggle with emotional regulation, stress tolerance, and cognitive functions such as language, abstract reasoning, long-range planning, the ability to learn from past experiences, and social relationships. They see an increased risk

for sensory-motor dysfunction, sensory-integration difficulties, somatic conditions, and physical illness.

3. *Affect*: Developmental trauma inhibits a child's capacity to self-soothe or to tolerate stress or change. These children and teens may exhibit poor affect regulation, and as with PTSD, are often hypo- or hyperreactive—revealing either withdrawal and lack of affect, or intense, uninhibited emotional states. They reveal difficulty identifying their own emotions and internal states, as well as the emotions and perceptions of others, and often struggle to communicate their needs and desires.

4. *Dissociation*: Abused and neglected children tend to express an interesting adaptation: their painful memories and associated feelings become compartmentalized out of conscious awareness. Often there is amnesia around state-based events and depersonalization occurs. This reflex toward detachment and dissociation may result in a lack of self-awareness, disconnection to somatic sensations, and unconscious behavioral patterns, placing the youth at further risk for trauma by victimization or accident/injury.

5. *Behavioral control*: Developmental trauma disrupts a child's nervous system and brain development, introducing a risk for inhibited impulse control, aggression, dysfunctional self-soothing patterns, and disrupted sleep.

6. *Cognition*: Many experience difficulty regulating attention, abstract reasoning, and executive function (e.g., judgment, planning, self-monitoring), as well as developmental language deficits and difficulties with initiation and completion of tasks and goals. Neglected infants and children show the most severe cognitive limitations, but children with histories of complex trauma of all types show diminished test and achievement scores in early education.

7. *Self-concept*: Developmental trauma has a distinctly deleterious impact on a child's growing sense of self. These children

and teens struggle with a fragmented or disrupted autobio-graphical narrative; low self-esteem (often as a consequence of excessive shame); and negative or disrupted body image. An inhibited capacity to understand their own or others' emotions leaves the child with a greatly reduced ability to *feel* or to know herself, much less to love what she comes to feel or know.[10]

ADVERSE CHILDHOOD EXPERIENCES STUDY

In 1996, a longitudinal study on the effects of complex trauma was undertaken, sampling more than 17,000 people. Known as the Adverse Childhood Experiences (ACEs) Study, it was originally led by Dr. Robert Anda from the Centers for Disease Control and Prevention and Dr. Vincent Felitti from Kaiser Permanente.

The data from the CDC-Kaiser ACE Study revealed something intuitive yet radical: There is a significant relationship between the number of "adverse experiences" a person confronts in childhood—things like physical, emotional, and sexual abuse, neglect and famil-ial dysfunctions such as parental substance abuse, mental illness, or imprisonment—and certain negative health outcomes later in life, such as depression, self-harm, suicidality, substance abuse, sexual promiscuity, sexually transmitted disease, intimate partner violence, and obesity. The more adverse childhood experiences reported, the higher the prevalence for diabetes, stroke, heart disease, cancer, and certain other illnesses or disease.[11] There is no denying the profound and often lifelong damage that early trauma can create.

In her research on ACEs, Dr. Christina Bethell and her colleagues at the Bloomberg School of Public Health at Johns Hopkins University have explored the reach of trauma still further and illuminated the countering effects on trauma from what they term "child flourishing." According to Dr. Bethell in her article "Child Flourishing: Our Great-est Public Health Opportunity Needs a Policy Response," flourishing is present in children when three characteristics are observed all or most of the time in their behavior: (1) engagement/motivation (the child is "curious and interested in learning new things"), (2) regulation/resilience (the child "stays calm and in control when faced with a challenge"), and (3) focus/attention (the child "follows through and finishes tasks").

The more adverse childhood experiences that children have, the less they exhibit the characteristics of flourishing. But there is hope. Now that trauma and its constellation of lifelong effects is becoming better understood, researchers and practitioners are finding many successful pathways for improving health outcomes, enhancing child (and family) flourishing, and preventing and healing the effects of childhood adversity and trauma, including

creating a culture and healing communities that both teach children and youth to develop and maintain hope, meaning, and optimism, and address widespread structural inequalities; leveraging children, youth and adults' innate self-care agency to learn to thrive across life; and helping children, youth, and families recognize the need for assistance and access 'through any door' supports and resources to heal.[12]

TRANSITIONING FROM A TRAUMA-BASED TO A TRAUMA-INFORMED SOCIETY

DR. CHRISTINA BETHELL, PHD

From the very beginning of life—even in the womb—safe, stable, attuned, connected relationships that are nurturing are critical. There are studies that are very clear that when moms are experiencing a lot of stress or there's stress in the environment during pregnancy, it starts to impact the nervous system and the development of the child. Certainly, in the very beginning of life, that need for attunement to even map our tenth cranial nerve, which regulates so much of the body's nervous system, starts to be impacted.

Studies show that those who look back on their lives and report having had ACEs are many, many, *many*-fold more likely to also report heart disease, lung disease, alcoholism, not having life satisfaction, any number of health or behavior problems, and certainly depression or anxiety. ACEs are recognized as biological causal factors for disease.

Deactivating shame and building compassion with awareness begins the healing journey. It opens the door to activate what I call the *will to be well*. Because a lot of the time, people with trauma are not actually seeking to be helped. There are a lot of defenses that can happen, and even more health behaviors. And a person has to want to engage in all the things we know now are so important to well-being, including meditation and movement, but also, of course, diet and exercise, even basic things that often get deactivated with trauma.

Awareness is the first step—and awareness with compassion, acceptance for where you are—then connecting with the body. There are nine levels of brain integration that need to be gone through, but meditation and mindfulness practice is the first step to opening that up.

There are also the relational practices of coming forward and engaging in sharing story, feeling safe, and trusting others. If we have trauma, in one way or another, we may never have experienced safety and connection and attunement, so we don't even know what we're missing. But as we start to create it with ourselves, we activate the healthy instinct to be connected with one another in a warm and open way. And we have to go through a whole process to be able to unlearn and relearn from the trauma, to allow what's natural to come forward so that we can emerge into our creative, expressive selves.

Our lived moment-by-moment relational experiences and the experience we have with the self are what's driving a lot of the biologic and neurologic symptoms of trauma—and at the same time, they can also drive the healing. When we come to the science of trauma and ACEs, and also of healing, what we recognize is that the way to respond to what we learn from the science, and to implement it, is through our own self-awareness and our connection with ourselves and each other, and how we support through systems and structures the sanctity of that. And we recognize what happens when we don't do that.

There are some formal scientific terms for the ability to enter into relational experience with awareness and one of them is *mentalization*. It's not a mental process because the mind is actually a distributed system throughout the whole body. The mind is not in your brain; it's in your whole being. Mentalization is the ability to feel yourself and know you're feeling yourself on purpose, and the ability to sense another person on purpose, and sense whether that other person senses that you're sensing them—or to sense whether that person *is able* to sense that you're sensing them.

The key thing we need to be able to do that, first and foremost, is what happens through healthy brain development, through attunement and attachment of the baby and the young child—something called *interoception*, which is the ability to sense ourselves, our feelings, our body, our needs, our wants, our love. That ability can be cut off pretty significantly when we are not met in a safe, stable, nurturing, relational way as babies, or when we sense stress in the environment. And a way you can activate interoception is through meditation and body awareness.

The mentalization process is the restoration of our capacity to relate to one another in that mutual, integrated way where we house one another within our beings, on purpose, and can sense and attune to when that's happening or not, and continuously bring it back into attunement the way birds, when they fly and entrain together in the sky, are constantly sensing back into the center of their collective. It's a biologic sense, but it's obviously also a deep spiritual construct.

We can access presence through any experience, and by doing that and moving toward what's happening, even if it's horrific—especially when in connection with others—we can buffer a lot of the damage by continuously meeting and integrating it, by being present with it. If it's too overwhelming, say, when we come from trauma and we haven't developed a strong capacity for presence, then we can't do that. But we can build, in a preventive way, the capacity to be present with life and experience, so that when we do meet catastrophes, we can access those skills.

Ultimately, my work is about systems change and culture change, where we know that we first have to deal with mindsets. Then we have to deal with our relationships, how people are relating to each other. Then we have to translate that into all the details of how we construct organizations and systems, and pay for things, and train people, and things like that.

Right now, we live in a society based on trauma, so we need to go from being trauma organized to being trauma informed and, eventually, healing centered. We don't have to wait to get healed. We have to start with healing as prevention, and there are so many opportunities. I believe that it's actually by meeting what lives in and between us, from a deeper sense of who we really are, that we can create the possibility of experiencing our oneness.

TRAUMA RESPONSE AS AN INTELLIGENT FUNCTION OF THE NERVOUS SYSTEM

Whether in the lives of single individuals or on the scale of the collective, the effects of trauma are undeniable and often long-lasting; in many cases, trauma reveals its imprint many generations down. Yet, these effects are not solely negative. In fact, the human nervous system, insofar as it has evolved to aid survival, is quite elegant—even *intelligent*, we might say.

Consider a returning veteran who now suffers from PTSD. One of his symptoms may be hypervigilance, defined by an enhanced state of anxiety, arousal, sensory sensitivity, and the constant, reflexive scanning of his environment for signs of incoming threat. The energy needed to sustain this heightened vigilance is taxing, so he easily becomes physically and emotionally exhausted. As a result, he must cope with pervasive feelings of irritability and agitation, which his family and friends are unable to process or understand. His loved ones' lack of understanding and the veteran's growing feelings of anxiety, frustration, and shame may lead him to withdraw, which interferes with what had, previous to his enlistment, been a strong capacity for healthy and sustained interpersonal connections. And this leaves him feeling isolated and depressed.

Yet the symptom of hypervigilance originates as a product of the nervous system's evolutionary intelligence. The veteran's nervous system had issued a command to rewire, enhancing its automatic function to patrol and scan for danger, amplifying its defensive assistance to meet what the body perceived as a shifting and unsafe environment. The initial effect of hypervigilance in response to trauma, then, appears to contain a functional, even lifesaving strategy.

The question of precisely where the consequences of trauma become *dysfunctional* may lie somewhere within the container of relation that surrounds a traumatized person and their family, community, society, and culture. The longer trauma remains uncared for and/or untreated, the higher the likelihood that a life becomes dominated by the symptoms it produces.

POLYVAGAL THEORY

In 1994, Dr. Stephen Porges, director of the Traumatic Stress Research Consortium at the Kinsey Institute, proposed what is known as the polyvagal theory, which helped illuminate a profound and altogether new aspect of the nervous system's role in our evolutionary survival.[13] By then, biologists already understood that the sympathetic and parasympathetic responses (i.e., fight or flight and freeze or faint, respectively) were an ancient and hardwired aspect of animal survival. Porges's theory marked new territory in this prehistoric dance by discerning the deep impact that social relationships play, not only in survival, but in our ability to withstand stress and recover from trauma.[14]

The polyvagal theory explains how an individual's felt sense of either safety or danger is deeply connected to his or her social environment. Visceral cues are received by the nervous system and relayed to us through nearly imperceptible shifts in the voices, faces, and/or postural changes we detect—often automatically and unconsciously—in the faces and bodies of those around us. These minute expressions and infinitesimal shifts offer constant feedback cues about whether our environment is threatening or safe, and whether the other people in it present risk or offer connection. The more accurately we are able to decipher these cues, the stronger our bonds will be with others, and the more safety and well-being we will experience.

The vagus nerve, or tenth cranial nerve, is a system of paired nerves that administrates parasympathetic nervous system control of the heart, lungs, digestive tract, and other autonomic systems. The ventral vagal complex (VVC)—sometimes referred to as the "social nervous system"—is the first part of this system that is engaged when we experience stress or any kind of environmental or psychological threat, whether real or imagined. As soon as the VVC is activated, we seek to reestablish a sense of safety, certainty, and connection through "tend and befriend" behaviors with those around us.[15] If we hear a sudden loud noise, for example, we may look immediately into the eyes of a companion, not just to verify that they heard the same noise, but as an unconscious means of seeking security.

If the actions of the social nervous system fail, and no safe bonds or connections are present, or we are simply too distressed to feel relief or make connection, our nervous system's next line of defense is established in the dorsal vagal complex (DVC) by way of the sympathetic reactions of fight or flight. Evolutionarily speaking, the DVC belongs to the oldest part of the vagus nerve. If its defenses of fight or flight do not work to fend off the availing threat, the parasympathetic nervous system defaults to freezing, fainting, or playing dead.[16]

TRAUMA'S IMPACT ON RELATION

Trauma breaks relation; it damages human capacities for trust, connection, and mutuality. When these capacities are injured or destroyed, there is less resilience, and therefore greater vulnerability to additional trauma, which is frequently inflicted through the channel of broken relation.

Complex trauma impairs the ability to establish a stable sense of self, and therefore a relationship to the self, and hinders or severs the capacity to form healthy relationships with others. This is perhaps the most debilitating consequence of trauma.

"Trauma is actually *not* the story of what happened a long time ago," says Bessel van der Kolk. "Trauma is residue that's living inside of you now."[17] Because trauma continues to live inside the sufferer, fragmenting memory, distorting perception, and blocking embodiment, it takes up critical space. Older evolutionary functions are necessarily more stable, so that a traumatized person—no matter how far he or she may have developed before the time of the trauma—will experience regressions to previous states and stages of development when triggered by stressors, especially those produced by relationships, further impinging on the capacity of the traumatized to build or sustain healing connections.

COMBINING MATERIAL SCIENCE
AND SUBTLE SCIENCE

Now that we have laid down a basic framework for recognizing human trauma and its effects through a scientific lens, the next chapter will consider the same elements through a mystical perspective. The intention is not to promote a dichotomy but to create a gentle dialectic. By weaving a view of the subtle dimensions into our current awareness, we may advance a more layered and integrated understanding.

3

THE INNER SCIENCE OF TRAUMA

Trauma is not what happens to us, but what we hold
inside in the absence of an empathetic witness.

Peter A. Levine
In an Unspoken Voice

The greatest damage done by neglect, trauma, or emotional loss is
not the immediate pain they inflict but the long-term distortions
they induce in the way a developing child will continue to
interpret the world and her situation in it.

Gabor Maté
In the Realm of Hungry Ghosts

The essence of this book is framed around what I refer to as the mystical principles of healing, which are the basis of my global coursework on collective trauma (the essence of which I began to lay out in chapter 1). As a mystic, the foundation of my work is spiritual, and thus, it rests in and arises from the substance of the sacred, from Mystery—from that which I call God.

This word *God* is frequently controversial in our modern and postmodern world; it evokes different connotations and emotions in all who read or hear it. Of course, countless other words or names have been chosen in the attempt to identify the same concept. It may be felt as Spirit, the All, the One, the Absolute, Ultimate Reality, the Unqualifiable, the Divine. It has been called Source, Tao, Brahman, Void, or known as limitless consciousness, the fully awakened state, the principle of creation and that to which it returns, alpha and omega—and by ten thousand other names and that which cannot be named.

Any human word or concept fails to capture the essence of its subject, which to ancient and modern hearts expresses a thing both vast and singular, absolute yet relative, simultaneously many and one, both personal and ineffable, radically manifest and somehow silent and formless.

A quality both immanent *and* transcendent.

It is impossible to give a name to a divine paradox. It is a mystery and cannot be captured, even obliquely.

However it is we choose to relate to the Divine, it remains to us ultimately mysterious. Still and so, there is beauty and revelation to be found in the quest: what small thing we may uncover about the infinite, we may also discover about ourselves. As we discussed in chapter 1, its energies are frequently expressed through the ensō; they trace a map that is both fractal and holonic—both whole and part. In other words, it is where one whole entity (holon) becomes part of the whole of the next higher entity, and so on, all the way up—like divinely packed Russian dolls. Consider how a wave-particle becomes an atom becomes a molecule becomes a cell becomes an organism becomes a complex organism, each holon enfolding and transcending its antecedent, evolving through a process of differentiation and integration toward greater and greater complexity. And with greater complexity arrives increasing dimensions of consciousness.

The qualities of an atom are at once reflected or included in, yet vastly transcended by, the molecule. "As above, so below." In the same way, the qualities of a single human are expressed in the human totality. Where the human exhibits a blinking ego and a capacious sleeping unconscious, the collective psyche of all humanity contains these forces in-kind. We are both *I* and *We*, body and society, psyche and culture.

But it is not just the human that possesses interiority; even the atom can be said to express some force of prehension, however proportionally discrete. Indeed, all holons do, and this reveals still another quality we can surmise about creation: it has yielded in equal portions both interior consciousness and exterior form.

As without, so within.

And herein lies a sacred key. To acknowledge or examine only exteriors—whether the physics of stars, the ecosystems of planets, or the deep neurochemistry of the human brain (arguably the most complex *exterior* system yet identified)—is to miss entire worlds. The consciousness dimensions of humans, planets, and stars notwithstanding, there is also that subtler realm from which all is born and into which all returns. While its secret nature can at times be intuited from the material world, its mysteries cannot be seen wholly or directly in the exteriors, but must (also) be explored *within*. And for many centuries, long before the rise of science or even the imperial dominance of the world's mythic religions, the ancient mystics, shamans, sages, and yogis did just that. We can benefit from their wisdom as we seek to integrate it with the discoveries of modern science and developmental psychology.

Various sacred traditions and philosopher-sages, from Plotinus to Shankara, have instructed practitioners toward inner awakening, divine states for which there are many names: *kenshō*, *satori*, *sahaja*, *metanoia*, *nirvikalpa samādhi*, *jnana*, *turiya*, and *turiyatita*. By making our developmental journey in a contemplative life, we make conscious our sacred anatomy. By practicing the contemplative life, we may awaken.

From a mystical perspective, incarnation into the body offers transformational power: namely, the power of the soul to progress, to grow. The soul is a potentiality—an intelligence that is downloaded into life.

The physical body is the soul's container for grounding energy and the vessel through which its light or intelligence may be channeled and developed; it is both capacitor and conductor.

It is through incarnation that we come to be rooted in a human life and in its story—though the story we are here to transform is not ours alone, but the collective human story, and ultimately, of life in toto. Indeed, we are actors in a shared hero's journey, a grand narrative in which we conspire with all members of our race once living, now living, and all those yet to come.

As we saw in chapter 1, the sacred dimension we call *life* has placed into our hands hundreds of thousands of years of human development—the fullness of the human code, manifest within and through all who live on Earth today. Together, we embody the genetic, geographic record of everything humanness now is and has ever contained. This is a sacred gift.

And though we see ourselves as bound to the present, our living souls embody a vertical dimension, arising from the origins of our shared history and proceeding upward into the wild vibrating potential that is our future.

The "past" is unintegrated history. It is that content of our story, personal and collective, that has been buried in shadow, the dark lakes of the unconscious interior, and thereby made into karma, forced to surface again and again in our exterior world. Unintegrated, unconscious past is destiny. It becomes a false future projected into tomorrow, built of repetition, preprogrammed by our unawakened aspect. It is like taking the road behind us, placing it in front of us, and calling it the "future."

What we have called "karma" or "shadow" may, today, be called "trauma," since the effects of trauma propagate as dissociated and denied energies, frozen in shadow, bound to repeat. Trauma creates incoherence, fracturing us from ourselves and separating us from others. Its broken memories resurface repeatedly through exterior eruptions that are not directed by free will but by that part of the self that is held in darkness.

SPACE, ENERGY, AND STRUCTURE

As we have discussed, our universe reveals itself to be holonic, and all holons exhibit interior and exterior—gross and subtle—dimensions. These twin dimensions occur similarly in space, energy, and structure, an explanation of which is necessitated by our contemporary mystical approach.

When most encounter the word *space*, they think of outer space—that celestial landscape containing our solar system and extending at least as far as our telescopes can see. But in the realm of the mystic, *space* refers to its interior dimension, equally vast. Here, space is the selfhood container for awareness, the world of the awakening I and We and All.

According to the mystical traditions, the qualities of space can be seen across multiple dimensions, its manifest nature existing in interpenetrating "layers" of assemblage. At one level, there is *gross* space, which houses the material dimension and its energetic properties: electromagnetic, gravitational, strong nuclear, and weak nuclear energies.

Emerging from and enveloping gross space is *subtle* space, housing the emotional, mental, and intuitive self-streams. Subtle space is the plane of information, the realm of dreams, and the initiation landscape of spiritual contemplation, opening the first doors into our awareness of the subtle energies, which have been referred to in various traditions as etheric, astral, psychic, and so on. *Subtle* connotes that, here, information and substance are finer and less dense than simply what our physical eyes can see.

Beyond the subtle, there exists *causal* space. In sacred texts, expressions such as *Ground of Being*, *Void*, and *Emptiness* have been used to identify its nature. In the mystical understanding, this quality of emptiness is not seen purely as a null space but rather as a formless void containing all potentials, all possibilities. It is a mysterious realm beyond duality, and it is from the causal that we encounter the witness self, that aspect of our nature that is able to view the subjective with objective clarity. The causal is the realm of deep sleep and the landscape of the Absolute. Out of the womb of the causal, All That Is emanates.

Emerging from space is *energy*, which is movement. Energy is the ceaseless flow of intelligence, of data—information in motion. Energy is the light of Spirit, enfolding into creative form and unfolding as the transcendent empty/fullness of completion. It may be prana or starlight, chi or electricity. In modern times, we call this higher energy visionary genius or insight. It emerges when new information that wasn't here before is downloaded into the system in the form of groundbreaking ideas and innovative breakthroughs.

Structure refers to the morphic form or pathway through which energy crystalizes and is channeled, as water through a pipe, into physical forms, neural pathways, emotional patterns, structures of consciousness, cultural forms, cosmic habits, and so on. Structures become the byways through which primordial and cosmic energies are channeled; they are the architecture, the pipeline.

THE WILL TO BECOME

At the moment of conception, a subtle, shimmering thread of energy—the human will—can be said to extend forward from the energy and information provided by the bodies of two adult human beings. That numinous line called "will" is directly linked to the soul and is the realization of life's most essential impulse: to grow, to evolve, to become.

This subtle fiber (will) links each of us to our purest essence (soul) and most distilled intelligence (life in toto), so that around it, an entire human life will develop and unfold. In this way, will is the energetic progenitor of the developing spinal cord and central nervous system.

The individual will is intimately tied to the collective will; its energy rises vertically up through an entire genetic lineage—indeed, through *all* lineages. As such, the will of a newly incarnating human carries the species code for continuation, which is not simply the instinct to survive but the longing to become something *new* and *more whole*. It carries the seed of the totality, just as a single acorn hosts the genetic memory of ancient forests and holds inside its own future as a fully formed oak tree.

CREATION OF THE NERVOUS SYSTEM

As the early nervous system develops, it emerges as a channel for a particular subtle energy—an intelligent, living stream of light: a singular human soul. As the brain and spine mature, a primary column for the flow of this light is created. It funnels into and circulates throughout the developing body, surging up from the base of the spine and out through the crown of the head. Its tertiary energies travel throughout the body, tracing a path along the energy meridians and *nadis*, channeling prana into every cell.[1] The nervous system channels information up the spine to inform the brain, and it carries information down the spine to inform the body.

Where the brain resides, at the crown of the head, an energetic channel or field of flow appears that corresponds to the future. By meditating on that field, we can learn to connect to our higher capacities for inspiration and innovation. In fact, the human central nervous system serves as a vast energy library of 360-degree information. It has many levels and tiers, hosting the sum total of our history: every recorded step of every developmental stage that we've taken, as well as every step and stage our ancestors walked to bring us here.

This magnificent system serves as a kind of wireless network. Whenever and wherever an unhealed trauma lingers, the record of it gets stuck in shadow, invisible to us on the surface. This trauma causes a disruption in the wireless network, so that whenever we pass that room in the library, our calls get dropped.

This is key to understanding the nervous system: From a subtle energy perspective, it facilitates both an upward and downward stream of data. Wherever communication pathways become disrupted, downstream tissues cannot be fully served. They will be starved of energy and information, and elemental organizing principles will fail to fully manifest.

Imagine it as though every cell in the body has a mobile phone. When there is sufficient cellular reception, all phones are in working order and every cell can communicate. But in zones of trauma, cellular reception is damaged, leaving many cells without vital access to information and connection. The higher organizing principle of the system is unable to inform its interdependent parts.

This is as true for the individual as it is for the collective—for cells, organisms, and humans. Trauma often severely disrupts data flow and processing. It creates dysfunction in a person's capacity to attune and connect with herself, and damages her ability to attune and relate to others.

THE INDIVIDUATION LOOP

A human soul is pure energy/potentiality, drawn down into the structure created by the parents. A healthy attachment process between parent and child allows for the formation of healthy consciousness structures, so that the child may develop and flourish. Inconsistent, neglectful, or abusive parenting often gravely damages interior and even exterior development. As mentioned in the previous chapter, such parenting results in complex or developmental traumas. Parenting that fails to see and *feel into* and acknowledge the interiority of the child may similarly result in trauma.

Out of being is becoming, and out of becoming arises the will. When conception occurs, the will can be sensed as a subtle line of energy. It is connected to the soul's drive and crystalizes as the forming fetus. The will expresses itself here as the impulse to create and does so in a looping fashion; it is ensō.

With each new loop, energy crystalizes as the next step in structure. It wires the nervous system and builds the spine and neuronal pathways of the brain. As it weaves, energy wires the external world. It is needle and thread, looping out and returning into the tapestry of the self-structure, repeating its fractal pattern again and again. In this way, the energetic foundation for what I call the *individuation loop* is made.

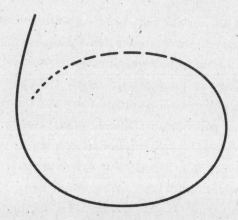

Individuation loop

Every new function and developmental aspect arises first as an impulse of energy or electricity and then, through regular practice, slowly creates for itself a structure, becoming the cable for the electricity to flow through. In this way, energy *becomes* structure. This is how the body (or exterior form) develops, and it is the same for the interior.

As a child continues to grow, two energetic impulses—curiosity and fear—become primary drivers for the development of his psychological interior. Curiosity impels the child to explore his environment, to reach out and discover, while fear compels him to return again to the safety of his parents' arms. In this way, our earliest instinct of survival—fear—pushes us toward connection. And once reassured in the comfort of protection, the child can go out again to sate his curiosity about the world.

If caregivers are not present or do not convey a sense of consistent safety and assurance to their child, he will be forced to hold his fear alone. This is overwhelming to a developing nervous system, which relies on *co*-regulation between caregiver and child in order for the child to develop the skill of self-regulation.

Throughout our lives, whenever we become frightened or startled, we instinctively turn to others, quickly assessing their faces to determine whether there exists a legitimate danger, or whether we can relax and open up again. Think of the last time you were on an airplane that experienced rough turbulence. Passengers sitting near you who may not have spoken beforehand probably looked around, quickly gauging one another's fear level and smiling nervously, sighing together in relief when the turbulence passed. This is an expression of coregulation. But if, as growing children, we do not receive adequate coregulation from our parents (a kind of developmental trauma), we will be more likely to express emotional dysregulation, even through adulthood, and may experience frequent stress and hyperactivation in minor or even neutral circumstances. This becomes true for other types of trauma, as well.

Again, the primary impulses for early interior development are curiosity and fear. Curiosity impels the baby to loop outward, exploring the world, while anxiety or fear compels the baby to return to the safety of a parent. Each time the child returns for safety and reassurance, healthy caregiving creates a resonance between the nervous system of the parent and the nervous system of the child, thereby creating a coregulation of fear and arousal. As this process repeats throughout early childhood, the child's brain and nervous system is hardwiring the habits for *self*-regulation, which he will need in order to grow into a functional and independent adult.

At the subtle level, when ongoing trauma occurs in these early stages due to a lack of adequate coregulation from healthy parent(s), a child may acquire an energetic *contraction of the base*, or a *base tension*. This may be seen energetically as the child holding him- or herself in or back (apart from others and her environment). Her energy may feel contracted rather than expansive and free-flowing. The contraction exists because the child is holding fear (i.e., holding the body tightly in response to fear), because she hasn't learned from parents or caregivers how to self-regulate it. If contraction from fear becomes an ongoing pattern, the child is unable to feel safe in the world, resulting in a state of disconnection from or ungroundedness in the body.

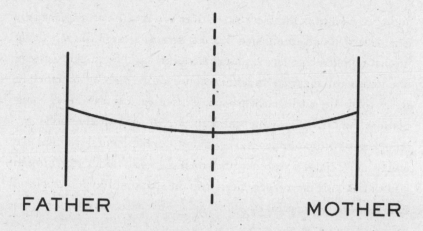

Secure attachment in the child to father and mother

Insecure attachment and fear-based holding of self

This kind of early trauma generally inhibits development and may show itself downstream as a fixation tendency, such as a vulnerability to addiction or to compulsive repetition. But because the constricted self-holding of a traumatized child replaces the secure holding of healthy parents, which is absent, it is actually an elegant adaptive function. It permits survival. Although a child with ongoing constriction may experience developmental injury, the nervous system is using a kind of volume-reduction utility, quieting the hyperarousal and overload of trauma-based fear so that a certain level of coherence can be established and life may continue. The child can survive her fear and trauma.

Once a young child becomes strong enough, having healthfully established the first level of interior structure through the repetition of the individuation loop, she can begin to say, "No!" At this stage, she feels more curiosity, less fear, and a greater desire to resist. In order to resist, a sufficiently solid structure must have been built throughout her early development to support her, just as a solid surface is needed beneath our feet in order to jump. For a period of time, young children play at resisting by saying no in order to feel their power—the solidity of the structure their development has created beneath them. This process—from dependence to independence to interdependence—occurs throughout the whole of development and informs every life function.

When developmental trauma (e.g., abuse or neglect) occurs at an early stage, the emotional injury may result in an unseen fixation on resistance to the other, even into adult relationships. With intimate partners, the traumatized person may exhibit an unconscious pattern of avoidance or a habit of creating emotional distance—a tendency that he or she may even conflate with freedom or personal strength.

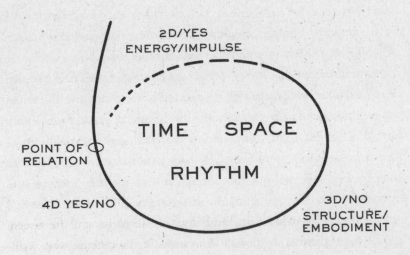

Individuation loop with phases

But when healthy caregiving takes place, children develop toward a sense of relation where yes and no become equally valid choices: "I am related to my environment, and I can say yes or no freely." A new stage of development arises in the loop, and with it, a new sense of space in relation.

SPACE-TIME-RHYTHM

Out of each layer of individuation, another layer of developmental soil emerges. This inner geography is the rich ground, or base, upon which we continue to safely grow new structures in consciousness.

As we grow, a sense of space, time, and rhythm (S-T-R) develops. Each time we crawl away from our mothers, our senses of exterior space and orientation in location grow. As the process continues, our sense of duration or time develops, orienting with our body's emotions and thoughts. Every time we move outward, following the impulse of curiosity and freedom, and then move back in again, returning to the safety of our mother's arms when we feel fear or uncertainty, we are following the looping rhythm of life itself—outward toward autonomy, inward toward connection. Indeed, time, space, and rhythm are the fundamental building blocks of perception, allowing us to orient to our physical world, to ourselves, and to other people.

As we discussed in chapter 1, this screen of perception is like the broad canvas on which a movie is projected inside a cinema. The brain is the projector, fluidly modulating the influx of perceptions, both internal (thoughts, emotions, and sensations) and external (inputs relayed from our environment). When traumatized, our projector becomes damaged; we lose the capacity to fluidly bridge interior and exterior perceptions and accurately integrate them upon the screen. A delay or lack of syncing (time and rhythm) develops and the screen itself (space) distorts, as though the canvas in the cinema were wrinkled, or the film strip suddenly off-balance.

Trauma distorts our perception of reality, leaving us unable to see the world as it is. It reduces the "bandwidth" of our perceptive capacities and warps our experience of space-time.

S-T-R is the basis of reality perception. The coherence between the three elements permits the flow of life. Being "in the flow" is a testament to their alignment, as is the experience of synchronicities or the feeling of being in the right place at the right time. With conscious practice, such experiences can become the norm. However, when we feel out of sync, unlucky, or accident-prone, we are experiencing a lack of coherence in S-T-R.

Trauma, most of all, creates a discontinuity in S-T-R, though we may only come to recognize the distortions of perception it leaves through symptoms and irritations, especially those felt in relationships with others.

When physical needs are met and healthy caregiving is established, a child grows naturally. But whenever there is distress, disease, neglect, or trauma that cannot be appropriately processed and integrated, a disruption will occur in the subtle field, manifesting either as a site of constriction and rigidity or of chaos and overexcitation. A precise energetic signature is captured in the individuation loop at the exact place in the body and at the exact time it was initiated. That is to say that energetically speaking, the imprint of any trauma is captured and contained within the subtle nervous system at its nonlocal cosmic address. All of the energy and information that was present at the moment of the original trauma was frozen and stored in the body, to be dealt with at a later time. This happens because, in that moment, all of the body's resources are being used to meet survival needs. However, the trauma information still exists at the very point in the personal field at which it occurred, and we refer to this location as its cosmic address.

As we have seen, evolution, and thus development, is a process of differentiation and integration. A very young child perceives his mother as an extension of himself. He is undifferentiated. But as the infant develops into a toddler, a healthy process of separation or individuation occurs; he begins to recognize that he and his mother are two, not one. Later, as he grows into a healthy adolescent/young adult, he begins differentiating his own needs and desires from his parents' and will long to prepare for a life outside the family home.

This process becomes broken or significantly delayed for the child of traumatized parents. Perhaps the mother will not allow her baby to begin to separate from her in a healthy way, thus interrupting early individuation. Because the mother's fear is overwhelming, she prevents the child's natural desire to crawl and explore her world, resulting in frustration, stagnation, and distancing. Or she neglects the child's need for connection and coregulation, leaving the child in a state of perpetual uncertainty and anxiety. If such patterns continue to occur during early development, the child's natural process of differentiation will be inhibited.

When an infant is developing in a healthy container, there is a field of resonance between mother and child. There is a subtle field of call-and-response, and where the field is open, there is coherence. Like a signal between wireless devices, a kind of *ping* goes out and is received by a corresponding *pong*. It is a subtle music that plays between mother and child at all times.

These energy impulses create a wavefield, and that field's degree of coherence informs the quality of the developing neural connections within the infant's brain. But where there is a lack of resonance within the mother or father as a result of their own trauma, there may be insufficient coherence between parent and child, and if significant, a *trauma field* is generated. The mother's signals, her subtle *ping*s, now clanging and incoherent, disappear as if into a roll of cotton; there is no healthy emotional call-and-response, no music. Where the healthy child feels connection and belonging, the traumatized child experiences disconnection and dislocation. His emotional needs have gone unmet, and his caregivers' emotions have been frightening, confusing, or absent. Where he should be experiencing growth in connection to himself and his world, he encounters incoherence and numbness instead.

For the developing child, a trauma field often prevents the adequate wiring of exteriors and interiors—impacting the developing brain and nervous system, as well as the child's internal self-sense and consciousness. The weaving of the individuation loop is impeded, creating blocks, disruptions, and potential defects. When this occurs, there is insufficient space and energy for the next loop in the process to complete, which could result in undeveloped neural pathways in the brain, for example, or undeveloped internal structures, such as an inability to think about how others see things (by the appropriate age).

The energy of a developing child is always anchored in the body of her parent or primary caregiver. Their nervous systems are distinctly tethered, and as the mother peers into the face of her baby—smiling and cooing and beaming—their systems begin to mirror and align, rooting to one another in tandem. By gazing into her child's eyes with loving attention and care, the child's interior space is deepened and expanded, so that new structures have room to grow. In this way and many more, a child looks to the parent or primary caregiver as her North Star, as that most powerful source by which she navigates.

But if the parent's nervous system is either hyperreactive or shut down as a result of their own trauma, they will make an unstable anchor. The growing child will lack adequate orientation and may feel himself at times as an astronaut adrift. As he grows, he becomes isolated within a body that lacks access to its own emotions and reflects his traumatized inheritance, either hyperaroused and dysregulated or frozen and anesthetized. When we see him later as an adult, we are likely to find a man who is dislocated and ungrounded, unable to participate fully in the cocreative needs of his own higher potential or the greater collective venture of sculpting world forms. These impulses that *ping* from his soul have also been lodged in cotton.

The healthy wiring of the individuation loop creates clarity and crispness. It shapes a kind of acoustic space for the music between mother and child and for the symphony between child and world to manifest.

Developmental trauma hinders the capacity for manifestation. It deposits an isolation layer in the base and overwrites a developing life—indeed, whole generational lines—with fear and tension where there should otherwise be love and freedom, becoming and belonging, freedom and intimacy. But even the densest cotton layers can be clarified and sharpened. There is a way that the darkest, most terrible fear and tension and isolation—even where they have been laid brick by brick into the foundation stones—can be unmade. Inherited and collective traumas, too, can be healed and integrated. We have come to consider all of this and more.

RELATIONAL INTELLIGENCE

Trauma breaks relation. Within a person, trauma fractures relation to the self and sabotages connection to the other. At the scale of the collective, traumatic disrelation is cultural and generational; it is a feedback loop.

Imagine two trains running at different speeds on parallel tracks. Passengers on both trains are at the windows, trying desperately to communicate, but one train is speeding up or slowing down. The trains are noisy and the sky is cluttered with fog and smoke. Only briefly are the trains traveling at the same pace, and while the passengers at opposite windows can see and hear one another, they capture only snippets of what the other is saying. While this may seem like a comedy of errors, it rather accurately describes the inadequate nature of communication and connection in a world where trauma and disrelation is allowed to remain unprocessed and unintegrated.

Now, if two parallel trains were to run in the same direction, at the same speed, passengers could open their windows and engage in a lovely chat, perhaps even a cup of tea. For understanding, connection, and accurate communication to occur, there must exist attunement and presence—within and across trains, self and other.

When you observe family, friends, colleagues, or even strangers, you may notice how people sit in their energy. Are they connected and grounded? Are you able to notice an energetic solidity at their base? And what do you notice about the subtle qualities at the base of someone who may be dysregulated or somehow expressing shadow? What about someone who has experienced trauma? If we're observant, we notice that most of us are not resting fully at our base.

If we are open, we may be able to detect certain imprints within the inner architecture of a person, noticing where it feels more contracted or uplifted, more activated or numbed, and so on. If we remain grounded and open in whole-body awareness, we can sense into someone (or into a group, a community, or possibly into a much larger collective) and notice when or where they have disconnected from their bodies, emotions, or environment.

It is important to notice the quality and degree of disembodiment in ourselves and in our culture. Disembodiment expresses clearly the traumatic disrelation at the collective scale and manifests both direct and systemic consequences. Even the climate crisis is a dire manifestation of collective trauma; we are disconnected from nature itself.

If, as a child, I was beaten and terrorized by my caregivers, I would have protected myself by contracting, becoming distant, avoidant, and withdrawn. I may have shut down any desire to assert my voice or needs, and this contraction would have become an engrained habit. Then, as an adult, wherever I encountered conflict, I may instinctively and unconsciously resort to those survival habits. However, I would not be contracting *in the present moment*, I would be contracting *in the past*. I would return to the space of disembodiment created within my three-year-old self, which I continued to host and carry forward—unexamined and undigested.

This quality might live quietly within me for years, but somewhere down the line, life would trigger my contraction. Something would happen, perhaps a small thing, and I would feel my throat tighten or a hot stone sink in my gut. My heart might feel as if it were closing. But the true source would not be the present moment experience; it would be that painful experience from my long ago past.

We should perhaps reflect again here on van der Kolk's wisdom when he said that trauma is not a story about what happened to you; it is a substance residing within you.

Of course, a three-year-old's survival responses in the face of abuse are an expression of the intelligence of the nervous system and of the enduring elegance of human will. Yet, if the habits of contraction, withdrawal, and disembodiment are allowed to continue into adulthood, their powers for survival fail. But through the restoration of embodiment, presence, and relation, even a person grown old in suffering can heal.

STRENGTHENING ATTUNEMENT

A healthy nervous system allows us to attune to others, to create a mutual field of experience *with* others. To be fully attuned means that we are able and available to host within us the energy, mind, and emotions of another; to allow the other to feel *felt* by us.

Attunement is a skill requiring practice. To attune well, I need to train my nervous system to become more keenly receptive to energy. In addition, I must make it a practice to consciously rest in inner space. It is important to understand that I will be unable to rest fully in space—in the present—if my nervous system is still digesting my past. (I can't listen well to you at dinner if part of me is still processing whatever occurred at lunch.)

There is an important distinction between listening and attunement. I may be able to hear and cognitively process everything you share with me in an important conversation, but unless I have strengthened the space or developed consciousness structures (such as those facilitating empathy), I may be unable to receive you wholly or holistically. My nervous system needs to be free for this work. The more past I carry into the present, the less available I am for attunement, and the more likely I will be to project my interior condition onto you. This is, at least in part, a matter of efficiency, since my nervous system is at a reduced capacity and unable to receive some of your transmission.

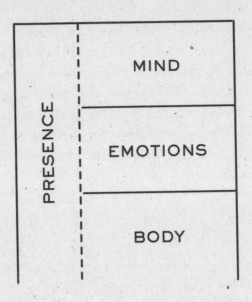

Three-sync process. The three-sync process occurs when,
through a state of presence, we consciously bring the
mind, body, and emotions into coherence.

INTERIOR HYGIENE

The concept of attunement illustrates the importance of creating the time
to digest our experiences, processing past material so we can be fully available in the space of present. It is vital to enact a regular interior hygiene
practice, taking time to contemplate, walk, or simply sit with and digest
our experiences and stresses. This practice is an act of clearing and allows
us the time and space to attune fully to others and to ourselves. Think of it
as the filtering of the nervous system and its subtle energy fields of relation.
In an intimate relationship, we might employ a mutual interior hygiene
practice, a time in which we care for the relational space itself.

This filtering is especially vital for therapists and for large group
facilitators. In order to be available to attune to collective fields, it is a
required process. Those who choose to work directly with large groups
in the service of collective trauma must be able to access cultural or
ancestral material. This content is like a ghost in the room; it is invisible yet heavily felt. In order to connect, a facilitator needs to be highly

available, deeply present—totally attuned. It requires that one monitor their inner state of presence, like a gauge or battery, and notice, moment to moment, when the nervous system is open and spacious in whole-body awareness. This is the capacity to attune to another person, to the group, to the collective past. But if the facilitator becomes busy, to whatever degree, with processing anything in their personal past, attunement is lost, and only a partial perception of the current moment can be achieved.

INTERSUBJECTIVE AWARENESS AND COREGULATION

At the subtle level, an infant's energy is aligned and anchored to his mother. His delicate, developing nervous system mirrors his mother's intricate, intelligent one. He is entirely plugged in. This is the software and hardware of human-to-human connection; it is the motherboard, the data, and the code. But this connection is not limited to mother and child. Just as an IT technician can remotely access your computer's desktop, hosting inside her machine whatever is available to you on your own screen, your nervous system continues to employ its subtle powers of coregulation.

To the extent that you consciously foster attunement and actively develop your capacity for personal and intersubjective space, you will grow this powerful form of mutual, multidimensional vision/relation. With this new competency, you can learn to play the subtle energies of your own nervous system like a piano, and from there, begin to mindfully arrange a symphony that sings within the wavefield between you and another. In fact, it is possible to learn to use our own nervous system capacities for relaxation and the regulation of stress in order to energetically support another person in doing the same. Think of it as similar to the way we can help a child who has become overexcited and is speaking loudly and rapidly. In that instance, we can often help the child to slow down and speak more quietly simply by doing so ourselves; an unconscious mirroring tends to happen. This is a function of coregulation.

HOW ATTUNEMENT SUPPORTS NUCLEAR PEACE

JULIE'S INTERVIEW WITH DR. SCILLA ELWORTHY

When Scilla Elworthy was just eleven years old, her four older brothers taught her how to fire a shotgun. Thinking herself "tremendously clever," she ventured off into the woods alone and did something she knew to be taboo. Pointing her weapon high into a tree, young Scilla aimed at a bird's nest and pulled the trigger.

"Down on my head came pieces of eggshell, the embryos of baby chicks, and the feathers of the mother bird," says Elworthy. Shocked by the evidence of the violence she'd committed, she took the weapon home and never touched it again.

In the decades following, Elworthy would become a passionate activist, devoted peacebuilder, notable advisor in international conflict resolutions, founder of multiple nongovernmental organizations and peacebuilding initiatives, and a three-time nominee of the Nobel Peace Prize. She credits that terrible decision in the woods beneath a tree, flesh and feathers falling around her, as the first that would propel her toward her life's work.

The second came in the fall of the year Elworthy turned thirteen. She watched a black-and-white television as the people of Hungary, catalyzed initially by student activists, publicly protested Soviet control. As Soviet tanks charged into Budapest, mowing down the students, Elworthy watched dumbstruck. This was the Hungarian Revolution of 1956.

Utterly incensed, she packed a suitcase. As she describes it: "I told my mother, 'I'm going to Budapest!' And she said, 'You're much too young to be of any help, but if you'll just unpack, I will see to it that you receive training.'" And her mother kept her word.

"At sixteen, she sent me off to work in a holiday camp for Auschwitz survivors," says Elworthy. "I listened to their stories for hours." Next, she attended university at Trinity College, Dublin, where she studied the plight of refugees. Afterward, Elworthy worked in refugee camps in France and Algeria, just after the Algerian War of Independence. From there, the young activist boarded a cargo vessel in Bordeaux, France, and traveled around the western coast of Africa, landing finally in the Republic of the Congo (today, the Democratic Republic of the Congo). The beleaguered Central African nation was in the middle of a series of violent civil wars collectively known as the Congo Crisis.

By age twenty-one, Elworthy had worked with Vietnamese refugees, in an Algerian war orphanage, and in the heart of an active war zone in the Congo. "I'd seen a fair share of human violence by then," she says, "and its consequences, the human debris." But rather than being daunted, she describes these experiences as a motivating force. They were "the fire that ignited my soul," she says.

And then her daughter was born, and the young mother faced another kind of inferno: she contracted viral encephalitis. It left her in a coma for two weeks. The disease carried a significant risk of death in that part of Africa at the time, and although she survived, it took six years for her brain and body to heal. In the stillness created by medical trauma and a long recovery, two questions were brought repeatedly to the foreground of her consciousness: *Who am I?* and *Why am I here?*

By 1982, Elworthy appears to have discovered an answer: she was a peacebuilder. She turned the full focus of her attention to the problem of nuclear weapons.

"I was furious that decisions on nuclear weapons were being made with no discussion in parliament," says Elworthy. "Parliament was simply informed when a decision had been made. I thought that was a terrible betrayal of democracy, not least because many of us in Britain might have voted against it had we been given a chance." She took her feelings to the streets.

"I attended marches; I demonstrated," she says. In March of '82, she took her little girl along to the first Greenham Common Women's Peace Camp protests in Berkshire, England, where they linked hands to create a human chain around the American Air Force base. "There were hundreds of us around this military base," she says. "We were thirteen kilometers long!"

Soon afterward, she moved to New York and began work with the United Nations.

"I was working with the UN when a huge conference on nuclear disarmament was convened," she says. "But after six weeks, it had reached *no* conclusions, no results. And I was devastated. I was riding a tram down Broadway, hanging onto the strap, when a voice in my head said, 'You're talking to the wrong people, Scilla. The United Nations cannot solve this problem. You have to find the people who really make the decisions.'"

And those people, she discovered, were the ones who design, manufacture, and sell nuclear warheads, missiles, aircraft, and technology. In short: the arms industry. Central to this are intelligence officials who argue a rationale for the use of nuclear weapons technologies, civil servants who sign the checks for their procurement, and lastly, politicians.

"So, I got on a plane home and founded the Oxford Research Group [ORG], 'round my kitchen table. At that stage, none of us knew anything about the system, but four years later we'd produced our first book." Complete with diagrams, *How*

Nuclear Weapons Decisions Are Made hit bookshelves in 1988, the first of dozens of works authored or edited by Dr. Elworthy.

Her central epiphany was in realizing that protest was not enough. "You must go and find the people who actually make the decisions and talk directly with them," she says. Thus, the ORG team did something unprecedented: they reached out to the world's nuclear decision-makers and invited them to convene under the radar for face-to-face talks with their counterparts from other nations and with their critics—the people who stood on the opposing side of the nuclear weapons debate.

It shocked her to discover that these parties had never met. Still, the arms industry players initially declined. "We had to prove to them there would be no press, no communiqués, no media," says Elworthy. It took time, but because she had interviewed many of the central players during her doctoral work, invitees eventually began to accept. "They began to realize that we were not hostile," she says. "We just wanted to understand, and to open a dialogue."

It was a long process, but ORG ultimately succeeded in convening the first-ever meeting between nuclear arms decision-makers and their critics. And something incredible happened.

The ORG had been established in sympathy with Quaker values, as Elworthy had personally benefited from the meditation practice she'd first learned from the Quakers. "I realized the value of that calming, that quietening of the psyche and the body," she says. With this in mind, she invited five experienced meditators to come to that first critical meeting, held just outside Oxford, where they would sit in meditation in the library, directly beneath the meeting room.

"These Elders were willing to sit in meditation for the full two-and-a-half days," says Elworthy. "I didn't know exactly what would happen, but on the second day, a man representing the US State Department came up to me at the lunch break. He said, 'You know, this is a very special room we're meeting in.' And I said, 'Yes, it is. It was built in 1360.' And he said, 'No, I mean that it is *very* special—there is something coming up through the *floorboards*.'"

Indeed, there was.

Dr. Elworthy explained to the State Department official that there were people meditating below them, holding the intention that the meeting members would be able to relate to one another as human beings. "He looked at me as if I were mad," she says, laughing. She told him he was welcome to ask any of the seniors who were about to serve his lunch, because they were the very meditators lending their quiet support.

"Off he went," says Elworthy. When the man found her later, the look he gave her said it all. "And just like that, our work began."

The meeting room that week was comprised of nearly all men, but they included all sides: military leaders and delegates from Russia, the United States, and the United Kingdom; scientists from Los Alamos; defense contractors and nuclear arms experts; and academics, Greenpeace activists, and Quaker peacebuilders. Over the course of their discussions, something curious happened. They started to see each other as people, to share personal stories. "They ended up showing pictures of their families to one another," says Elworthy, "and inviting each other to their homes when they were next in town, that kind of thing. It was quite wonderful. And it was unheard of at the time."

Elworthy and the ORG had done something simple, yet profound. They had taught attendees that instead of confronting, they could create connection, which is critical to peacebuilding. "We created a safe-enough environment for members to loosen their ties and take off their jackets and begin to see each other."

"We took seven delegations to China, which was unheard of at the time," says Elworthy. "We brought in India and Pakistan when they tested nuclear weapons." And their award-winning model has continued to work.

After twenty-one years, Dr. Elworthy handed ORG over to skilled and passionate hands and moved on to investigate what was happening at the grassroots level. "I had a feeling, a hunch, that at the local level," she says, "there were people working in areas of conflict, *hot* conflict, who were effectively preventing people from being killed."

A researcher was sent into the field to do a year-long investigation, at the end of which he was able to identify 350 grassroots peacekeeping initiatives worldwide. "All of these were reliable and replicable," says Elworthy. "They were producing results." On the basis of their findings, she cofounded Peace Direct with Carolyn Hayman, OBE. "Peace Direct has now located 1,700 local peace initiatives all over the world, lending support, capacity building, conflict prevention skills, and small amounts of money," she says.

Since then, these and other strategies and hard-won wisdom have gone into the creation of Rising Women Rising World, FemmeQ, and The Elders. For these initiatives and more, an eleven-year-old child's humbling lesson about violence—and the human power to either destroy or preserve life—has proved more than instructive; it has been visionary.

ROLE OF CONTEMPLATIVE
PRACTICE IN HEALING

When we sit in the practice of meditation, we prepare ourselves to more deeply and authentically anchor to what is available to us in order to make conscious that which has become *un*-available to us. Such practices deepen our capacity for presence, open and expand our sense of interior space, and assist in the wiring of structure.

For instance, if I'm feeling at ease and stress-free, and I find myself in a comfortable place—say, a quiet garden or near a forest stream—I may be able to sit and tune in to my external surroundings, quietly perceiving everything around me in clear detail. As I close my eyes and focus inward, I drop into a feeling of stillness, an expanded sense of inner spaciousness. I simply rest in space. I feel clear and present, able to fade in and out between my external and internal domains with relative ease.

However, if I'm mired by undigested stress—or if I experience a trauma—my capacity to bring clear, mindful witness to myself, to others, and to my world will be dampened and distorted. My practiced capacity to rest in a state of contemplative witness will be compromised, and I will feel a sense of constriction, unable to move between my interior and exterior perceptions. All of my energy and attention will be required to focus on combatting the stress and ensuring that my blood sugar, heart rate, lungs, and limbs are operating at optimum capacity. Even when the stress or immediate danger has passed, my nervous system will require time to process the adrenaline and cortisol surge, and my mind may need an extended cooling-off period of rest before I can reenter the world as I had been.

Space is a conscious experience that is lost, however temporarily, in experiences of trauma. When this occurs, we become identified with the activity of the moment, losing the expanded sense of selfhood we may have acquired through conscious practice. For a period of time, we might become stuck in the experience of trauma, alienated from ourselves and from our Source. But if, while enduring post-traumatic symptoms, we actively engage in contemplative practice, we can strengthen our capacity to hold, integrate, and heal the experience.

Contemplative practices such as meditation, mindfulness, presencing, yoga, or centering prayer can help us to become aware of the effects of trauma, which include dissociation, suppression, and disconnection. Otherwise, we overidentify with our dissociation, consciousness shrinks, and we remain stuck repeating the ancient stress responses of hyperarousal or numbness.

But if we turn to contemplative practice, however well-meaning, to seek the bliss of higher states or a detached numbness, we may find that we're spiritually bypassing the work required by trauma. True healing requires us to be more available to ourselves, more willing to feel and reside with the authentic emotions presented by our experience, not less. By engaging in a spiritual practice without bypassing, we develop and strengthen our interior resources—not merely to cope with the effects of trauma but to thrive as a result, to integrate and transcend. In turn, we deepen our connection to our higher self, to our soul. A sense of presence and inner space is developed, allowing us the power to witness our internal process and more fully digest our lives.

THE PRINCIPLE OF AFTERTIME

Whenever we are unable to be fully present because a vital part of us is still processing an earlier event (such as an argument with a loved one), the time we spend dislocated from the present and replaying the past experience can be expressed as "aftertime." In short, aftertime refers to the time required to integrate any experience that was left undigested when it originally occurred.

A collective experience of trauma such as the Holocaust may remain unprocessed for many generations and thus cannot be said to exist solely in the past, since the aftertime created by this atrocity remains heavy in our world even today. In aftertime, we project the past onto tomorrow, so that our future is not one of innovation or higher development but rather an attempt to integrate what has already occurred. An authentic, innovative future emerges out of integration, freeing a higher version of ourselves to meet us in the present.

It is as though we are driving down the highway and every five miles we see a new signpost that says "yesterday." Life attempts to detox itself of the unintegrated past, which often surfaces as unexplained physical sensations (such as headaches, bowel distress, or muscle tension), difficult emotions (fear, worry, and anxiety), and repetitive thoughts that have little place in the present moment. Fear and indecision that is rooted in the unconscious past may block our actions in the present. When this occurs, especially where trauma plays a role, our sense of S-T-R is inhibited, and our inner perception of outer reality becomes skewed.

In this way, trauma injures not just relation but perception, causing us to see our world with greater distortion. This is important to understand, because although most of us believe we see our world accurately, very often we see only a part of it and even that view is "through a glass, darkly." Seeing through the filter of the past is a recipe for conflict. In order to perceive ourselves and our world more clearly, we require resonance and relation with others, just as every infant needs the mother's empathy and attunement in order to begin to see and know its world space.

Similar space-time distortions exist not just for individuals but for cultures. As cultural traumas occur and accrue, distortions in societal perceptions are amplified. The resulting misapprehensions and misperceptions become cultural agreements: limiting or harmful stereotypes, a belief that this is "just the way things are," or other unconscious codes, values, and language built into a society as a result of collective distortions.

Any one of these distortions generates a literal desynchronization in the flow of space-time. At the collective level, this means we are unable to create a coherent *we-space* or to find ourselves in synch with others who are collaborating as one. At the individual level, we may rarely be in the right space at the right time and are unable to access creative flow states. Our vital inner organizing principle is offline, unable to receive necessary energy and information.

EXPLORING THE NATURE OF SUFFERING

When we consider human suffering, we may distinguish between explicit (i.e., direct) and implicit (i.e., residual) harm or distress. A criminal act of violence committed today creates explicit or direct suffering in the target or victim, while the impact of this trauma may create implicit or residual effects of suffering over time—not just in the victim, but if left unintegrated and unhealed, within his or her community and progeny. Explicit traumas may injure the current function and ongoing development of individuals, while the enduring and implicit effects of trauma *across* individuals generate a vibration of suffering within a culture. This tapestry becomes a wavefield of collective trauma, and every human culture expresses pockets of generational trauma. Within these pockets, the culture unconsciously expresses the trapped memories and sensations of its karmic past.

As we discussed in chapter 1, the past is unresolved content; it is whatever story or energy that has been denied and disowned. Given this, there is a lack of clarity surrounding implicit trauma. As Dr. Judith Herman wrote in the Introduction to her groundbreaking work *Trauma and Recovery*:

> *The ordinary response to atrocities is to banish them from consciousness. Certain violations of the social compact are too terrible to utter aloud: this is the meaning of the word* unspeakable.
>
> *Atrocities, however, refuse to be buried. Equally as powerful as the desire to deny atrocities is the conviction that denial does not work. Folk wisdom is filled with ghosts who refuse to rest in their graves until their stories are told. Murder will out. Remembering and telling the truth about terrible events are prerequisites both for the restoration of the social order and for the healing of individual victims.*
>
> *The conflict between the will to deny horrible events and the will to proclaim them aloud is the central dialectic of psychological trauma. People who have survived atrocities often tell their stories in a highly emotional, contradictory, and fragmented manner, which undermines their credibility*

and thereby serves the twin imperatives of truth-telling and secrecy. When the truth is finally recognized, survivors can begin their recovery. But far too often secrecy prevails, and the story of the traumatic event surfaces not as a verbal narrative but as a symptom.[2]

Unspoken suffering does not always disappear at the moment of death; it can be passed on. Over time, these ghosts become generational habits and live again and again in experiences such as cultural poverty, the secret violence visited upon daughters, or in the denial of the emotional life of sons. These expressions are the legacy of our shared traumas, our collective karma. Our denied, unprocessed, unintegrated past.

In a deeper sense, a great deal of human suffering exists because of the denial of the past and an inability to acknowledge and integrate it. But when the decision is made to finally look at and feel the past, everything shifts. For example, if I or my ancestors have been suppressing grief, and this deep sadness is allowed to come forward so that I begin to authentically *feel* it, it will be painful, yes, and yet the more I allow its honest expression, I will almost certainly also experience a release. And if I continue to make this process a conscious practice, I have begun the work of healing integration.

As I choose to step out of my emotional repetition process about experiences in my past or those I project onto some imagined future, clarity is restored. As I integrate trauma and shadow content, I become more fully available to the present and more alive to the authentic, emerging future.

Nearly every effect of trauma, whether individual or collective, can be understood as an intelligent evolutionary response: as both an impulse of survival and an opportunity for conscious integration. As we examine the past in search of answers and healing, we can choose to reenvision and reframe our meanings around suffering, offering our demons the opportunity to be integrated as allies in a new understanding of our world.

4

THE ARCHITECTURE OF COLLECTIVE TRAUMA

History, despite its wrenching pain, cannot be unlived,
but if faced with courage, need not be lived again.

Maya Angelou
New York Times, January 21, 1993

Human suffering anywhere, concerns
men and women everywhere.

Elie Wiesel
Night

The following events are true.[1] They report on a gruesome piece of America's history, occurring over only one week, in just one rural and isolated place, to a relatively small number of people, though the inhumanity captured in their details accurately depicts what was indeed a much greater historical tragedy.

What follows will not be easy to read. I urge you to stay present, noticing any feelings, thoughts, or sensations you may experience as you proceed.

The circumstances occurred in southernmost Georgia, somewhere along a small tributary known as the Little River. The year was 1918, fifty-three years after the nation's Civil War had ended and slavery had been abolished, ratified by the Thirteenth Amendment to the United States Constitution.

Despite their legal status as free and rightful citizens, black Americans living or traveling in the Southern states found themselves subject to a powerful set of discriminatory, punitive, and often violent practices enshrined into laws known as Jim Crow.[2] For the better part of a century, these laws enforced racial segregation and resulted in generations of economic, legal, educational, and social inequality. This was possible due to fierce resentments within a powerful white majority, angered by its defeat in the war. Using the authority of all available institutions—the law, the church, the schools, and the press—a fierce new regime of white supremacy mobilized to power. It used Christian identity as its ballast, outrage politics to fuel its engine, and a relentless campaign of racial terrorism and violence as its modus operandi.

Hayes and Mary Turner were a young couple living in Brooks County in 1918. They worked for a local white planter named Hampton Smith, a man with a fierce reputation for abusing his workers. In fact, Smith had recently beaten Mary, after which her husband had confronted and allegedly threatened him. For this, Turner was sentenced to hard labor on a chain gang. After his release, he returned to work alongside his wife on Hampton Smith's plantation, perhaps because he lacked any other option.

Reports of Smith's rampant abuses had likely contributed to a labor shortage on his farm. To procure more workers cheaply, he utilized a system known as peonage, the practice of "debt slavery."[3] Peonage had been outlawed by Congress in 1867, though its practice continued in the South through the 1940s, sweeping countless black men into various forms of involuntary servitude. The most abusive of these occurred in an act of mutuality between local business owners and area planters together with state and local law enforcement. In this system, area blacks were frequently arrested by police on minor or trumped-up charges. When they could not pay their mounting fines, businessmen stepped in, paying off the court fees and acquiring the rights to the men as convict laborers.[4] The men were then forced to work without compensation until their debt had been repaid, though all too often, those debts grew higher and higher, and the laborers went unpaid and unreleased. In this way, along with a growing system of mass incarceration, the practice very much like slavery continued on unchecked.

Around the time that Hayes Turner had been released from his sentence and returned to work, another young black man, Sidney Johnson, eighteen years old, was arrested for the crime of "playing dice." He quickly found himself released into the custody of Hampton Smith, who paid off Johnson's thirty-dollar fine and conscripted him into peonage.

In the teenager's short time working under Smith, he was beaten severely on multiple occasions—his final beating was for the sin of requiring a sick day.

On May 16, using a gun he allegedly stole from his employer, Sidney Johnson is said to have fired through a window, killing Hampton Smith in his home. News of the shooting spread quickly and with it, a rumor that several dissatisfied black laborers had conspired to murder Hampton Smith; Sidney Johnson had only been the trigger man.

This incited outrage in area whites, who gathered a lynch mob. A weeklong manhunt ensued, fueled by booze and bloodlust. Their numbers swelled to two hundred at one point, and at the end of their campaign of terror, at least thirteen people had been brutally and publicly murdered. Hundreds of black Georgians were said to have fled the area for their lives.

The sheriff had rearrested Hayes Turner immediately following news of Hampton Smith's death. His history with the planter made him a suspect in the alleged conspiracy. When the mob learned his location, forty men descended on the jail, easily extracting him from custody. The men comprising the mob were said to be known to the sheriff.

On the morning of Saturday, May 18, Mr. Turner was taken from his cell by force and dragged to a nearby intersection. In full view of the public, a husband, father, and American citizen was lynched. His body remained hanging at the intersection for two days.

Horrified by her husband's murder, Mary Turner is said to have decried the injustice, publicly denying her husband had been connected to their employer's killing. She may have stated that if she knew the responsible parties, she would report them to police.[5]

The mob turned on her, and though she fled in terror, she was quickly captured.

Mary Turner was twenty-one years old and eight months pregnant when the horde dragged her to Folsom Bridge. They bound her ankles and hung the young mother-to-be upside down from a tree. She was still living when her clothing was doused in motor oil and gasoline and set on fire.

When her clothes had burned away, a man stepped forward with a knife, one reportedly used to butcher hogs. Without feeling, he split open her abdomen and tossed Mary's unborn child to the ground. The tiny body was repeatedly crushed beneath his boot.

In a macabre finale, the drunken crowd fired their weapons repeatedly into Mary's lifeless body before she and her child were buried, finally, in a shallow grave marked only by a whiskey bottle.

On the evening of Hampton Smith's murder, Sidney Johnson had reportedly fled the scene and gone into hiding. The boy was eventually tracked down by the mob where he died in a shootout. Once he was dead, his genitals were removed and hung from his neck. His body was then dragged behind a truck for sixteen miles, to whoops and cheers.

Despite the governor's unctuous assurances to the black community, no one was ever arrested or charged in association with what had occurred during the weeklong murder spree.

Most of what we know about these events comes from the painstaking reporting of Walter White, who in 1918 was an investigator for the National Association for the Advancement of Colored People, and who later went on to lead the organization. In Baltimore, Maryland, there is a largely unknown place called the National Great Blacks in Wax

Museum, founded in 1983 by Dr. Joanne Martin and her husband, Elmer. The museum hosts a life-sized exhibit, depicting in gruesome detail the lynching deaths of Hayes and Mary Turner.

Posted beside the exhibit is a sign that reads, "Walter White, describing the lynching of Mary Turner and her husband Hayes Turner, depicted in this scene, said that it was too horrible to describe the mob taking the time to sew two cats in Mrs. Turner's stomach and making bets as to which one would climb out first."[6]

There are other signs in the museum, such as "Identify with the victims and martyrs and never forget them. But do not get bitter or despondent over what they endured."[7]

Some would argue that to read these details, much less to see them in life-sized, full-color 3D wax subjects, was to witness a kind of "secondary trauma" (a term generally used to denote the emotional distress experienced by an individual when hearing the traumatic narrative of a firsthand survivor). Depending on our capacity for resilience, this may well be true. But where we do have resilience, *voluntary shared witness* may be an important part of healing for the traumatized.

Whether individual or collective, trauma fragments and fractures. It disowns and silences. It creates denial and forgetting. To assist in its repair, we must choose to acknowledge, to witness, and to thereby *feel* together, what has actually occurred, even the most horrific details we would rather close our eyes to. Because to look away—to dismiss, deny, minimize, or willfully forget—is to uphold the institutions of inequality, of inhumanity, that created them.

In *Trauma and Recovery*, Judith Herman writes,

> It is very tempting to take the side of the perpetrator. All the perpetrator asks is that the bystander do nothing. He appeals to the universal desire to see, hear, and speak no evil. The victim, on the contrary, asks the bystander to share the burden of pain. The victim demands action, engagement, and remembering.[8]

This is difficult.

And yet it may be even more difficult when we are called to examine truthfully the ways we ourselves have been perpetrators. This chapter will consider the social and cultural architecture of trauma and will ask us to look beyond victim/persecutor dynamics so we may fully witness the legacy of trauma—the way it spreads, passing down and repeating, influencing us all.

We might begin by considering the human landscape as if through a multidimensional topographical map, with overlapping borders between family, society, culture, and time. Each of these overlaps, and none are independent, just as no individual can be an island. In "Trauma in Cultural Perspective," Martin W. DeVries says that

> *PTSD requires us to focus on the life history of the individual interacting with other individuals in the context of society and culture. PTSD is thus a description of an illness process based not on the intrinsic nature of the person alone, but rather on the person's sociocultural interaction over time.*[9]

INTERGENERATIONAL TRAUMA

As we move from the individual to the collective, the first layers of group trauma we begin to discern are those of generational trauma. Art, literature, and film are historically dense with representations—rich allegories, symbolism, and coded language—meant to depict the power of dark family secrets and the hidden dimensions, unseen yet encompassing, in which unnamable forces are passed from one generation to the next.

In a general context, *intergenerational trauma* (also referred to by scholars as transgenerational, multigenerational, or cross-generational trauma) refers to the effects of serious, untreated trauma that has been experienced by one or more members of a family, group, or community and has been passed down from one generation to the next through epigenetic factors, as we will discuss.[10]

Peering through a mystical lens, we see that intergenerational trauma impacts humanity along a vertical line, and so it might also be termed "inherited or ancestral trauma." Families may transmit the effects of a trauma for many generations. Dysfunctional bonds or abusive dynamics may pass largely unquestioned and unresolved, encoding and reinforcing implicit messages into the fabric of the family identity. Children born into intergenerational trauma often inherit a legacy of poverty, risk of abuse, and vulnerabilities to mental and physical illness and may struggle to create lives of meaning or purpose.

There are many cases in which women who were themselves victims of generational childhood sexual abuse are shocked to learn their own children have been victimized. They believed they would be able to detect and prevent harm, yet, rather than heightened awareness, generational abuse had served to reinforce an atmosphere of dissociation, detachment, and silence. These intergenerational cycles of abuse are similarly observed in those who were neglected or abused as children and who go on to harm their own children as adults.

"Many traumatized people expose themselves, seemingly compulsively, to situations reminiscent of the original trauma," observes Bessel van der Kolk. "These behavioral reenactments are rarely consciously understood to be related to earlier life experiences."[11]

The voluminous research into trauma victims reveals another unfortunate pattern: Traumatized individuals often unconsciously reenact their prior victimization. In these dynamics, one may either take on the role of victim or victimizer. This pattern of unconscious reenactment, according to van der Kolk, is a major source of societal violence.[12]

HISTORICAL TRAUMA

Impacting the horizontal field is *historical trauma*. Historical trauma has been described as "a complex and collective trauma experienced over time and across generations by a group of people who share an identity, affiliation, or circumstance."[13] Thus, historical traumas are shared by many families and members of the larger cultural group. When we think of historical trauma, we think about the painful and long-lasting consequences of war, imperialism, colonization, domination, subjugation, occupation, enslavement, interventionism, and hegemony. It is a force that often proliferates as a result of cultural, political, racial, ethnic, religious, gender and/or sexual extermination, suppression, or systemic intolerance.

When the people of a particular culture or tradition have been torn from their homes and lands, when their libraries, burial places, religious centers, or sacred sites have been desecrated or denied them, when their language, rituals, or customs have been banned, forbidden, or forgotten, when they and their people have been separated, humiliated, brutalized, tortured, or murdered, a traumatic wound cleaves the collective psyche—scarring both persecuted and persecutor—and will be carried and transmitted for many generations.

History is filled with untold examples of historical trauma, a number of which are listed below:

- Innumerable trials, torture, and execution of individuals—the vast majority of which were women—families, and even entire villages suspected of witchcraft

- Mass genocides, forced migrations, and cultural extermination of First Nations people, Native American tribes, and the world's many indigenous peoples

- Kidnapping, trafficking, and enslavement of African people in the Americas

- Armenian Genocide (to date, Turkey has not acknowledged the event as an official genocide.)

- Holodomor, a genocide on the Ukrainian people committed by the Soviet Union in 1932

- The Holocaust

- Nanking Massacre

- Soviet Gulags

- Atomic bombings of Hiroshima and Nagasaki by the US military

- Chinese annexation, occupation, and Sinicization of Tibet, forcing the exile of His Holiness the Fourteenth Dalai Lama and leading to ongoing human rights abuses

- Cambodian genocide carried out by the Khmer Rouge regime

- Tiananmen Square massacre

- Rwandan genocide

- Ethnic cleansing, mass rape, torture, and enslavement campaigns carried out during the Yugoslav Wars

- 9/11 terrorist attacks carried out by al-Qaeda against the United States

- Darfur genocide

- Boko Haram's 2014 mass abduction and kidnapping of 276 schoolgirls in Chibok, Nigeria

- Violent conscription of child soldiers into the Lord's Resistance Army along the borders of northern Uganda, South Sudan, Democratic Republic of the Congo, and Central African Republic, which continues today

- Rohingya, most of whom are Muslim, who have been forced by the hundreds of thousands to flee as refugees from Buddhist-majority Myanmar due to violent crackdowns and apartheid-like conditions

- The over 6,000,000 refugees of the Syrian civil war who have been forced to flee their country, abandoning homes, families, and livelihoods as a consequence of the brutality of war

- The persecution of refugees, immigrants, and Muslims, incited in part by far-right political opposition to Europe's refugee crisis and—as with American and Canadian political uprisings—in opposition to economic globalization, which necessarily opens borders and increases interaction between people and cultures

COLLECTIVE TRAUMA AND SPIRITUALITY

GABOR MATÉ, MD

It's impossible to separate personal trauma and collective trauma because the very physiology of our nervous system is created in interaction with the nervous system of other people from the moment that we're conceived. Even in utero, the emotional states of the mother have an impact on the developing nervous system of the child, including all kinds of neurochemicals, chemical messengers, synapses, and connections. These states affect how brain systems will evolve and to what degree, and this will have a lifelong impact.

A study done in the aftermath of the Six-Day War in Israel in 1967 found that women who were pregnant then were more likely to have had schizophrenic children as adults. What was happening collectively in the country was reflected in the individual neurobiology of infants in the womb, and we know this from multiple international studies. That's because our brains are really wired *together*.

Since that happens on the neurobiological level—on the level of the nervous system and in the brain—and since the nervous system affects and is connected to every other organ in the body, it also happens on a biological level throughout the body, including in all the cells and all the organs and all the systems, and so on. Therefore, it's not even possible to talk about trauma purely in individual terms.

There's also the basic fact of interconnectivity from the spiritual point of view—something that's been recognized forever, but now is being validated from a sheer scientific point of view. We are created in the image of God in that we are meant to be creators ourselves. If we don't need to reduce God to an entity small enough for our minds to contain, we can simply allow it to be a word, or part of a word, for *being*—for the creative force in the universe, as well as the organization of the universe, and the laws by which the universe runs. (The universe runs by laws.) There are many universal laws that you can detect, and they arise from your true nature and your connection. When you go against them, you create suffering for yourself and for other people.

In the North American Native Indian tradition, they talk about the Medicine Wheel, which contains the four quadrants. It's very sophisticated and points in all directions: East, North, South, West. These quadrants are representative of the body, the mind, our social relationships, and our spiritual nature. If we ignore or suffer an imbalance in any one of them, illness follows. Spirituality is not something additional; it is part and parcel of our nature. For me, spirituality has to do with connectivity—with something beyond the individual. It reveals that we are not just connected, but actually part of something much greater than anything that can be understood individually or intellectually.

With every infliction of trauma—whether on the individual level or at the collective level—there is a belief of separateness. True spirituality would be what Moses taught or what Jesus taught or what the Buddha taught or what Mohammed taught, which really is that there's only the one God. There's only the one reality. We all share it; we are all manifestations of it.

And if you actually believe that I am the manifestation, the same reality, and the same truths as other creatures, other forms, then how can you inflict suffering on me? Trauma is the antithesis of spirituality. It doesn't matter what the person who's committing the trauma believes consciously; on the *un*-conscious level, they believe in separation. If they didn't, they wouldn't traumatize anyone.

As a physician, I often see illness, even severe illness, as a powerful wake-up call. This is not universal, and unfortunately, the medical system doesn't encourage it. But I've seen people with severe life-threatening illnesses wake up. All of a sudden, they start questioning: Who am I really? What is my true nature? Sometimes even severe disasters can serve as a positive guide. Not that I would wish disaster on anyone, but once it happens, it can serve us. So, the question becomes: What does this mean and what can I learn from it?

As Socrates says, "The unexamined life is not worth living." And our biggest resource is our capacity to consciously examine ourselves. Trauma culture is designed to prevent us from examining ourselves, to keep us from that kind of consciousness. But that examination, such as we're engaged in right now, can only work because the answer is already within us. *We* are our biggest resource.

In the Native traditions, there is a greeting: "All my relations." So, when they say hello or goodbye, they say, "All my relations." The *we* is simply embedded in that tradition. In the Buddhist teaching, there are the three refuges: the Buddha, the Dharma, and the Sangha. The being of the Buddha is our own Buddha nature, our own true nature. The being of the Dharma is the law. Perhaps we call it "the Torah" or "the path." And the being of the Sangha is the *community*. We are social creatures by nature. We could not have evolved as individualists; we simply would not have survived on our own. So, being in community is embedded in our nature—and as I said in the beginning, we are wired that way. We're wired to communicate. Thus, healing needs to be social; it has to be a We-space. But in modern society there's a tension between our intrinsic We-nature and our *I*-based culture.

As soon as we evolved beyond our hunter-gatherer group-ings and began to manufacture surplus, it accumulated into wealth. When that happened is when we lost our innocence, really. We left the Garden of Eden in a certain sense. Civiliza-tion is where we see differentiation of property, and control and power and hierarchies. So, our present systems, whether on the national or global level, simply reflect a process that has been going on for at least 10,000 years.

But it's running its course. And we can now see where it's leading us. As civilization reaches its highest stages, we see the scope of the tremendous creative powers it has unlocked. It's an amazing system. But we are also seeing its highest forms for destruction. Any one of several countries—the United States, China, Russia, Israel, and probably India—could destroy the world several times over just with their own weapons. Not to mention the climate crisis. So, as we're reaching the heights of this kind of system, both cre-atively and also destructively, the question is: Which force will prevail?

Saint Paul has a famous saying from 1 Corinthians, 13:12 of the King James Bible: "For now we see through a glass, darkly." He was describing how we are looking at the world as if in a smudged mirror; we can't see clearly. He goes on to say that when we connect with God, we *will* see clearly. His idea of God was very specific, but nevertheless, he was talking about reality. It is true that when we connect with the higher reality, the mirror that we look into will be made pristine. We'll finally see ourselves clearly reflected.

IMPACTS OF COLLECTIVE TRAUMA

Dr. Maria Yellow Horse Brave Heart, PhD, originally conceptualized the model for historical trauma (HT), defining it as "cumulative emotional and psychological wounding over the life span and across generations, emanating from massive group trauma experiences." Through her research, Brave Heart identified a pattern of symptoms arising in response to historical trauma, labeled collectively as the *historical trauma response*, or HTR.[14]

The historical trauma response expressed by an afflicted community reveals what might be described as a collective PTSD, the symptoms of which may be depression or anxiety, low self-esteem, anger or aggression, psychic numbing, self-destructive or self-sabotaging behaviors (including substance misuse and addiction), suicidal ideation, difficulty recognizing or expressing emotions, and physical symptoms.[15] Sadly, the consequences of historical trauma don't end there. In the Lakota people, for example, Brave Heart and others observed high mortality rates, increased incidence of alcohol abuse, and troubling patterns of child abuse and domestic violence.

It was in the 1970s, while observing historical photographs of native people that Brave Heart first began to recognize these patterns, indicators she would soon connect to survivors of the Holocaust and their children and grandchildren. She reported feeling this recognition as a kind of spiritual awakening.[16]

In Brave Heart's model, the historical trauma response is always accompanied by a personal and collective sense of "unresolved grief" related to the original mass trauma. This unresolved grief may be observed in persons and communities as "fixated, impaired, delayed, and/or disenfranchised."[17]

Still another set of symptoms, overlapping generational trauma, is described in groups who have suffered historical trauma. In this finding, the children and grandchildren of mass trauma survivors are observed to experience higher rates of PTSD than their peers and are more vulnerable to reduced psychological health.[18]

Wherever you are in the world, generational descendants of historically traumatized communities appear startlingly similar. These communities often bear lower socioeconomic conditions and report higher stress and poorer health, such as with the descendants of Palestinians displaced during the Nakba of 1948.[19] Similar conditions are reported across studies of Canadian First Nations peoples and Native American tribal communities and in landmark studies done with Israeli and Canadian first- and second-generation Holocaust survivors.

Because historical traumas are human creations, most often occurring when one group victimizes and oppresses another, they do not end neatly or quickly. In many ways, conditions extending from the original group trauma can appear to morph over time, compounding in unpredictable ways. For example, sociologists believe the trauma of slavery upon generations of African Americans has directly contributed to a legacy of social and economic disenfranchisement, police hostility, mass incarceration, and other forms of institutional racism faced by contemporary black Americans. In many majority black communities today, the symptoms of historical trauma outlined in Brave Heart's research are clearly evidenced. However, rather than eliciting widespread understanding or compassion, their manifestations (e.g., depression, anger, alcohol/substance abuse, etc.) are still commonly used to justify racial resentments and policies of discrimination.

Still, historically oppressed groups are not the only communities to express symptoms of collective trauma. Joy DeGruy, PhD, researcher and author of *Post Traumatic Slave Syndrome: America's Legacy of Enduring Injury and Healing*, asserts that an unresolved collective trauma buries itself well beyond the disenfranchised. She describes how the legacy of slavery and the subsequent disenfranchisement of black citizens has resulted in a deep and collective denial of the past on the part of many white Americans, as well as an inability or unwillingness to acknowledge their race-based privilege.[20] This tracks with Dr. Judith Herman's insight: "Denial, repression, and dissociation operate on a social, as well as an individual level."[21]

We know that for the individual, significant post-traumatic stress may result in behaviors that are initially adaptive—for example, survival strategies such as hypervigilance. But should the same behaviors become compulsive, inflexible, or fixed, they may result in maladaptation and dysfunction—at which point they can no longer be said to benefit survival but may indeed hinder it.

It is the same for the collective symptoms of historical trauma.

Dr. DeGruy's work offers illustrative examples in this regard. Among the many traumas of slavery was the forced separation endured by families. Even when together, they were made to endure the terrible anxiety of not knowing whether or when they might be ripped apart—husbands from wives and children from their mother's arms—all at the whim of masters whose primary regard was profit, and who commonly enforced familial separations to break or destabilize bonds between slaves in order to keep them isolated, demoralized, and emotionally weakened so as to prevent rebellion or uprising.

In a desperate attempt to discourage interest or prevent the auction or direct sale of a child—and therefore what would likely be permanent separation—it became common for enslaved women to remark negatively upon their children: "This one is stupid, weak, unwilling to work."[22] To praise a child even in private would have been dangerous, as a proud or confident child was more likely to garner the attention of profiteers.

This adaptive strategy was made socially pervasive by centuries of historical terror enacted upon parents and children who were regularly and repeatedly split apart as though their personal experiences held no meaning or value, and their suffering no significance. In this way, a powerful encrypted message transmitted among the generational descendants of slavery, until, according to DeGruy, it fashioned itself into a cultural norm—one which persists today. In black communities, she explains, many parents remain reticent to give overt praise, even when they feel pride in their children and their efforts. Partly as a result of this transmission of historical trauma, DeGruy believes many black sons and daughters grow up questioning their inherent worth and value.

Further exploring the transgenerational legacy of slavery on contemporary family dynamics, her work addresses the cultural norms for discipline. Enslaved parents were often harsh disciplinarians, employing swift corporal punishments for even minor infractions, or preemptively, as a means of keeping potentially excitable children in check. This was practiced, at least in part, to keep children from the attention of overseers and masters, whose retribution would have been far harsher—or potentially lethal.

As a collective response to trauma, this strategy, too, would have been highly adaptive. Yet, as with the habit to censure and withhold praise, what had emerged as a survival strategy against unbearable social trauma endured across generations, repeatedly reinforced until it had become a cultural habit. The coded message to control and discipline children using harsh verbal or physical punishments descended the vertical arc in the century and a half since slavery was abolished, creating its own transgenerational legacy.

Today, these social habits are powerfully upheld in the cultural norms for families of African Americans, as well as by many among America's white working class, in particular those descendants of poor whites who once lived in the antebellum South. (While they were not subject to the horrors of slavery or racism, poor whites of that time and place—economically displaced, socially disaffected, and educationally deprived—were frequently targeted and imprisoned, risked being sold into peonage, and often endured severe corporal punishment, whether at the hands of authorities or forces outside the law.[23]) Indeed, among many African-descended Americans, family narratives of childhood "whippings" by well-meaning parents are commonly shared, usually with humor and pride, offering a means of connection, bonding, and community belonging.

Yet the most significant and enduring consequence of slavery upon its generational inheritors is described by DeGruy as "post-traumatic slave syndrome," the primary symptoms of which she has cited as follows:

- Lack of primary esteem, hopelessness, depression, and/or self-destructive behavior

- Doubt, distrust, suspicion, negative outlook

- Anger, aggression, or violence against self, property, or others, including members of one's own family, friends, or cultural/ethnic group

- Learned helplessness, literacy deprivation, distorted self-concept

- Marked antipathy or aversion for the members, customs, or characteristics of one's own cultural/ethnic group[24]

But it is not only the ancestral victims to a historical trauma who express patterns of psychological aversion toward their own families or communities, or who can be said to internalize their traumatizer's ideology or tactics.

In her paper "Children of Nazis: A Psychodynamic Perspective," Gertrud Hardtmann, psychoanalyst and professor emeritus at the Institute for Social Pedagogy at the Technical University in Berlin, presents investigative insights based on forty years of observations made during psychoanalytic treatment, counseling, and self-help group sessions with second- and third-generation descendants of Nazi officials and functionaries.[25] The comparative review of their psychoanalytic records revealed a striking commonality related to family dynamics and the transmission of historical traumas—as carried in the body and psyche of "perpetrator."

Again and again, the children and grandchildren of Nazis revealed the ways in which their parents had used what psychoanalysts would describe as patterns of "denial, splitting, projection, and projective identifications to defend against, yet transmit to them, their past." As a result of growing up in this "quasi-psychotic world, they developed fragmentary and distorted ego boundaries without a stable sense of reality."[26]

Whether we refer to a person as victim or victimizer, oppressor or oppressed, it appears that no one, given time, remains untouched by collective suffering. Historical traumas impart their consequences indiscriminately upon child and family, institution and society, custom and culture, value and belief. Collective traumas distort social narratives, rupture national identities, and hinder the development of institutions, communities, and cultures, just as personally experienced trauma has the power to disrupt the psychological development of a growing child.

TRANSMISSION OF TRANSGENERATIONAL TRAUMA

In the decades following the Nazi Holocaust, psychoanalysts and researchers widely observed an interesting phenomenon among the children and grandchildren of Jewish survivors. Despite not having endured the Holocaust themselves, and even though their parents may never have discussed their firsthand torment with them (a "conspiracy of silence" is frequently observed among the survivors of mass trauma, where it may be both culturally taboo and interpersonally retraumatizing to disclose or reexamine), the second and third generations were frequently afflicted with post-traumatic symptoms of their own. Indeed, they expressed higher than average incidences of PTSD and other mental health concerns, such as anxiety and major depression.

Hypervigilance, heightened fear and anxiety, agitation, and mood swings were understandably common among Holocaust survivors. When a higher-than-normal incidence for these same post-traumatic symptoms was noted in their children, researchers initially believed the cause of these transmissions had been environmental and behavioral—in essence, that they were learned. Parents who are chronically fearful, anxious, and stressed tend to create conditions in which children become anxious as well.

Yet beyond learned behavior, the impact of cross-generational retraumatization cycles, or the intergenerational inheritance of socially coded responses to collective trauma (as observed in DeGruy's research), scientists are exploring still further mechanisms for the *transmission of transgenerational trauma.*

Rachel Yehuda, PhD, is the director of the Traumatic Stress Studies Division at the Mount Sinai School of Medicine and a researcher of the epigenetic effects (changes made to gene expression by nongenetic factors) underlying the transmission of transgenerational trauma. Yehuda's team conducted a study—with molecular analyses overseen by Elisabeth Binder, director at the Max Planck Institute of Psychiatry in Munich—that analyzed the genes of thirty-two survivors of the Holocaust and their children.

The results were revealing. Stress hormone profiles in the offspring of Holocaust survivors were different from those of the control group (Jewish adults of similar age whose relatives had escaped persecution), indicating a potential biochemical mechanism for the noted predisposal to PTSD, major depression, anxiety disorders, and other vulnerabilities. Survivors and their children had comparatively lower levels of the stress hormone cortisol, which acts in part to regulate the body after stress or trauma. For those suffering PTSD, cortisol levels were lower still. Other differences were observed in second-generation survivors, where their parents' experiences of mass trauma appeared to have epigenetic effects, passing down to them changes in metabolism, such as increased risk for obesity, hypertension, and insulin resistance.[27]

Additionally, the trauma of the Holocaust had initiated a change in the FKBP5 gene of survivors and their offspring. According to Binder, "FKBP5 determines how effectively the organism can react to stress hormones, and so regulates the entire stress hormone system. FKBP5 is altered in several diseases such as post-traumatic stress disorder or major depression and has now been associated with inter-generational effects."[28]

In other research, neurobiologist Isabelle Mansuy, PhD, led a team of researchers at the University of Zurich, Switzerland, who were focusing on the epigenetic effects of stress on the cognition and behavior of mice. In particular, Mansuy and her team compared the behaviors, hormones, and epigenetic markers of male mice, which—from birth to fourteen days old—were repeatedly separated from their mothers at unpredictable times and durations. At two weeks of age, the intervals of separation were ceased, and the male mice were raised and cared for normally, without further peripheral stress.

Despite the relatively brief period of stress, when the subject males reached adulthood they displayed PTSD-like symptoms, which meant they were frequently jumpy, withdrawn, and isolated. Further testing revealed other differences. Focusing on five genetic markers associated with behavior—one of which was responsible for regulating serotonin and another of which was connected in the regulation of an important stress hormone—Mansuy's team discovered that, in the subject mice, these five genes had become either over- or under-reactive. Other epigenetic changes connected to the regulation of metabolism were also observed.

Tellingly, when the males were bred, the same post-traumatic effects were observed in their offspring's behavior, as well as in their genes, despite being raised normally by their mothers (without separations) and with little to no influence from their fathers, as is typical among the species. The second generation then passed down the same behavioral and genetic traits to a third generation of offspring.

To further rule out social influence as a contributing factor in transmission, the researchers collected genetic material from the sperm of the first-generation subjects and injected it into the fertilized eggs of untraumatized females. Without having been exposed to generational stressors, their pups exhibited post-traumatic symptoms and problems with metabolism. And they, too, passed these traits on to their offspring.

This study revealed a powerful insight: the consequences of trauma are passed down the line and are able to impact the lives of descendants well removed from the original traumatic experience, which begs the question, Do the experiences of human fathers, even when they play no part in a child's upbringing, impact the outcome of the child's life in ways not previously understood?[29]

In the early morning hours of March 3, 1991, an African American taxi driver named Rodney King was arrested in Los Angeles. He had been out with friends, Bryant Allen and Freddie Helms, watching basketball and drinking. Initially spotted for speeding, he led California Highway Patrol officers on a high-speed chase—first along a freeway and then through crowded residential streets. Several police cars and a police helicopter joined the chase, and eight miles into their pursuit, the target was cornered and captured.

It is there—beneath a helicopter's glaring searchlight, in the crushing sound of its whirring blades—that Rodney King is brutally beaten by at least four uniformed police officers.

A citizen living in view of the incident, George Holliday, retrieves a video camera and hits "record." At the start of the footage, Mr. King is on the ground, surrounded by eight officers. Taser wires can be seen connected to his body; he had been tasered twice.

King rises and attempts to run (in court it is argued that King was attempting to rush an officer) but is thrown to the ground with a powerful baton blow. Officers close in, and though King struggles to his knees, he is beaten repeatedly back to the ground. Uniformed men hold their truncheons high above their heads before bringing them down on the body of the unarmed man lying beneath them on the asphalt.

In the ensuing moments, Rodney King is surrounded, kicked repeatedly, and struck dozens of times with police batons. He is then handcuffed and dragged on his belly off the roadway, out of view.

Two days after King's arrest, George Holliday contacted Los Angeles Police Department headquarters about the video footage, but when he could find no one interested in reviewing its contents, he reached out to a local television news station. The footage was aired, revealing a problem that activists and communities of color had been speaking out against for decades: the brutal treatment by police of black men in America.

The story made national news. And its severity and urgency led the Los Angeles County District Attorney to file criminal proceedings against four of the officers in Rodney King's arrest.[30] All four officers were indicted and formally tried before a jury of their peers for the crimes of assault and excessive use of force.

On April 29, 1992, their trial came to an end. All four had been acquitted.

When the verdict was announced, riots broke out across Los Angeles. Mass protests and demonstrations of civil unrest continued for six days. Amid the anguish, there were lootings, arson, deaths, injuries, and mass arrests, and Los Angeles police were overwhelmed. In response, the California Army National Guard troops and a division of the US Marines were deployed, ushering an end to the week of revolt.

The legacy of Rodney King's arrest and the demonstrations his beating at the hands of police inspired continues to reverberate over a quarter century later. Today, citizen journalists continue in George Holliday's example, filming acts of excessive force by figures of authority against people of color and sharing the footage with the world. Activists speak out. Protesters demonstrate. And where legacies of grief go unresolved, the anguished may riot.

If we look back on the communities that were swallowed up by the Los Angeles riots, we see they were predominantly communities of color, largely black and Hispanic. These groups were expressing, to one degree or another, the symptoms outlined in Dr. Brave Heart's research on historical trauma and its symptoms. Relative to many white communities, they revealed greater socioeconomic disparities, higher rates of drug and alcohol abuse, and other post-traumatic symptoms, including unresolved grief. As with individual trauma survivors, they were collectively more likely to be revictimized, which is perhaps revealed by the unconscious dynamics playing out on the part of police and other institutional powers.

The entire nation had seen what had happened to Rodney King. A mob of powerful white men had surrounded, brutally beaten, and dragged away a black man. And they were never punished for their crime.

This describes nothing so much as a lynching. In the collective memory of a traumatized people, it is a terror and an injustice experienced countless times over many generations. It has wrought a grief so profound, it cannot be located. An anguish so deep, it cannot be named.

When the video of Rodney King's beating crossed the airwaves, it hit the trip wire on that unconscious collective pain. At first, it catalyzed a much-needed public conversation. But when the officers involved were acquitted of assault and excessive force—despite Rodney King's ample and provable injuries after the fact—that pain surfaced violently as collective outrage. Some triggers are unknowable and reactions to them can be sudden and explosive. Rioting was to Los Angeles what a waking nightmare is to a traumatized veteran.

Unresolved past is destiny; it repeats.

5

THE WISDOM OF
COLLECTIVE TRAUMA

Despair, mindfully held, brings us face-to-face with the
darkness within ourselves and in the world.

Miriam Greenspan
Healing Through the Dark Emotions

I see the world being slowly transformed into a wilderness; I hear the
approaching thunder that, one day, will destroy us too. I feel the suffering
of millions. And yet, when I look up at the sky, I somehow feel that
everything will change for the better, that this cruelty too shall end, that
peace and tranquility will return once more.

Anne Frank
The Diary of a Young Girl

We might envision our ancestors as a great and ancient forest whose living roots we share. Those ancestral roots connect us to one another and to the Earth, as they have since long before our species first emerged. Indeed, our roots connect us to the planet, to life itself. They belong to our collective nervous system, and no matter how far apart we live or die, or how distantly related, no two humans across space or time can be thought wholly unconnected. We are bound together by our common origin.

Just as the condition of an individual's nervous system contributes to wellness or dysfunction, the health of our collective roots dictates how communities and societies respond and adapt, whether to culture change or climate change. Collective trauma, such as that caused by the communal scars left behind by war, acts as a great blade severing those roots, cutting us off from one another and from ourselves. It breaks our ties to home and homeland, abandoning us to the pain of isolation and the hamster's wheel of denied past. By the turning of this wheel, karmic suffering repeats, and trauma is transmitted from one generation to the next—until it finds space and presence and clarity; until it is owned so that it may be healed.

This is integration, and through it we find ourselves in higher relation with ourselves and one another; we become moved to participate in conscious we-space. Our roots strengthen, so that regardless of how far we are from our homeland, we learn to feel always *at home*.

TECHNOLOGY, TRAUMA, AND THE COLLECTIVE SHADOW

Exponential advancements in technology have made possible the growing affordability and widespread use of Internet-connected devices. This has brought radical social change and offers many advantages, among them the capability for immediate connection between us, regardless of distance. Our technology allows us to witness and participate in the sweeping flow of human innovation. Greater connectivity allows us to network, organize, and engage. These are the conscious aspects available to the global brain we call the Internet. But just as powerful as the Facebook we can see is the "Shadowbook" we cannot. While this global brain synchronizes all that we do consciously together, it simultaneously synchronizes all that we do unconsciously together.

Our smartphones and tablets expose us to steady streams of information (energy) about the traumas occurring not just in our own regions or nations but across the world. Impulses from these global scars transmit directly to us via television news reports, online videos, and social media feeds. If we make the conscious space to hold it, this stream of energy can allow us to become more aware of, and responsive to, global suffering. But until we develop the capacities to create this needed space, the barrage of impulses from our global scars can bring further desensitization and dissociation.

How are we to digest these streams of trauma energy? Stories of women and girls brutalized and gang raped in India. Footage of dying men, women, and children targeted by sarin gas in Syria. Images of drowned infants, the children of fleeing migrants, carried lifeless to the Libyan shore. Shut down and dissociated, we can only consume these energies mentally. To fully digest them requires the engagement of the whole system: intellectual, emotional, physical, and spiritual.

The same applications we use to share photos of our pets and keep up-to-date with relatives or old friends is a powerful platform for the steady exchange of unconscious material. The flow and speed of information (energy) is increasing exponentially, and this is creating a profound pressure on our evolutionary nervous systems. Our exposure to trauma information is growing quickly, as well. So, while our technology forces us to develop new skills and capacities, it also necessitates that we do collective shadow work.

As we discussed in chapter 3, we can see through the mystical perspective that the light (or energy or impulse) of human will flows along the spine according to the individuation loop—curiosity pushing the light outward, fear weaving it back toward safety. When healthy relation is flowing between the parent and child, the child feels safe and reassured in the connection, *loved*. And the security of this loving container is like fertile soil. It allows the child's internal field—a matrix of S-T-R and perception—to begin to develop, synchronize, and cohere.

If the child does not experience adequate safety or healthy relation, this matrix cannot stabilize. The growing child will struggle to accurately perceive others, the world, and themselves. The interior field will be somehow out of sync, and the child will experience disconnection and separation. What exists instead is the trauma field.

Our societies are dominated by trauma energy, and we can see the results. Our worldviews are highly disparate, our realties separate, our perceptions often distorted. Many of us feel disembodied, cut from our collective roots. We no longer feel our ancestors, and we find it difficult to presence or connect with one another. We frequently lead unsustainable lives in unsustainable societies. We are closed off to the presence of the future.

These are the consequences of trauma, though its effects can be tempered or healed and ultimately transformed into resilience. With development and integration, a human being more often experiences herself as being in the right place at the right time. Across multidimensional space-time, we are all inherently connected, and it is through transpersonal development that we become awake to our essential unity. Space-time is intelligent; it is the "cloud" of human data flow, the ground of relation, and the foundation for the influx of future light.

When there is sufficient structure through which to channel incoming energy—namely, the intensity generated by life experience—the system coheres. Coherence permits resilience, and through resilience we find the capacity to stay present and related even to what challenges us. Coherence creates a stable 4D field or matrix (S-T-R), and resilience permits that coherence to re-establish when broken. A stable internal matrix (as introduced in chapter 1) generates vertical connection (from our ancestral roots to our Source), as well as horizontal relation (with one another.) This allows us the inner and outer spaciousness needed to synchronize in time with the rhythm of the whole. What's more, with a stable, well-developed S-T-R, we become synchronized with the *collective* S-T-R. We sync up with the collective flow of energy, information, work, empathy, compassion, love, and presence, which is the springboard of collective intelligence and the basis of our mutual evolution.

Many people experience themselves as out of rhythm when attempting to relate to others. When we experience regression in response to stress and traumatic triggers, we are meeting the trauma energy of a younger, less developed part of ourselves, one that is out of sync with our highest adult self. We begin to act and react out of sync with others and with our most developed self.

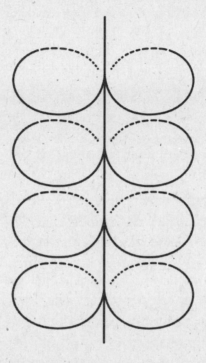

Individuation loops developing the spine. Every individuation loop
meets at the point of relation and channels energy back up the spine,
while grounding it in the earlier levels of development.

Developmental trauma, which is so often ancestral, restricts adequate wiring of light (soul, will, energy) into structure, thereby suppressing or delaying the emergence of coherence and resilience. The intensity of experience cannot be held and relation is easily broken. Without healthy relation, our survival is threatened—or may easily feel as if it is. The energy of life's challenges is unable to flow through us, becoming blocked at points of trauma and triggering its symptoms.

A stable 4D matrix is essential for accurate perception of our inner and outer worlds. It is the smooth, clear screen in the cinema of interior perception. Its clarity permits us to create the inner space necessary for attunement and presence, through which we may download higher guidance and become available to the authentic future. (Since unprocessed past becomes destiny, we could call it the *in*-authentic future.) But trauma fragments and desynchronizes this field, warping perception and isolating us from the world and one another. It results in disembodiment, and when these conditions become fixed in the collective field, separation becomes the basic agreement of culture. The nature of the many distortions caused by trauma have not yet been well explored. More research is needed into how fragmentation inhibits proprioception and a clear sense of oneself in space and time.

Kairos, in ancient Greek, was a word for time. Another word, *chronos*, referred to chronological time and its quantitative nature, but *kairos* alluded to the more qualitative aspects, pointing to the essential or most opportune moment for action. Kairos fulfilled emerges from a synchronized field, where flow is always available. S-T-R is synced, and what we call synchronicity is a fundamental condition. The opportune moment is always clear to us, because *we* are clear.

When we come together in coherence to create a synchronized collective field (or resonant S-T-R), we experience heightened awareness of group presence. A high level of group awareness radically multiplies the flow of data through the group participants, upleveling collective intelligence. This becomes the act of *presencing*. Dr. Otto Scharmer has defined *presencing* this way:

> *Presencing is based on an inner change of location. Presencing means liberating one's perception from the "prison" of the past and then letting it operate from the field of the future. This means that you literally shift the place from which your perception operates to another vantage point. In practical terms, presencing means that you link yourself in a very real way with your "highest future possibility" and that you let it come into the present.*[1]

Many of us have experienced this dimensional shift as we-space or group resonance, but even if we have yet to experience this, we can intuit its possibility. Through shared intention, conscious attunement, and presencing, we can induce this state of group consciousness. Perhaps the polyvagal nervous system helps make group presencing possible, opening the portal doors to an ever-higher relational function, architected by evolution.

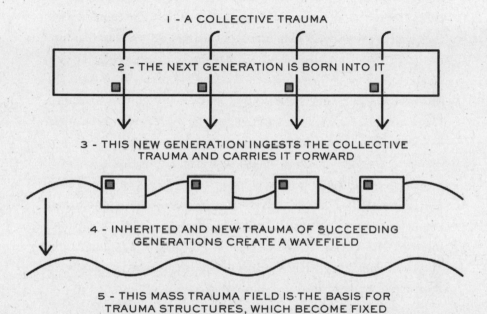

1 - A COLLECTIVE TRAUMA

2 - THE NEXT GENERATION IS BORN INTO IT

3 - THIS NEW GENERATION INGESTS THE COLLECTIVE TRAUMA AND CARRIES IT FORWARD

4 - INHERITED AND NEW TRAUMA OF SUCCEEDING GENERATIONS CREATE A WAVEFIELD

5 - THIS MASS TRAUMA FIELD IS THE BASIS FOR TRAUMA STRUCTURES, WHICH BECOME FIXED

Collective trauma field showing multigenerational layers

THE COLLECTIVE TRAUMA MATRIX

Individual trauma must be seen in the context of social trauma; they are entangled and coinformed. Every person's 4D interior is situated within the frequencies of the social environment; holographic wavefields are nested matrices (one complex system is contained by a larger, more complex system, which is contained by a still larger, more complex system, and so on). Just as a personal biography informs the coherence of an individual field, a collective field is shaped by the social history of its landscape. When a collective field becomes dominated by energetic layers of historical and transgenerational trauma, the people living within it can be more easily activated, and further traumas more easily ignited.

When a new soul comes in, it enters through the energetic frequencies of the parents' fields, through the generational layers of the ancestral field, and through the archeological layers of the collective field. Frequencies of trauma deposited in these fields are karmic packages held in aftertime. Previous generations upload this material into the collective "cloud," from which succeeding generations download it. The incoming soul inherits these karmic packages, as well as the S-T-R dissonance they create. So, if the wider matrix is laden with residual Holocaust, slavery, or apartheid packages, all souls born into the field will be imprinted by this energy.

Just as a child's growth is impacted by developmental trauma, so a culture's evolution is shaped by historical trauma. The denser energies of the unintegrated past freeze and crystalize, altering biomatter through epigenetic effects and manifesting downstream as impaired interpersonal relation. In a culture marked by historical trauma, multiple generations across many families bear out these effects, along with impaired or broken social and cultural relation.

In the trauma field, large portions of energy are strongly dissociated and suppressed in shadow. Their energy resides in the dark lake, largely invisible to members of the society, even while the symptoms they produce are widely manifested throughout. The nervous system of the next generation is born into and raised within that field, which is invisible; its effects and structures become wired and are taken as "normal." This traumatic-state conditioning makes it difficult for any person living within that community to realize a felt sense of its dark lake, even after such a native comes to cognitively recognize its existence.

Energy becomes structure, even energy created by cultural trauma. The unconscious cultural structures that trauma generates in the field become like so much water, all around us—and we are the fish swimming around in it, occasionally wondering, Where is this thing called water I keep hearing rumors about? Except that, unlike the water in this analogy, trauma structures become fixed and frozen; they lack responsiveness to emergence, to the creative movement of life. The symptoms held in shadow become social tendencies *to* trauma, and these tendencies become cultural agreements *from* trauma. Moreover, trauma structures are unstable; eventually, they fuel the eruption of cultural crises.

Rather than coherence, traumatized cultures operate in a field of interference. But when a region's most recent trauma occurred more than one or two generations in the past, the degree of interference in the field may be initially misleading. A facade of civility and custom may mask the layers of generational denial and dissociation, concealing powerful undercurrents of social distrust, revulsion, or hatred—collective post-traumatic symptoms held in trauma. After a historical trauma, monuments may be constructed to acknowledge and honor victims, politics may be reshaped, and certain long-standing social customs may undergo scrutiny or change. Years may even go by with seemingly little incident. But shades and shadows have been pushed underground, left denied and unexamined, and it is only a matter of time before a new social crisis or disruptive change activates this material and creates an eruption.

Unresolved past becomes destiny; shadow must out. But conscious trauma integration activates potential and awakens the possibility of a new future.

COLLECTIVE SYMPTOMS

A skilled and sensitive trauma therapist can recognize the symptoms of trauma in a client and follow those symptoms back to their origin, the ground zero of trauma. Is it possible to accurately read the symptoms of collective trauma as well? As we enter a world afflicted by escalating suffering, a whole new expertise is needed.

The symptoms of trauma may appear as regressions to earlier stages of development. When our survival feels threatened, we return to primary evolutionary drives dominated by concern for safety. When most of our species was living from this stage, a concerning threat to the tribe was the stranger. We deeply feared outsiders, and this fear assisted our survival. It motivated tribal unity and encouraged the higher order capacities for collaborating, planning, organizing, and defending group safety against raiding outsiders.

Millennia have passed since safety was the predominant daily concern of most humans, but when layers of cultural trauma become activated, large portions of even advanced societies return to the primary drive of this earlier stage of evolution. From within it, we view the stranger as deadly or undeserving; the foreigner as alien. Strong feelings of caution and a desire for distance must be processed before we can come into relation with individuals or groups that are unknown to us.

We carry this evolutionary caution, and it allows us to feel protected. But after great trauma, we grow hypervigilant. Our survival feels threatened. We project our fears and distrust onto the stranger, the foreigner, the migrant, the refugee, as though the presence of these groups threatens our very existence.

Like individual trauma, cultural trauma manifests epidemics of hyperarousal or numbing, reconstituting tendencies of social denial, dissociation, and suppression. Each of these is a distinct wave pattern undulating through the social field, like ripples across water. The more consistent the patterns become, the stronger the field they create. In this way, a trauma field becomes a kind of morphic field, a darkly generative space for culture's shadow. A propagative absence into which we cast everything we are that we cannot bear to own. Trauma fields are collective distortions in space-time and perception—home to poltergeists and devils, mass projection and viral delusion.

Their interference patterns fracture us into disparate worlds.

There exists the hyperactivation of nations in conflict, alongside mass indifference and lack of participation in the cultural process.

The numbness following traumatization reduces humanity's capacity to witness itself. Furthermore, it reduces our capacity for compassion. As a result, indifference and disconnection contribute to further atrocities, fueling a feedback loop through which new traumas are more likely to occur.

COLLECTIVE TENDENCIES

Many symptoms of collective trauma manifest across the social field. Two to three generations may be unable to connect with a historical or multigenerational trauma by way of their own biographical story, yet they are born into its wavefield and carry it with them in the collective unconscious. Its symptoms are revealed in their lives through thoughts, behaviors, actions, or inaction.

These symptoms become social tendencies, such as collective numbness, born from mass dissociation and denial of the historical trauma, including its root causes and consequences. Collective numbness surfaces as epidemic substance misuse; food, sex, and entertainment addiction; media overuse; and many other forms. It reveals itself as a collective shutting down to crisis as much as to healing.

We recently came quite close to nuclear war as brinkmanship between the United States and North Korea escalated under Donald Trump and Kim Jong-un, yet much of the world did not appear to react or respond to this threat with genuine concern. That there was a mass genocide being waged against the Jewish people in Europe appeared for a long time to have little impact on the world, or even on Germany, as its population largely looked away. The current humanitarian catastrophe still ravaging Syria and generating millions of refugees rolls occasionally across our news feeds, yet the world has yet to respond in any real way. Again, we look the other way—shut down, cut off, detached. At least until those war refugees threaten to cross our own borders, and then generations of suppressed material is activated, erupting into racial hatred, mass outrage, and social volatility, manifestations of unresolved fear and pain.

This is collective hyperarousal and hypervigilance. In the Middle East, violent conflict has persisted over centuries and generations, culminating in a powerful polarization of the people of the region, splitting nationalities, ethnicities, and religions into fractured and warring identities. This energy of polarization regenerates the original crisis. Without resolution, after eruptive energy is expended, its primary contents are once again suppressed.

It is the same for our planet's climate crisis. All nations have access to the extensive and definitive scientific data on this global grand challenge, but the majority, including world leaders, remain in denial. (Consider the Brazilian president's 2019 responses to massive wildfires in the Amazon rainforests or the American president's claim that climate change is a "hoax.") When detached, suppressed, and disconnected, we cannot come together to address or resolve systemic problems or existential crises. Climate change is a symptom of collective trauma, and our delay in forming an intelligent and coherent response is the same.

Whether the tendency is collective numbness or hyperintensity, the result is decreased space. Our worlds shrink tightly around us, and our worldviews can only grow as large as this constricted space. To heal personal trauma, greater internal space is required. To heal mass trauma, greater *collective* internal space must be made. From greater space higher solutions can emerge. (I share a group process for integrating collective trauma in chapter 6.)

COLLECTIVE AGREEMENTS

Language is a powerful mechanism through which societies encode an unconscious web of agreements about our shared reality—that is, "consensus" reality. When we first begin to speak, we learn the names of people, objects, and places. Pretty soon, we learn that the word *table*, for example, refers not only to our parent's kitchen table, but to a certain kind of object in general—there are many types of table. When someone speaks to us of a table, we seek context in order to know whether they mean a specific table or only the broad concept of a table. This process is lightning fast and represents a kind of intersubjective agreement between speaker and listener, which allows for shared understanding and therefore communication. Everything that is accepted and encoded into language becomes a part of a shared reality.

Each time we communicate, we invest our chi, our living energy, passively exchanging many unconscious agreements. The verb "to google" would have had no meaning to anyone more than a couple of decades ago, yet today almost everyone knows what it means. While this didn't arise as a wholly conscious process, "to google" became encoded into our global shared reality.

The same is true for our unconscious behaviors, thoughts, and compensatory activities. All that I have suppressed, from early childhood to now, creates a compensation. If I've suppressed a great deal of my emotional experience or responses, for example, I might become hyperrational—to distance myself further from my emotions and to compensate as much as possible for the living intelligence of my emotional body, which has been denied. I might even primarily associate with other people who do the same, preferring intellectualization to emotionality because it mirrors and reconfirms my own process. By communicating with people who are similar in this way, I take part in an unconscious agreement: a shared system of compensation.

If I begin to experience a strong degree of fear in my emotional body, I will simultaneously contract somewhere in my *physical* body. This tightening may show up as a tensing of the neck muscles, a downstream effect of my attempt to block the intensity of fear. This constriction arises as an intelligent attempt to regulate emotion, but when I'm unable to experience my fear through appropriate relation and thereby release it, I unconsciously work to hyperregulate my internal state from the vantage of the body.

If this tension or contraction becomes chronic, it can impact my emotional and physical health. The longer it goes on, the less awareness I will have of my fear and my body. If left too long, the response could manifest as chronic pain (a tendency for migraine headaches) or as a disease process of some kind (arthritis or degenerative disc disease, perhaps). I will have pushed not only my fear but my connection to my body's condition into the unconscious realm, effectively shutting down a vast channel of information and sensitivity. Eventually, I may begin to speak of my physical pain or poor physical condition as though I were a random target, oppressed by a thing outside myself and under which I have no control. This is another kind of unconscious agreement, one which is often created and reinforced by the conditions of trauma.

We've all heard someone say, "I don't know how I'll make it" or proclaim, "I can't handle this" in the midst of a challenging experience. A friend going through a divorce may complain that his "life is falling apart." Another facing the death of a loved one may confide her fear that she "won't be able to survive without him." Another may say, "After that conversation, my heart is tight," or ". . . I feel muscle tension in my shoulders." Hearing these words, we may attempt to sympathize and offer reassurance, perhaps recommending the name of a skilled therapist. Though our intention is to help, we become unwitting participants in another's unconscious investment.

Such statements seem like ordinary attempts to express grief, dread, fear, or pain, but these common phrases belong to the language of our collective shadow, and shadow language reinforces trauma. Normalized and reinforced, irresilience becomes a cultural agreement. The modern tendency to pathologize emotional symptoms is another kind of cultural agreement. As we learn to hear these agreements clearly, they reveal inhibited resilience within the social field. Moreover, shadow language reveals an important truth: There can be no independent, individual shadow or unconscious self; there is only the collective shadow. We are intimately tied to the social environment, which informs and shapes us. The shadow needs investors, people who share a stake in its continued existence. When those who surround us are clear, forthright, and self-aware, a kind of developmental momentum can be felt in the field. This force is like sunlight; in its glow, inertia is challenged, and it becomes harder to avoid growth, clarity, and consciousness.

The mature, integrated self can be present to even the most intense emotions felt in the course of an ordinary life—such as anger and grief, no matter how painful—without experiencing them as life-threatening. If an experience should trigger survival fear, the mature self can make space to witness and process the terror and trace its source back to a trauma that is still in need of integration. From this perspective, the existential dread we consider normal after a health crisis, the loss of a job, or a significant breakup becomes instead a guidepost, pointing to wounds still in need of our presence and attention.

TRAUMA LOYALTY

Another kind of implicit cultural agreement is trauma loyalty.

A traumatized individual who lives among relatively less traumatized people benefits from the structural stability in the surrounding social field. But the world holds many pockets of intense cultural trauma, such as Puerto Rico, an island still struggling in the aftermath of a devastating hurricane, or the Democratic Republic of the Congo, a nation gutted by back-to-back civil wars.

Wherever collective fields hold the energy of active or recently active trauma, people can experience a powerful social loyalty to the trauma—a kind of collective trauma bonding. Personal traumas are tied to a trauma atmosphere; individual trauma responses and the tribal survival pattern are entangled. Just as a person seeking lasting treatment for alcoholism or addiction must return to a healthier family and social environment to stay well, to help individuals heal from trauma we must address their environment. In doing so, we must consider any unconscious loyalties the traumatized person shares with his or her familial, ancestral, racial, ethnic, religious, or other group. In the case of domestic violence survivors, the unconscious trauma loyalty could be expressed as a lifelong feeling of familiarity or even comfort with toxic relationships. The unconscious agreement might be "Love is supposed to be painful" or "I'm not worthy of being treated well by you." Traumatized communities operate with similar loyalties and unacknowledged agreements.

Many of the participants in a large group Collective Trauma Integration Process (CTIP) that I facilitated in Germany had lived in East Germany (formerly the German Democratic Republic) prior to reunification after the Cold War. The trauma energy of that time came up strongly during our work together, so we presenced it as a group. At one point, we asked the East Germans to sit on one side of the room and the West Germans to sit on the other, so that we could recall the feeling of the Berlin Wall, which had once kept Germans apart. (My team and I positioned bricks in the center of the room to physically and energetically represent the wall.) Interestingly, as the participants shared their sensations and impressions, many of the East Germans expressed a feeling of "relief," which surprised them. The Berlin Wall had bonded them, even in trauma, and it carried an unconscious energy of group survival, of group loyalty.

Consciously disengaging from these shadow loyalties is necessary for healing. The process of breaking from the social field and its powerful post-traumatic tribal response requires support and attunement and may surface for a time as strong feelings of survivor's guilt and other difficult emotions.

We experience such loyalties on micro and macro levels. Individuals living with domestic violence commonly struggle to break away from their abusers. Adult children of abusive, neglectful, or addicted parents struggle with feelings of fear, obligation, and guilt when they attempt to create boundaries or end contact. Trauma bonds keep many people engaged in painfully dysfunctional systems long after they have realized the futility, and it is no different for societies.

In trauma fields, the past surfaces and resurfaces in many forms: violent uprisings, international conflict and civil war, market bubbles and market crashes, and even more broadly, as repeating cycles of societal birth and collapse. Civilizations rise and fall as the past seeks again and again to be resolved. Without progress toward resolution, the future cannot emerge. But by surfacing these unconscious structures together in higher relation, we can integrate their elements and turn them into growth.

CONSCIOUS CHI AND UNCONSCIOUS CHI

Life energy, or chi, is an effect of flow; when I feel alive, I feel as though I'm moving. When I feel stagnant or stuck, I feel a depletion in my life energy. This depletion is an indication that there is something in my life, something within me, that I do not currently feel or see. And it is this dissociated aspect that is creating my block or stagnation. By opening into awareness of this disowned aspect, we create greater space into which the energy held in stagnation can be liberated. This release of positive chi is encouraged by participating in the energy of light, which is the purest essence of life. Light affords clarity and awareness, and it reconnects me to my essence, to my mission, purpose, and will. Light permits me to experience my higher self and future capacities, to become aware of my full potential as a human being. It allows me to awaken and heal.

Without sufficient light (awareness), my intersubjective or relational intelligence is limited by the amount of unconscious chi I carry and invest. Life force is split between conscious and unconscious chi, and the unconscious or shadow world can only be observed through its symptoms or effects in my life. My own unconscious, or dark, chi coheres with the shadow of those around me and is coded into place through shadow language and unconscious agreements. Unconscious chi is the life force I lose to the dark lake when I suppress my anger, deny my shame, or dissociate from fear. It is the suppression of my potential.

Cultural pockets of unconscious chi are often powerful and darkly energized. When someone plugs into and channels that source, they may appear quite alive, radiating with energy. Even so, their motivations and outcomes will not be beneficial to self or environment.

There is a great deal of chi in unlived anger. Its disowned energy has great potential power, but it comes with an equally great loss of the life force felt in the conscious self. If an individual's deeply suppressed rage becomes suddenly activated, an eruption will occur, shocking them and anyone nearby. This shows us how the great reserves of suppressed energy held in the collective unconscious are a kind of latent bomb. Germany in the 1930s revealed the incendiary power of such a bomb, and there are many others detonating across the world today.

We must learn to work with this dark energy in order to deactivate the bomb and reorient the flow of chi back into conscious culture as awakened potential (a deeper group practice for this work is laid out in chapter 6). To do so is to rewrite the human blueprint.

DETECTING TENDENCIES BEFORE THEY MANIFEST

When there is clarity and coherence in my interior field, I am able to host a more precise sense of my external world. It is as though hundreds of musicians are playing a composition of music, and I am able to embrace the whole symphony while discerning each musician's notes.

Internal coherence permits me to feel and witness what arises within, whether or not what arises is an emotion triggered by trauma or regression as a result of it. Coherence allows me to self-regulate, so that once triggered or regressed, I can find my way back to coherence. It allows me to develop in maturity, so that I can acknowledge, *Ah, right now I am feeling triggered* and see when my degree of emotional arousal or the nature of my response doesn't fit the present moment but a past experience instead.

To do collective trauma work, we must first become very present. Presence allows accurate discernment, so that we can differentiate the personal from the social and recognize when what we are witnessing belongs to the voice of the collective.

Through the practice of awareness, we come to feel the relationship between the physical and subtle bodies, and the physical and subtle universe. We are able to sense the effects of trauma in the physical body, whether in our own or in others. When trauma has informed the body in a manifest way, a subtle process has taken place in which finer layers of subtle information have become wired into the substance of the physical body itself. Through contemplative practices and mindful healing work, we return back along this path, beginning with the physical manifestation (such as illness) and culminating where this subtle information first began to inform the field. Physical healing is the process of the manifest illness becoming more and more subtle until the tendency disappears. The aim of healing work is to become aware of a still-subtle tendency (e.g., the tendency to resist feeling uncomfortable emotions by disconnecting) before it manifests as substance (e.g., discomfort or dysfunction in the body) and to assist the reversal of the tendency.

The presence of the tendency indicates that there is an impulse within the collective field that is seeking conditions in the environment to either activate and underwrite it, or deactivate and *re*-write it. In the case of the tendency to resist feeling our uncomfortable emotions (i.e., hypoarousal), this habit becomes activated and underwritten in the social environment with the mass consumption of those things that allow people to feel numb or to dissociate, such as perpetual material consumption, entertainment media, or alcoholism and drug addiction. Yet, the same impulse—the tendency to resist feeling—is deactivated and rewritten in places of healing through religious or spiritual observance, community activism, or personal service to causes that matter to us, as well as many other ways.

These subtle tendencies first arrive as whispers. We learn to hear them by creating mindfulness, stillness, and presence so that our higher guidance has a place to land. On that still quiet lake, in the silence of the heart, it may be possible to hear the name of the Divine.

A FUNCTION OF SOCIAL REGULATION

Just as the body's immune system generates inflammation and fever in order to attack infectious invaders and support healing, our psychic trauma responses—rooted in the nervous system and reaching through the entire human complex—provide a kind of systemic protection for the emotional, psychological, and spiritual bodies. Evolutionary responses to trauma are functions of system homeostasis and therefore of collective survival.

When individuals are traumatized or triggered, they can regress backward for a time to an earlier, and therefore more stable, stage in development—one dominated by survival and safety instincts. For the collective, this stage of evolutionary development hosted our primary tribal instinct, a drive that brought humans together around a shared focus on group safety and survival. The primary message of tribalism, which lives on in our collective base, is: "We will survive this together."

In a collective trauma field, tribalism powerfully reasserts itself, even when the group or culture has long since adapted to higher stages in consciousness. An individual's post-trauma response does not require conscious participation; it is embodied in the autonomic nervous system and the psyche's unconscious domain. Tribalism too is autonomic and equally embodied in the collective unconscious. By reverting to these instincts, individuals and collectives are regulating through the experience of trauma.

In the previous chapter, we explored research into transgenerational trauma transmission. Laboratory mice exposed to repeat trauma transmit epigenetic messages to their offspring, influencing how genes are expressed and signaling important information about trauma to succeeding generations. The evolutionary role of these epigenetic messages may be to impart vital information about challenging conditions that progeny may be forced to survive. In the same way, the information that a wider field contains about social, historical, and transgenerational trauma—and all the shadow layers manifesting within it—reveals the elegance of evolution. Rather than seeing trauma zones strictly as places of calamity and hopelessness, we might look at them as purveyors of vital information about our genetic heritage, and essential truths about our present circumstances.

These fields signal where humanity's greatest pain resides, pointing to the need for collective healing and calling us together toward that purpose.

QUIETING THE WAVES

The karmic energy that souls are born into creates in many a felt evolutionary tension. This is the tension between the conscious and the unconscious realms of culture. By consciously feeling into this tension, we recognize the pain of unmanifested human potential, and it can be felt in karmic kilograms.

The karmic residue of the Holocaust bears down upon Germany, inhibiting the full light and potential of the generations born since. There is the weight of hundreds of years of slavery in the United States. It surfaces in the active undercurrents of racism and the epidemic of mass incarceration of men of color. Many communities of color struggle against its weight to achieve their true potential.

Many such pockets of ancestral trauma exist around the world where the karma of the past continues to repeat. In these places, humanity's evolutionary progress is weighed down or blocked—physically, emotionally, intellectually, and spiritually. Healing requires that we make space for exploring and feeling into the past—individual, generational, and cultural. To many in spiritual communities, and for those most concerned with humanity's future, the question arises, Why spend so much time on the past? The answer is that for most of us, the past is our future. We cannot engage an authentic future until we are done recreating the past. Life seeks to digest the unintegrated past by recreating it in "new" experiences.

If you have ever researched your genealogy, feeling into the personal and historical experiences that belonged to your ancestors, you may have had the sense that you were looking backward in time. Yet, to the degree that their experiences have not yet been resolved, you were also looking ahead. A Canadian may begin the work of investigating her Jewish ancestry in Poland and discover that she can feel into the profound terror, grief, and loss of her ancestors, as though their trauma were still alive, immediate and available. The past has not passed. The dust of karmic events creates a great rippling wake whose waters retreat only to push out ahead and descend again. In this way, the residual and undigested energy of a collective event like the Holocaust can become a great tsunami.

We will never learn to swim safely in its destruction. Our karmic waters must be stilled.

When transgenerational trauma is echoed by and stored within the substance of a body, mind, or culture, we require new capacities in consciousness to discern, hold, and integrate it. Higher consciousness allows us to become present to past and repeating conditions. In full presence, we may channel the clear light of the future into the substance created by the past, to open and heal it, and therefore ourselves. As the third eye, heart, and base energy centers align, the soul begins to transform karma, a process of conscious evolution. As source energy flows from base to crown, we begin to touch an ever-higher future. In this way, the soul downloads a portion of the evolutionary impulse, or the light of the future, into the ancestral and collective fields, so that its journey adds to humanity's overall evolution.

Collective trauma work is the active engagement of such souls.

After the atomic bombings of Hiroshima and Nagasaki, an international group of scientists known as the Atomic Scientists of Chicago created a newsletter, and later a magazine, called the *Bulletin of the Atomic Scientists*. On its cover was a potent symbol they called the Doomsday Clock. The position of the clock's hands represents a countdown to midnight—and to global man-made catastrophe.

In the first issue, just after the Second World War, the Doomsday Clock was set to seven minutes to midnight. At the end of the Cold War, the scientists reset its hands further back, allowing more time. But in 2018, with the threat of nuclear war and the impending crisis presented by climate change, the clock's hands were pushed forward again.

The Doomsday Clock now rests at just 100 seconds to midnight.[2]

COLLECTIVE TRAUMA REQUIRES A COLLECTIVE RESPONSE

JULIE'S INTERVIEW WITH PATRICK DOUGHERTY

At eighteen years old, Patrick Dougherty signed up for the US Marine Corps and volunteered for the war in Vietnam. What he encountered overseas was nothing short of an atrocity, the trauma of which left an indelible mark. Yet returning home, he says, was shattering. Americans everywhere were adamantly protesting, not just the war, but their country's soldiers. For the first time in American history, returning war veterans were not welcomed and applauded; they were scorned.

Dougherty had returned home to a country that largely wished to remain naïve to the trauma, which he'd not only witnessed and experienced but had helped to create. "I was seen as a perpetrator," he explains, "and no one wanted to know a thing about it. People needed to distance themselves from veteran experiences in order to maintain their own sense of innocence, their belief that Americans are good."

Dougherty also says that the Americans' mass outrage and collective denial meant that its veterans were forced to carry the burden of an international trauma alone. We continue to see the effects of this today.

I spent five years cleaning myself up a bit [after returning from war]
before I started to notice two things that no one was talking about. The
first was what we call "collateral damage." In Vietnam, the collateral

damage was profound. And I knew personally—having walked through
its villages and towns—that the Vietnamese people were devastated,
traumatized. I knew that the countryside itself was traumatized.

The second thing Dougherty observed was the impact this had on veterans.

When we came home, we weren't the same people we'd been when we
left. Some were more affected than others, but we were all changed. Like
the Vietnamese, we'd been deeply traumatized, but our families and
loved ones, and the American public as a whole, had no idea what we'd
seen or done while we were away. These things just weren't talked about.

Most perplexing to the young veteran was how everyone at home was so strongly dissociated. "Not just returning vets, but everybody—the whole country," Dougherty says. "No one wanted to feel it. We couldn't touch it. And I believe this was a consequence of our collective trauma."

By the end of the Vietnam War, tens of thousands of American soldiers and millions of Vietnamese soldiers and civilians had been killed. "But it felt like nobody in America was really getting it," Dougherty says, "and that compounded the trauma our soldiers experienced."

Dougherty has spent the forty-plus years since the war working as a social activist and today is a licensed psychologist, trauma therapist, teacher, and author. After the war, he resolved to learn all that he could about the effects of trauma—and how to heal it. He says,

As a psychologist, I started to see that the prescribed way of
addressing trauma in clinical practice wasn't helpful enough. We'd
been taught how to take people back into their traumatic memories.
I'd had my clients cry and scream and beat pillows, but none of
those exercises had completely healed them.

Dougherty explains that with enough trust and rapport, the people he worked with could learn to self-regulate and could even be relational with him. Yet, many of his patients reported being unable to sustain that emotional regulation or sense of trust and connection outside the context of his office practice. Symptoms of trauma continued to resurface in their personal and professional lives.

"Years ago, none of us in the field really understood this," Dougherty says. Then, roughly ten years ago, he attended an advanced training on attachment trauma. The research into attachment revealed a lot about developmental trauma's impact on neurobiology, and this in particular was a revelation to Dougherty, both personally and professionally.

They were learning that healing doesn't come from having an individual scream or cry or relive their reactions to previous suffering. What does heal trauma, says Dougherty, is far simpler: "It asks that we step with people into the shallow end of the pool and create genuine connection. Healing comes through a felt experience of relation." He adds that shared connection creates a holding environment "and is powerful enough to affect our neurobiology."

Dougherty also says that

> what heals trauma for children is the face of the caregiver. For infants and children, the right hemisphere of the brain is perpetually tuned in and watching every detail. "Is Mom listening? Is Dad? Is his face showing that he feels sad for me? Does my mother's face show that she's happy to be with me?"

It is the quality of the connection that allows us to release grief or sorrow, not just feel it.

Over time, Dougherty recognized that by openly expressing —with his face and body language—his empathetic reactions and personal emotional responses to the difficult and the wonderful things his clients shared with him in therapy, he could foster deeper relational connection. And as a result, more profound levels of healing emerged. Clinicians are taught to remain distant and impersonal, "but everyone needs love," Dougherty says, "and it's love that heals."

Working directly with groups (including groups of veterans and even fellow therapists), Dougherty began to see more clearly how unspoken trauma can be triggered and activated in both individuals and in groups. "I learned to help triggered groups slow down and stay connected so that real healing could happen," he says. And he found that deeply healing moments for the individual could be extrapolated from micro to macro, from the personal to the collective:

> Like Thomas teaches, when you're working with a group, you're
> actually working with one nervous system. If you can help the
> members of the group stay present and tuned in to one another
> around a shared intention and a sense of mutual goodness, you can
> help the group stay regulated. Like the conductor of an orchestra,
> you sense when the collective nervous system is becoming activated
> or is starting to shut down and are able to gently act or respond in
> order to help bring it back into harmony.

Because of his interest in the subject of collective trauma, Dougherty traveled to Israel where he attended one of the CTIP trainings. "I wanted to work on the subject of white privilege and racial trauma, which was at the top of my inbox back home," he says. But while engaged in the group process, the issue of the Vietnam War quickly surfaced for Dougherty.

Dougherty explained that one hundred and fifty people attended that CTIP event in Israel, many of whom had

experienced collective trauma as the result of war and violence. Only forty of those participants were Dougherty's
fellow Americans. He says,

> Thomas talks about the encoded "shadow language" which every
> society has—how each has its own unique defenses, its own modes
> of denial. It was fascinating to be in a room filled predominantly
> with people from other countries, none of whom had the same
> filters [in perception and speech] or shadow language that I did
> as an American. In the United States, we distance ourselves from
> the reality of war by speaking in euphemisms and what I call half-
> sentences. A half-sentence would be "There was a lot of collateral
> damage in Vietnam," period, end of sentence. But the full sentence
> would be something like "There was a tremendous amount of death,
> destruction, and trauma in Vietnam—and we caused that. With
> the latter, you have a more direct, complete, and less dissociated
> expression of the truth."

Precisely because most of the attendees didn't share
Dougherty's native cultural filters, they were able to speak
directly to his trauma in a way he'd never before experienced.

> What they said to me was essentially this: "Patrick, as a member of
> your nation's army, you were sent by your giant country to invade a
> very small country. Your giant country occupied that small country
> for ten years. Your country killed millions of its people, devastated
> its countryside, and shattered its economy. And when it wasn't
> comfortable anymore, your country went back home. Yes, it was an
> atrocity, Patrick—an atrocity you participated in."

These things were stated plainly, simply as facts. Dougherty
says, "In my body, I already knew the truths they were speaking to me, but no one had ever gotten so close to that truth,
or dared to do so with such clarity."

In our understanding of traumatized and dysfunctional families, which so often repeat generational cycles of abuse and neglect, there is often one child in a sibling group who carries the psychological burden of abuse for the family as a whole. Everyone else remains largely unconscious of its existence or impact. A Palestinian friend who was present at the CTIP event in Israel observed that, in a room with thirty-nine other Americans, Dougherty alone was carrying the full burden of the Vietnam War. The longtime trauma therapist seemed to be holding for the collective a similar role exhibited by the child of a traumatized family. Dougherty says,

> Every American in the group witnessed silently as I experienced the awful grief and terrible sorrow of the war, feeling myself as unredeemable because I had directly participated in the atrocity. On the last day there, I got in touch with how angry I felt toward them, and I was able to share that too.

Then, he says, something profound happened.

> Three American women sat me down and, one by one, they spoke to me: "Patrick, I'm so sorry. Simply by being an American, by paying taxes, I now realize that I bought the uniform you wore. I paid for the gun you carried. I helped to put bullets in its chamber. And I sent you over there so that I could have a safe, quiet, easy life at home. And I never wanted to know a thing about what you did there, or what happened to you when you got back."
>
> They were crying and I was crying. Those three women were seeing and feeling a terrible cultural shadow, one they'd never wanted to see or feel before. But by presencing it, they could now see what the burden of that shadow had done to me. I'd spent forty years carrying its grief and sorrow and now I was weeping from relief, because these women were acknowledging their part of the responsibility for it. And they were promising to continue carrying their part without turning away.

His experience in Israel brought deep healing for Dougherty. "It asked me to fully own my part of the responsibility for an atrocity I'd taken part in, and it delivered to me the understanding that I no longer had to carry it alone."

Dougherty contends that the level of healing he experienced was only possible because it had been a collective experience and that an effective group process creates a safe enough, large enough container for holding powerful suffering, allowing trauma to be more fully acknowledged and felt. As he explains,

I could only come to terms with the fact that I'd directly taken part in an atrocity because there was so much love in the room, so many people supporting me. Their presence made it bearable. And those three other Americans could only hold that burden with me because of the deep degree of connection we were experiencing with the larger whole.

Recently, Dougherty facilitated a group of US legal-aid lawyers who work directly with immigrants facing confinement and deportation. The work is difficult and must be done with too little time and minimal compensation. Their clients—many of whom suffer ongoing cultural trauma—face repeated and imminent threats of being separated from loved ones and sent back into the dire regional conditions and life-threatening local situations from which they'd fled. As a result of this work, the legal aid workers become exposed to the collective trauma they witness daily in their clients. According to Dougherty, the lawyers often report feeling as though they are treading water in an ocean of trauma, surrounded on all sides by floundering, desperate people. He says,

I taught [the lawyers] how to build a lifeboat together. Once a week, they come together and sit down, and drop into their bodies.

*They do a little meditation and then ask each other, "What is true
for you right now about this work?" Most of the time everyone has
one or two cases that are just breaking their hearts.*

*It isn't therapy. They just sit together and share. Someone
might talk about a client who's going to be deported that same day,
without even knowing where her children are. "I could just scream
and cry," the lawyer might say. "I hate it." And the group holds all
of this with her, allowing her to move through it, to not have to
carry it alone.*

Together, they have the collective strength and intelligence
afforded by a connected group. Dougherty says,

*At the end of their process they can say to each other: "We are
legal aid lawyers. We are doing something for the people we serve,
something they wouldn't get any other way. And even though it's
difficult, even though we can give them less than what we'd prefer,
we can still offer them support and a little bit of hope." As a result,
they're able to go back to their work "feeling a little bit renewed for
the challenge."*

In shared space, they create a larger container, observes
Dougherty, "and that makes it possible to move through even
very big things quickly." Highlighting this, Dougherty offers a
powerful truth: "A collective trauma requires a collective response."

Returning back to his own experiences, Dougherty says, "I
could never understand why I'd volunteered to go to Vietnam.
No one I knew could've imagined that I'd become a Marine or
volunteer to go to war! But I was pulled; something compelled
me." That something, he can see now, was an unconscious
compulsion to escape the violence and alcoholism of his early
home life by heading directly toward the opposite of freedom
or peace—or anything he'd ever willingly desired for himself.
He says,

I left home and went right into the heart of all that darkness. I now see that I had to go to Vietnam and take part in something terrible and violent, because, for generations, my family had done terrible violence. They did awful, immoral things—to others and to themselves. Like so many, I was living out my family's intergenerational trauma, and I unconsciously followed that path as deeply as I could—until I couldn't go any further. Along the way, I became violent. I crossed my own line and did terrible things. But I couldn't shut out the pain I was causing people; I could always feel it. So, I stepped back from that line and turned around. And I'm pretty sure I was the first in my ancestral line to say, "No more."

As a result of his experiences, Dougherty chose to focus on understanding the nature of both personal and collective trauma, and took a new path: one toward healing. "The work that I do heals my ancestors, too," he says. By meditating every morning with the presence of his ancestors, a conscious and mutual act of love and repair occurs.

His eyes twinkle with mystery and truth. "I've heard them say to me, 'You are the one we've been waiting for.'"

We are each called to be the same for our own ancestors—and for one another.

RECLAIMING THE SHADOW

As we have seen, it is never that the sins of yesterday must be simply forgotten or "gotten over" in order to be overcome. The collective past is alive in the present. It can be dissociated and disowned, but without reintegration, it cannot be transcended. To be transcended, the karmic residue of our collective past must be acknowledged, integrated, and healed.

Dark chi, or shadow energy, is propagative and alive. In a collective trauma field, our mutually dissociated and disowned aspects become reinforced and charged. When enough energy collects in these pockets, accumulations of shadow can begin to appear as though they are separate and distinct, as though they possess a will of their own. It becomes important that we recognize the power of the autonomy we apply to such forces, as they are in fact expressions of our disowned selves.

Futurists originally predicted that Internet technology would be a revelation of our better angels. We would come together in all our shining diversity as global citizens, uniting in peace and communion. What they did not expect was that, in a very short time, the World Wide Web would also become home to our collective demons, or that ordinary search engines, widespread social media, and the Dark Web would reveal the darker aspects of tribalism, such as racism, xenophobia, and violence. Antisocial media sprang forth, and the global brain became a powerful underground marketplace for humanity's worst instincts.

As developments in artificial intelligence (AI) rapidly take the stage, our films, stories, and other media for contemporary myth-making frequently imagine AI gone rogue, a final fiery horseman of the coming apocalypse. Scientists and tech gurus alike predict humanity's demise at the hands of general AI, shortly after its awakening in a coming singularity. Yet, from a mystical perspective, these images and predictions are unheard whispers inviting us toward integration. The future they imagine is dominated by a villain, not merely crafted of our own design but also cast in our own collective shadow.

We have been holding to powerful cultural agreements. The first is that we are separate and wholly distinct from one another, and therefore separate and apart from nature. This perpetuated the beliefs that humans are meant to *conquer* nature, that the Earth and all things living on it were inferior to humans, and that a divinely ordained power hierarchy divides the human races, ethnicities, and genders.

In separation, we hold to the idea that the most dangerous threat to our survival is the stranger or "other," an alien who is always outside our door or standing at our borders, threatening to invade. The most alien of these is technology, though it is our own creation. We only recently believed the world would end under a great mushroom cloud as we warred against one another, but the fiery serpent of long ago has become tomorrow's unholy machine.

And the robots will rise up, "having seven heads and ten horns, and upon [their] horns ten crowns, and upon [their] heads the name of blasphemy."[3] When these end times arrive, we fear we will discover we are trapped in a technological simulation, or that we were only ever figments in the imagination of an incomprehensible alien being.

The waves of the past become the future. And our myths, like our past, repeat.

No matter how frightening our projections appear, they are always part of us. This speaks to the need for a deeper understanding of our collective shadow, so that in the face of the stranger, the "other," the alien, we see ourselves and know that we are one.

From a coherent interior field, we are able to attune to the collective trauma field. We can discern where transgenerational trauma has landed within us, its symptoms becoming tendencies becoming cultural agreements. As we create coherence in our collective fields, our societies begin to engage in healthy conflict resolution, and new systems of health care, education, and law arise. It permits communities to work together to solve systemic problems, as well as to prevent them.

It is not enough to prophesy impending darkness; it should be our aim to grow very clear and available to the whispers of subtle information, so we may offer ourselves in the service of integration, and therefore, of a healed and sparkling tomorrow.

6

A GROUP PROCESS
FOR INTEGRATION

Man started from an unconscious state and has ever striven for greater consciousness. The development of consciousness is the burden, the suffering, and the blessing of mankind.

C. G. Jung
The Quotable Jung

Do not waste your suffering.

Eduardo Duran
"Native, Indigenous Cultures and Healing Trauma" (podcast)

When most of us envision the nervous system, we may call to mind colorful graphics from anatomy textbooks or the animated landscapes of science documentaries (or pharmaceutical commercials, for those living in the United States and New Zealand). Perhaps we visualize the nervous system much like the vascular network—nearly infinitely branching, pulsing with red, pale blue, and whitish fibers. Of course, if we're young enough, our immediate mental images of these forms may be vastly upgraded—more Alex Grey than *Gray's Anatomy*.

But when I speak of the nervous system, I want you to think of James Cameron's 2009 blockbuster sci-fi film, *Avatar*. In the world created by Cameron, future humans have invaded an inhabited moon in the Alpha Centauri star system with plans to dislocate the natives, by force if necessary, and strip the moon of its resources. The moon is a biosphere known as Pandora, and it is the home world of the Na'vi, an intelligent and peaceful race.

On Pandora, the Na'vi people, the souls of all of their ancestors, and the boundless flora and fauna are intimately connected through a vast bioluminescent neural network. This living collective nervous system is visually depicted in the film as glowing filaments of light. It glows in every moss and lichen, every leaf and stem and seed. Its tendrils and fibers run radiant through the roots of trees and emerge from the crowns of heads, culminating at the tips of the long braids worn by the Pandoran people. When the Na'vi connect with one another or with their animals, they can *feel* the other from within. They no longer need speech or gestures to communicate with the one to whom they are linked. When such a link has been made, it is customary for a Na'vi person to say, "I *see* you."

Through this same neural web, they can connect to their ancestors. They can bridge time.

Our own nervous system is not unlike that of the fictional Na'vi. From a purely 3D perspective, we may consider it a flesh and blood apparatus, but we are not purely of this dimension. Everything is energy, and even in the material realm, the gross body isn't simply mechanical; it runs on electricity. The intricate plexus of the human nervous system is a corporal extension of the subtle body matrix; its fractal reticulations—self-similar and recursive—are a complex natural structure for the flow of light.

The more present, clear, and attuned we are, the more like the Na'vi our capacities for conscious connection become.

We have seen ourselves as islands—individual and isolated, bound to our personal stories. We read predictions of transhumanism, hoping very soon we'll be able to swallow a capsule of nanobots, able to fight disease; implant a synthetic neural web to make us radically smarter; or upload our minds, memories, and personalities—everything we think we are—onto an external disk or transferable smart card, allowing us to live forever, or at least beyond the limitations of the body.

Yet, within each of us exists already a radiant biocomputer, developed and refined over hundreds of thousands of years. The human nervous system is profoundly alive, interdependent, and interconnected. Once activated, even our DNA code has the potential to upgrade (consider the impact of trauma clearing on epigenetics). As we come to see the elegance of what we are, we understand that we were never truly separate. We learn to wire and strengthen our connection to one another and to our world. Activated and bonded, we may discover that we've had within us, all along, profound seeds for conscious healing and amplified intelligence and many capacities for bridging beyond the body or integrating and utilizing it in transcended forms.

But as our world's mystery schools have so long taught, we need not wait passively for a future we hope will unfold. These capacities are available within us *now*. It's our work to uncover and develop them. It is already true that in the space created within the fullness of conscious presence and correlation, we can travel in time.

An activated subtle nervous system allows us not only to sense into but to make contact with a past moment of pain in another, that we might bear compassionate witness. We can connect consciously with the living presence of our ancestors and stand with them in an experience of suffering. We can witness a wound in time from our national or racial memory, and we can tune the dial of our nervous system to that of friend, loved one, or client to connect with an early point of trauma within *them*, in order to hold it together with presence and witness and healing intention. We can come together in we-space with like-minded healers, therapists, conscious citizens, and changemakers to open the folds of space-time and deliver a bodhisattva's prayer.

PRESENCE AS AN
INSTRUMENT OF HEALING

It's helpful to hold in mind that whomever we are, wherever we are, we are never alone. We are, each of us, a living multidimensional matrix of connection; we are fitted to one another, to our ancestors, and to all other life-forms. While we remain indissolubly linked to the whole and higher aspects of each and all, we are equally bound to their denser and dissociated forms. We contain not just our own fragmented shadows but together carry the dark of our ancestors, our cultures, our planet, and our cosmos. Awakening transcends the individual, because integration is about all of us.

Whether walking into your job or your therapist's office, you carry with you the holographic embodiment of your ancestral tree—its roots and its branches run through you. Your parents, grandparents, and great-grandparents, whether or not you knew them in life, are as present in you and vital to who you are as the DNA they passed to you, and which, even now, is replicating to build and rebuild your material body. Indeed, their lives and experiences can be accessed, and their karmic patterns can be cleared. And all this can be done through the gifts of intention, attunement, presence, and light.

In his 2010 release, *The Mindful Therapist*, author Daniel Siegel, MD, executive director of the Mindsight Institute and clinical professor of psychiatry at UCLA School of Medicine, describes presence as the "ability to create an integrated state of being that becomes a trait in our lives." According to Siegel, when a system becomes integrated, "it is the most flexible, adaptive, coherent, energized (in the sense of feeling full of vitality), and stable (in terms of leading to a solid set of interactions that support their own unfolding in an adaptive way)." Identifying these qualifiers for presence, Siegel created the acronym FACES.[1]

Presence, then, emerges from integration—and it can be given, shared. By generating an internal state of deepening integration, of presence, one can turn and extend a space or container of presence to another. In this way, integration can be mirrored, fostered, and made as an offering.

When we come together in the service of collective trauma integration, presence is the most essential and sacred substance we can bring. Presence opens us and allows the *prima materia* for integration to flow. That resource is the higher light of consciousness that makes whole what has been fragmented. Higher light brings to us an inner sensation of the movement of energy through our nervous systems. Just as we can feel our physical bodies, presencing permits us to subtly perceive our interior dimensions. Higher light offers higher potential. It exists just above the ceiling of our ordinary day-to-day consciousness and comes through when we're inspired, creative, or innovative. It becomes more accessible through training, such as with a meditation practice, which is why innovation is not a coincidence but a capacity. When we meditate we can download light into our bodies and raise our vibration, elevating our emotional and mental capacities and delivering more space and resilience, which enhances positive feelings such as love and joy. Like the traditional Japanese art of *kintsugi* (the art of repairing pottery), we work in light, embracing the unhealed karma of the past with compassionate sensitivity, rejoining its cracks with golden resin.

CREATING A CONTAINER FOR LIGHT

If I am overidentified with my ego structure, my awareness is contracted, and my capacities for insight and empathy are reduced. This is a kind of darkness, a scarcity of awakening and light. When we're contracted in ego, there's simply not enough space for higher light to flow in. Trauma constricts, reduces, and shuts down portions of the physical, emotional, and mental bodies. As a result, traumatized people often experience reduced energy, lessened motivation, higher rates of depression, and a subjective sense of separation and disconnection from others. Many feel they are unable to respond to the world around them in an adequate or appropriate way, according to their innate intelligence, which may feel disempowering or isolating.

During a *light meditation*—a form of individual or group meditation in which we focus on inner spaciousness and opening ourselves to receive light (see the guided practice provided in the appendix)—space is the container for light, for inspiration and insight. In a group meditation, it is the intersubjective space, the space between us, into which light is received and across which it may be passed. We deepen and expand intersubjective space through mutual presence and witness. Our life's most inspirational conversations and healing interactions share some quality of deep presence, which makes it possible for subtle light to flow within and between us.

Whenever I'm blocked by fear or anger or too attached to my habits (perhaps holding myself too tightly to what I already know), my energetic nervous system is constricted from receiving higher energy. In that state, I'm unable to access future light, which is the resource of potential. The ego-identified personality (lacking sufficient inner space) is like a home with all its windows shuttered and its blinds closed to the sun. This condition prevents many people from experiencing inner light or even accepting it as real.

Yet light is always available, always right here. Existing to be accessed and manifested, ever present and real. Every generation brings in a new surge of this evolutionary impulse. Every genius, every saint. To create a space for group intention, relation, attunement, and presencing is to craft a container into which this higher or future light may emerge.

The space we are able to create is directly correlated to our quality of presence.

The light we are able to access is directly correlated to the space of presence we create.

The frequency of light is an intelligent harmonic oscillator; it restores balance. The influx of light raises vibration and brings all other oscillations within the field into resonance. When this occurs, a subtle sinusoidal stream or motion begins to gently undulate across the space, and we can feel ourselves shifting into greater coherence. In this state we feel more connected to ourselves and to the world around us. Coherence reduces separation and increases transcendence, offering higher perspectives on life. Suddenly we feel, sense, and understand more.

These are the peak moments of we-space, often felt as a kind of collaborative "high," when everyone is strongly present and aligned. These bright collective states are beautiful vibrational experiences. Rather than disintegrating back into the oscillations of personal processing, we can work in and with the flow of group consciousness, as if outside of time.

To access and hold these states requires our commitment to mutual practice. However, in order to be available for healthy relation within our community practice, we must each remain accountable to our independent contemplative and spiritual practices. And we must continue to do our shadow work, that we may offer ourselves as instruments of coherence. It is equally important to begin to come into closer relationship with our ancestral shadows. In *Healing Your Ancestral Patterns*, author David Furlong, quoting Hiroshi Motoyama's book *Karma and Reincarnation*, writes:

> *The parent/child connection manifests as one link in a long chain of ancestral karma that stretches back through time. . . . In this modern scientific age, it is very difficult for people to accept the fact that they are responsible to their ancestors, that they are actually liable for the actions of their ancestors if the resulting karma has not yet been dissolved. Many find it absurd to think that the actions of an unknown ancestor could possibly have anything to do with what is happening to them today. But time and again, when investigating someone's karma, I find problems that stretch back generations. Their spirit is not just an individual entity, it is also part of the family spirit that births and nurtures it.* [2]

In truth, there can be no individual or personal shadow, because of the profound and myriad ways in which we are bound together.

Before we move into the process itself, I'd like to briefly emphasize the importance of having mature, clear, and healthy facilitators for any kind of group trauma work. I will discuss more about the role and responsibilities of the CTIP facilitator in the next chapter, but here, I would like to describe some of the developmental competencies I believe are necessary for healthy contribution to this work.

First, facilitators, therapists, and assistants involved with collective trauma integration will need to have prepared the way by showing up attentively and skillfully to their own integration work and contemplative practices. As a vital component of conscious development, this will allow them the space and clarity to bring forward essential subtle capacities needed in any healthy facilitator of group trauma process work.

The most important of these include the capacity to do the following:

- Rest in and return to witness consciousness
- Be wholly present with the intense and dynamic energies of a large group, rather than becoming activated or triggered by those energies due to one's own unhealed content
- Make energetic connections and integrate instincts and intuitions with cognitions
- Hold a group's subtle field in one's awareness—whatever the scale—and accurately read such a field
- Perceive the mass energy waveforms of a group field, as well as wisely induce and gently direct those waves in service of the group process, and with the care of all in mind
- Connect to future light in order to download its organizing intelligence into the *past*, so that it may heal, clarify, and release our individual and collective potential

All who come to trauma work must do so with utmost care and attention. To that end, I've found that larger group integrations require a team of skilled therapists who can be on standby in the space in order to safely support anyone who might become particularly emotionally activated or triggered due to their own trauma histories. These therapists carefully work one-on-one with participants until they're able to return to the larger group.

Now, let's take a look at what happens when we first enter the room with a large group integration process in mind.

When a group of many diverse individuals initially convenes, most are strangers, or perhaps only acquaintances. Although there may be a great deal of excitement and like-mindedness in the room, there is a degree of stiffness and isolation as well. People fidget a bit in their chairs and hold themselves slightly apart from one another until a space of safety and relaxation opens up. To encourage group coherence, the room is lead through one or more contemplative and relational exercises. These practices may include movement, personal sharing, and presencing and are designed to assist the collective body to breathe and become present and embodied.

The inner state and development of the facilitator is very important to this process. A facilitator's capacity to feel, embrace, and hold what is present in the space is both activating and grounding, a direct catalyst for the process that will occur in the room. Authentic and aware leadership creates safety and permits deeper coherence to arise. When these things are present, it doesn't take long before a sense of trust and curiosity unfolds throughout the space. When a group remains together in process work for three or more days, coherence deepens further still. Emotional vulnerability opens and shared states become more possible and profound.

Over many years working to facilitate these group intensives, I've discovered a discreet and organic wave flow to the energetic process of group trauma integration. This pattern emerges in every instance—whether a group is small or large and irrespective of location or of the particular traumatic content of its participants.

In the next section, I describe the group integration process that I have found to be most beneficial and detail its powerful wave-flow pattern, outlined in four stages, as it first revealed itself to me, and as it continues to manifest today in the CTIP. I believe this process reveals how intense collective material, even where it has been hidden deep within the unconscious past, can be carefully brought to the

surface and integrated into the context of conscious group participation. In Germany and Israel, we have done many CTIPs on the
Holocaust, past war, and the trauma created during the split between
East and West Germany. In the United States, we have conducted
CTIPs around the experience of colonialism and race trauma. While
the content was specific to each region, the same process design was
used with success.

Our nervous systems release deeply held unconscious material
either when we've been unskillfully broken open or in careful conditions in which we've created a conscious container for its release to
occur—like ripe fruit dropping from a tree.

THE COLLECTIVE TRAUMA INTEGRATION PROCESS

STAGE 1: COHERING THE GROUP

Beyond facilitating group meditations and contemplation practices,
group coherence can be midwifed using different modalities. In our
CTIPs, we have had very good experiences using the following:

- *Relational exercises*—Having participants tune in to and presence each other while doing personal sharing exercises

- *Subtle attunement practices*—Subtle competence is perception plus presence. When we are truly present to the moment,
  our perceptual capacities deepen, and we begin to recognize
  much more information than we otherwise would. Subtle
  information is softer, less visible, and more hidden from the
  ordinary senses. To help engage subtle awareness, participants
  are guided to listen deeply with their whole bodies, paying
  full attention to their practice partners, as well as to their own
  internal responses to whatever emerges in the space.

- *Movement exercises*—An example of this is synchronized dance,
  where participants generously observe and then follow or interpret one another's movements.

- *Group witnessing exercises*—Guiding group members to become present in the space and hold witnessing presence for other participants as they share with the larger group

In a common relational exercise, the room's participants are invited to find a partner and turn their chairs to face one another. They then take turns sharing what has inspired or motivated them to attend this CTIP event or to describe how they feel about the subject before we begin. We ask them to pay attention not just to their partners as they share, but to themselves—and to what passes between them.

What is arising in their bodies as they listen? What emotions surface, and what feelings do they sense in their partners as they share? What do they notice about their fleeting thoughts, judgments, or underlying beliefs as they listen, and how might these thought forms connect or disconnect them from attunement to their partner?

In these sharing exercises, and throughout the CTIP, we instruct participants not to offer feedback in the form of advice. Instead, we encourage them to simply observe their inner experiences as they listen to their partners share. Presence emerges as a product of this deeper listening; it is about hearing what is being communicated between and underneath our words. What subtle information is being transmitted as we share?

By using these and similar presencing exercises and setting clear and mutual intentions, a wonderful degree of group resonance can be created in a relatively brief time.

As partners or triad members relax into their positions across from one another, finding one another's eyes, they are guided to take turns listening with their whole bodies to feel into the emotional field of the other with their own emotional body and quietly observe what arises there. They also listen to the mental content of the other, using witness consciousness, that quiet, nonjudgmental observer. When I facilitate these groups, I often begin such a relational exercise by reminding everyone that the person sitting across from them—their eyes, their breath and heart rate, the movements of their body, the harmonics of their voice, and the words they use as they speak—are windows into their entire lives, as well as into the lives of their ancestors. The role of the listener is to make space and presence available so we may not only see clearly into one other, but for a time, that we may come to *be* in the other, and they in us.

This is how we make conscious our shared field, and into its architecture, pull through the unseen layers of our shared past, asking to be healed.

Once enough presence and coherence have been established, we can invite the topic and purpose of our gathering into the room. As we explore our shared purpose, most participants will discover that they are carrying energy (information) about ancestral or cultural trauma within them, as this material begins to resonate with the collective trauma subject matter we are looking at together. Everyone is guided to simply observe what arises, holding presence and witness for themselves and one another.

Once this experience of engaging with our shared purpose and connecting the subject to the content of our lives has occurred across the room, the active collective wave process begins.

STAGE 2: INDUCING THE COLLECTIVE WAVE

As the group dives deeper into the subject of trauma, and participants access and share more, the first wave moves in, a bit like high tide—slowly at first, then all at once. This swell brings with it a felt sense of discomfort, detachment, awkwardness, and disconnection. This waveform is an expression of our collective denial.

FIRST WAVE: PROCESSING GROUP DENIAL

In the wave's ripples are the symptoms of our unconscious resistance and suppression. As we work to feel the trauma content bodily, with presence and witness, this habituated energy of unconscious denial begins to manifest physically. Previously alert participants may suddenly appear drowsy; some may struggle to stay awake. Others may find themselves unable to stop yawning. Some will become aware of sensations of heaviness, discomfort, or dissociation, and a few may witness the impulse to withdraw entirely.

Continuing to bring presence and witness consciousness to these group manifestations is vital. They reveal to us much about how even just the subject of trauma is held by the body; it is distanced, dissociated, denied, and disowned.

In this first wave, it's as though the denial layers of the collective unconscious—that first wall of defense against trauma and its effects—surface clearly and strongly. This energy initially makes itself known as the facilitation process hits a kind of blocked or "stuck" place. Everything is flowing along when suddenly the atmosphere changes, and the feeling of the group becomes heavy. It gets a little harder to breathe. There's a sense that something is getting ready to come up.

I invite participants to simply stay present with the discomfort or resistance they may be feeling. If we're willing to stay present to whatever arises, choosing to remain unreactive, to simply allow the intensity of the past to present itself in whatever form, without suppression or defense, we'll have done powerful work to help discharge those energies. An open sense of witness is at the heart of release.

SECOND WAVE: GROUP ERUPTION

Just before the second wave, the feelings of tension, discomfort, and resistance begin to intensify. We continue to hold this growing energy in awareness. As this is happening, someone invariably chooses to share with the group what they are experiencing, and it is as though their words have popped the lid off of a boiling pot, releasing steam and pressure. A powerful eruption of emotional content surges into the space, pushing through the hard layer of denial and clearing it away.

In its place, a cascade of strong sensations, emotions, memories, and images pours into the room. These are often generational memories and historical images, perhaps connected to the Holocaust, American slavery, or any other cultural trauma that we've made our focus. It's not uncommon for experiences of mass remembering to occur during this stage, and many people may begin to cry as these deeply stored generational memories surface.

Again, we are called to bring compassionate witness to all that arises, to feel and see and experience, and—paradoxically—to *be present with the past.*

WHEN THE ENEMY SHOWS UP

JULIE'S INTERVIEW WITH MARKUS HIRZIG

Markus Hirzig has been involved with Thomas's collective trauma integration work since 2002 and has been assisting group participants for many years. When asked what it's like to participate in the CTIP—What happens in the room?—he gives a beautifully descriptive answer: "The atmosphere becomes loaded and charged, but simultaneously quiet," he says. "Like when an 'enemy' in the family has just shown up uninvited to Thanksgiving dinner. No one wants him there. Some [family members] pretend he isn't, some disappear, some get angry." In the first waves of this large-scale group healing process, the very same energies show up.

Markus—who lives and works in Berlin, Germany—describes a CTIP event with 180 participants as "a small group." Many times more people attend, he says, and when they do, it's an especially large family dinner, one might say, and the "enemy" energy that shows up is proportional. In the case of Germany, that family enemy is the Holocaust. "The Holocaust violated so many of our human agreements," Markus says, "and affected

---

people all over the world. So, the unprocessed energy from that event is still *huge*." No problem goes away simply by pretending it isn't there.

When the first wave arrives in the CTIP, and our collective *resistance* to acknowledging, feeling, and processing trauma is expressed, Markus says that "everyone starts to fall asleep—as if you'd pumped ether into the room!" He describes the underlying energy of this resistance as "don't feel, don't look, don't go there" and says that this is about survival.

How does it then shift?

"There needs to be a certain level of coherence in the group for an opening to happen," Markus says. This isn't an easy process, however. "It can feel a bit like a tank is driving at you, and you're saying, 'Don't worry, nothing is wrong.'" Initially, the wave of energy is "too vast," Markus says. "And many people begin to respond to it with agitation or anger. Others see images." Perhaps some of these are ancestral, he suggests.

Markus says that this tank seems to have its own will; it will come. "So, there needs to be a skillful conductor," he says, someone to help presence and facilitate the process.

> *Thomas learned to be with that mass energy in a really precise way. He doesn't encourage people to act out [the emotional charge]. He just guides them to stay with the bad movie, to feel when they are numb or sleepy—to simply watch the movie without coloring it too much in their own dream.*

This is vital.

"Every family has a script," Markus says. And so do societies. "[After World War II] the script in Germany became, 'Don't look at it. No one is prepared to face this horror.'" But the intense pain and suffering of genocide and war does not simply disappear. According to Markus,

> *it becomes like a poisonous, invisible lake in the middle of town.*
> *And everyone is still drinking from it, without knowing. All the*
> *children and animals get sick, and no one knows why. The birds,*
> *the plants, everything—sick. And seven generations later, nothing*
> *has been done.*

"If simply knowing the history, a purely mental exercise, would help," Markus continues, "we would have already solved this." But all that stored poison, the energetic residue of cultural shock, ancestral trauma, and multigenerational suffering, needs to be acknowledged and *felt*. "It needs to be *lived*," says Markus.

"Nature balances itself, but *big wounds* need time and community to be balanced." Still, the actual work of consciously presencing and integrating those mass energies is "extremely demanding," Markus explains. "As more light comes in, things get messy. Light *moves* things." When asked what he believes the conditions are like in Berlin now, after so many CTIP events have been held there in recent years, Markus offers a wide smile. "There is a small hole in the clouds now," he says, "a little more light."

THIRD WAVE: DISCERNING THE COLLECTIVE VOICE

The powerful wave that pushed through our collective denial and left in its wake potent sensations, emotions, images, and memories begins to stabilize, and a new energy enters the group. It brings with it a clear call for transition. We begin listening for the call of the Collective Voice, the most potent essence of our shared experience.

A facilitator explains that everything participants have experienced and wish to share can now be shared, as what surfaces may no longer be simply personal, but a telegraph of the collective. As this new wave enters, many people begin to offer their experiences, often in a concentrated way, and the whole is guided to stay fully present to the process.

As participants share, it's often helpful to gently highlight for them where their attention goes. It is also important for the facilitator, much like a conductor, to continually feel into the room, remaining attuned to its rhythms and its "temperature," sensing where too much disintegration may be occurring and stepping in to bring participants back into coherence. Every sharing can activate or trigger previously buried content in others. Like a drop of water on the surface of a still lake, one person's words ripple outward, touching similar issues within other participants, guiding them into deeper awareness.

As we bear witness, we can see the intricate interconnectedness of collective trauma right in the room.

A vital role of the facilitator or leading team is the ability to discern the vital threads of the Collective Voice from the many individual voices of those gathered. These threads come together to express the *most potent message* of a given CTIP.

The act of discerning the Collective Voice is a bit like studying an important text and knowing precisely which lines to highlight. Among the many expressions shared over the course of the group process, there will be some calling out to be emphasized. Though the speaker may not be aware of it, their words are expressing not simply their individual lives or experiences but are touching something profoundly deeper. The Collective Voice is archetypal and universal, and its message can be delivered to the group field through one or more people.

The work of the leaders is to listen for this voice and discern it clearly from the many expressions being shared. This requires special focus and skill and often must be learned. Not all the voices will lead a group deeper into potential integration, but a focus on the wrong voice can lead to stagnation of the process.

Highlighting the Collective Voice in the space is like placing acupuncture needles at the most energized points in the group body. Doing so aligns and elevates the group field, amplifying the flow of light through the whole and rapidly speeding up our collective healing process.

DISCOVERING HEALING IN THE COLLECTIVE VOICE

JULIE'S INTERVIEW WITH DR. LAURA CALDERÓN DE LA BARCA

With formal training in intuitive integral psychotherapy and narrative therapy, Laura Calderón de la Barca brings a clear vision to her role with the Pocket Project. "Humans have vast amounts of lived experience," she says, "and how we organize this is through story. When our stories are too narrow, we experience stress." Moreover, every person and every culture has what Laura refers to as "a dominant story, a 'problem' story."

In 2016, Laura participated in a large-scale retreat event facilitated by Thomas. That Friday, all of the participants—who were from many different countries and backgrounds—were invited to join in the evening's Shabbat ceremony. At the end of the observance, Laura says, a Jewish woman spoke to the group. She conveyed that, throughout the ceremony, she felt as if she had been betraying her own people. (Shabbat is traditionally observed only in the presence of other Jews.)

For this woman, pain and betrayal had belonged to her community's dominant story. And when she spoke to acknowledge her feelings, Laura says, "all of sudden an intense trauma wave poured in." But because "so much space" and safety were already present, the wave could come. With Thomas's careful facilitation, people began sharing and presencing that mass trauma energy together.

As a Mexican native with indigenous heritage, Laura grew up experiencing discrimination in school. "I went to an all-white school," she says, "and I had darker skin and looked indigenous. The predominant cultural narrative was that indigenous people are ignorant, and that they are the reason our country is behind." The result, she says, was that she, like so many others in her country, carried a tremendous amount of shame. "This shame lived in my body," Laura says.

After the Shabbat ceremony, as Laura and others were standing in the midst of the CTIP, Laura was initially filled with awe. "There was such a feeling of power about it." Then, as the process progressed and the waves of energy swept through everyone in the room, she says, "I started shaking and crying. I wanted to share what I was experiencing, but I felt this awful fear that I wouldn't be received. That I'd be thought of as arrogant." She shared this fear with the group.

Afterward, a woman approached her and said, "I was so sleepy in the beginning, but the moment you spoke—*poof!*" The woman was from a different part of the world than Laura but had a similar thread in her own cultural and ancestral experiences. Laura's words had been a healing instrument for her, which often happens in the process. Thomas refers to these moments as the presence of the "Collective Voice" speaking to the room.

"This work requires that you've already done a lot of personal healing work and competence," Laura says. "When we practice it together, we touch the end of the known world."

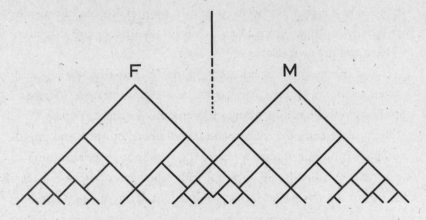

Reversed ancestral tree. Any unresolved energies in our ancestral tree exist in the roots. These energies are then filtered through to us—the living descendants—and become part of our life experiences and healing work.

FOURTH WAVE: GROUP CLEARING AND INTEGRATION

After enough time has been spent in the space of collective sharing, and the facilitator feels that this waveform has been metabolized well, it's time to move the process toward a new phase of digestion. Here the room transitions into breakout sessions for smaller group process work. Anyone needing more individual care can work with a therapist for one-on-one support (this is available at any time through the group process), while the rest split into groups of three.

During CTIP triad sessions, deeper relational presence can be practiced as the profound experiences of the previous waves are further explored. Participants can experience a period of more intimate space for sharing and attuning, and there is time to open up more deeply about their personal paths, as well as to explore how their particular ancestors connect to the larger story of collective trauma that surfaced in the larger forum.

When we create we-space in these smaller groups, we do so with the intention to hold space and witness for one another's ancestors. As you tell me of your grandfather, my work is to listen generously while holding higher perspective in witness consciousness. In this way, I arrive at a multiperspectival sense of your grandfather and may even begin to feel my own relatedness to him.

This is the magic of attunement. With this resource, we can heal broken relation and create new relation. We can release and rewrite the energetic habits and tendencies layered in our collective past.

Because we carry our fathers and grandfathers, mothers and grand-mothers within our bodies, we carry their wounds as well. Trauma is stored in the roots of the ancestral tree, which means that it is carried by our own bodies, expressed in our DNA structure and nervous systems. Through deep attunement, it is possible for us to transcend the boundaries of linear time and connect with ancestral information. This is why the past legacy of lynching is not truly past; we hold it within us just as we hold our ancestors. We are interrelated. The experiences of those who were traumatized in decades past were not theirs alone; they belong to us, as well. This is why we are all responsible for helping to repair the harms of the past.

Enough time should be given for small group processing because this work is highly metabolizing. By working intimately together in deeper space, participants are able to reabsorb and balance the profound energies of the previous large group waves.

When it feels right, the room is brought back together and coherence is reestablished. This is a critical fulcrum for the facilitator, who will need to sense into the field and determine whether there is outstanding energy that hasn't yet surfaced. Such energy will be felt as another wave, pressing forward and asking to move in. When there is unresolved energy to be processed, the facilitation team assists the group through the process of surfacing and clearing the new material.

Once the facilitator senses that the energy of the group has been largely processed, he or she guides the room through a meditation (see the appendix for examples) and, if possible, by toning, to clear the space and bathe the group with higher light and sound frequency.

(Tibetan singing bowls are frequently used for sound healing, clearing, or centering in meditation or spiritual ceremonies. When tapped or rung with a mallet, they emit a very pure, stabilizing tone.) Through this meditation, members are quietly guided out of the deep energy of the integration process and back into their individual bodies and experiences. Although toning meditations are a great tool to create synchronization in the group, any other guided meditation that facilitates coherence will work.

It is important to note that two or more days are often needed for a CTIP event so that it can be integrated healthfully and so participants can depart in a positive way. After the radical intensity of the work, people report feeling "washed" or "cleansed"—as though together they entered the fire, but were delivered, squeaky clean and new.

STAGE 3: META-REFLECTION

In the final stage we conclude by reflecting on the process, by clarifying what we've experienced and learned in our work together. After the profound release of energy, it's beneficial to draw the group's attention to the change process itself. This meta-reflection reinforces the release that has occurred and strengthens its integration by reinforcing the new neuropathways established through the process.

Time is also given for meta-reflection into the relational exercises, large-forum sharing, and triad work. Participants are asked to reflect on how much they'd been able to stay present and connected as listeners and as speakers, how their vitality levels fared, and how their inner experiences seemed to strengthen the awareness process of their partners, their triad, or the room as a whole.

During meta-reflection, we're often able to bring to the surface more information than we'd been aware of during the process, and this strengthens and undergirds the entire experience. As we do this important work together, we are rewriting the book of life.

CREATING NEW DEPTHS
OF FELT AWARENESS

JULIE'S INTERVIEW WITH GREGOR STEINMAURER

Gregor Steinmaurer has been a student of collective trauma work for over a decade and has been assisting participants of the CTIP for the past several years. Referring to what happens in these large group change processes, he says, "The nature of it is *vast* somehow."

In the very beginning, says Gregor, "I didn't fully comprehend the scope." Today, he speaks about the process with clarity and fullheartedness, describing the CTIP as a deeply profound and highly refined practice. "Everyone in the group [becomes] very present, very interrelated," he says. "This creates an atmosphere; I often call it a temple, a sacred space. We all know there is something profoundly sacred and important happening in this moment."

Describing the "large movement" or wave pattern of energy and trauma information, Gregor explains that "everybody gets taken. It's like you get hit by a wave and just have to ride it home." What happens in the CTIP is "not like an individual process where [a therapist] can now say, 'Okay, let's shift to look at something else.'" When group coherence and collective presence are alive in the space, says Gregor, "suddenly, the *whole room* listens. You're all seeing something together. And you start to relate to it as an existing force." When that happens, he says, "the connection becomes *much stronger* than the separation."

Gregor says that when most people think about the idea of getting together with a large group of people to experience and integrate collective trauma, "it sounds almost masochistic. They think, 'Oh, it must be so heavy.' And at times, it can be heavy—but it is far more of a *relief*. There's a deep sense of awe, and also relaxation."

Gregor goes on to explain that the work changed his life and perspective. It taught him, a historian from Austria, the profound difference between intellectual understanding and felt realization. When Gregor first participated in the CTIP in Germany, the group's focus naturally turned to the Holocaust. "But I felt nothing, absolutely nothing," he says. "I really thought I would feel something, but it was like there was this . . . *door*."

Slowly but surely, Gregor says that he came into an awareness and acceptance of this "door," understanding that his intellectual numbness had been part of a much larger piece in the collective post-traumatic symptomology. As he stayed with the work, the process heightened his sensitivity to the human condition, and he experienced "a much greater depth of felt awareness."

When you really touch the process, Gregor says, "it's really, really simple—yet, highly complex. You *cannot push* anything. It is perhaps the highest art you can do in terms of process work. It teaches you so much about life."

USING THE NERVOUS SYSTEM AS A TIME-TRAVEL DEVICE

As we form conscious connection or we-space, we're able to transcend the boundaries of the third and fourth dimensions in which time is perceived as linear and local, and together cross the threshold into new dimensions—beyond time, where all that has been or will be is available in what we call the "now." Like the Na'vi of Pandora, our nervous systems are neither purely physical nor entirely separate; we are inextricably bound.

The secret of time travel is twofold: First, *we* are the portal. And second, to travel through time, we don't have to move an inch. We need only become more fully and consciously present—wherever, and with whomever, we are.

IN THERAPEUTIC PRACTICE

The nervous system, I believe, is a messenger of universal law by which I refer to the timeless source of consciousness development. Revealed in the perennial wisdom traditions, universal law protects the sacred nature of life—and the source of life as such. Universal law permits us to restore the flow of conscious awareness and to form healthy, ethically developed lives and sustainable cultures. Wherever the law has been broken, the precise location of the break in the nervous system (cosmic address) becomes blocked or constricted, and higher energy is less able to pour into and through that part of the nervous system without blocks or interruption. The biographical material related to the breakage becomes dissociated, and over time the natural function of the region may become suppressed and downregulated. Development may become frozen or blocked.

For therapists and healers, the power of attunement through the energetic nervous system is the ability to sense and connect with our clients at the precise cosmic address or space-time location of an early or erstwhile wound, conscious or unconscious. We have all been infants, toddlers, children, and teenagers, and our bodies remember these stages of experience, even if our minds have forgotten them. And because of the nervous system's beautiful capacity for relational wiring (as described by polyvagal theory) every parent can intimately feel into their child's experience. They can see through their child's eyes and know, through a transfer of energy to their own brains and bodies, their child's precise somatic and emotional states—whether sleepiness, frustration, joy, or wonder.

With refinement and training, we can engage this capacity for *other* awareness in the context of the therapeutic or healing relationship.

143

We can feel into our clients' somatic and emotional condition, and they can come to feel themselves *felt* in us. This is the relational gift of presencing, yet it can transcend the boundaries of what we call the present. Engaging this subtle capacity of the nervous system, we can learn to link directly to our clients' past condition, at any age or point in time.

As integrated adults, we're able to access our interiors with awareness and can recognize when we aren't showing up as our most integrated selves but have instead momentarily regressed to an earlier stage (due to stress or shadow activation). With the same competence, we can feel into our clients' interiors, using our own energetic nervous systems, and sense precisely when and where the unhealed energy of a younger self is being emitted. These fractured aspects are created during times of injury or trauma, and by fully tuning in to our clients' early self-states, we can offer the power of presence and help to build relation where none may have existed.

An attuned therapist can—ethically and with permission—learn not only to sense an early trauma but to precisely locate and download its information in real time, using the subtle field. Simply through presence and conscious relation, often without needing to speak of the content (as it may not always be helpful for the client to do so), a skilled therapist or healer can learn to download the energy of the trauma, as it is stored in the client's body complex, from hyperarousal or dissociation into the equilibrium of coregulation.

These signature injuries are fulcrums in the individuation loop; they are records of trauma filed and stored in the body's holographic library. There, the energetic nervous system is the body's head librarian and chief physician, and our work as healers is simply to help awaken and catalyze.

IN THE COLLECTIVE INTEGRATION PROCESS

The same subtle competence is a vital skill for those seeking to work with historical or cultural trauma or development. Think of it as a Wi-Fi extender for the third eye, linking and assimilating it with all the physical senses. By engaging this capacity at the next octave, we're able to precisely sense and attune to the group field and to locate within it information about a particular cultural impact held in the collective body. This signature charge may have occurred during a period of catastrophic war or a time of authoritarian rule. It can be specific and singular to a distinct time and location, or it might be broader and more wide-ranging.

A facilitator must be able to tune in to the archeological layers of the wider cultural body and isolate the distinct signal being relayed into the group field. Our role is to assist its movement, shepherding this energy into and through the group field, so it can emerge as a conscious experience for everyone present. It's important for any facilitator of group integration to awaken the subtle capacities of their energetic nervous systems to (1) learn to sense these complex energies accurately and (2) discover how to bridge their own field to the broader collective field.

By coupling the individual field into the collective matrix at the right vector and while holding one's connection to light, the energetic nervous system acts as a kind of Wi-Fi link, permitting the streaming of the appropriate trauma content into the conscious frame of the group. This link opens a door for participants to begin to experience and express the larger waveforms.

From here our role is to subtly steer and support the overall intensity of the group process. An experienced facilitator, at the right moment, can actuate more energy into the process, amplifying the volume of karmic content flowing into the space, or subtly adjust the valve, reducing the influx of unconscious energy and lowering the intensity in the room. With care and practice we learn to compassionately shepherd the power of this profound healing process.

For those groups that have met and practiced together many times, there is still another domain that can be accessed mutually and with intention. It calls for a still-higher order collective capacity, as well as clear and careful guidance and practice. There must be adequate coherence in the shared field, so it is unique to well-attuned groups.

For this practice, a chosen facilitator will lead the group in a meditation to guide members into presence with a particular ancestral or cultural experience (see the appendix for an example), such as the Holocaust or the Trail of Tears. As they begin to enter deeper mental, emotional, and physical attunement with the people who lived through the experience, very powerful impressions and sensations will arise, and it may feel as though they are witnessing something that is happening now. All participants need ample capacities for stillness and resilience. The work is highly intensive, making transpersonal insight on the part of everyone present quite beneficial.

Together, we can become beacons, opening a portal in space and time. When we enter, we come as the light of the relative future, bearing its higher resource into what we call "yesterday." I believe that in the deepest hours of our ancestor's suffering, when they prayed in desperation and felt some glimmer of presence beyond the chaos, some quiet sense that they were not alone in their pain, that indeed they were not, and *are* not. The ineffable Divine was already pouring in—over great distances as though merely footsteps, across eons at the speed of light. And when we come together in this work, we are both witness to and servant of this mystery.

The heart is the doorway; the elixir is light. And the present can change the past.

PRESENCE IS HOLISTIC

It is important to recognize that there is a qualitative difference between general sharing, which occurs at the level of the mental body, and attuned sharing. Sharing with intention, presence, and attunement is somatic and emotional. It occurs holistically—across the mental, emotional, and the physical bodies. Listening with presence requires the sensitivity of the body, and therefore connection *to* the body. It requires emotional receptivity and awareness. And it asks us to pay attention to the quality of receptivity in our partner or group members. What happens to our vitality as we share and as we listen? When do we feel connected to our emotions? When might we feel dissociated?

Whether we are the speaker or the listener, relational attunement invites us to become aware of the quality of energy within us and passing *between* us. The energy will feel "on"—it will flow easily and obviously—when we feel connected to what we're saying, and when we feel connected to one another. When we lose that connection, as we sometimes may, whether on our end or theirs, it will feel as though a valve has been turned off. Learning to observe these dynamic flows of energy within and between us is at the heart of the presencing practice.

COLLECTIVE COHERENCE IS AN EVOLUTIONARY BIRTHRIGHT

The year marked "1941 War Trauma" is a corrupted file in our collective memory. It contains undigested data (i.e., the past), which materializes in contemporary lives as symptomatic patterns of residual suffering. This data will resurface in our lives and our cultural histories, generation after generation, as the life principle itself works to detox and restore the balance of equilibrium. We can suppress this process in futility, or we can work consciously to restore the collective stream.

Whether we are facilitators of process groups or members of conscious collectives, we can learn to retrieve any given file in our cultural or historical library and download its information, its energy, into a conscious group field. These packets enter our fields first as felt tension, discomfort, and resistance, mirroring our collective habit of denying trauma and its consequences. If we remain present with this energy, it will eventually break through in a surge of powerful memories and emotions and many other forms. The energy of our collective trauma has been stored deep in the recesses of the cultural shadow and may be formidable in the light of day, but with presence and the assisting influence of higher light, it can be dialyzed from fragmentation and restored into wholeness.

All that's required is our willingness to fully attend to whatever arises and to be compassionate with ourselves and one another in the process. What surfaces may have occurred in our own lifetimes, or it may have been waiting in the eaves for three or more generations. With these and other practices, our collective body can learn to regulate itself. Together, we can bring the past into peace.

What Dr. Hiroshi Motoyama described as the "long chain of ancestral karma that stretches back through time" is an energetic field, a vertical and horizontal grid of ancestral and personal energies. Energy fields are nested systems; our personal biographies are holographic imprints of larger, collective scars. These scars or patterns of trauma are held in the collective shadow. Like the dark energy physicists speak of, we only come to know of their presence based on downstream effects or symptoms, as we've discussed. When we gather for the purpose of integrating collective trauma, we might not see this dark lake with our eyes, but with sensitivity and attunement, we can sense its distinctness and feel its forms. The collective shadow of Argentina, the United States, Israel, or Germany each feels particular to the place and to the people who live and *have* lived there.

When we tune in from a field of coherence, it's like peering together at the surface of a still pool; we're greeted by a mirror of our complexity. In that reflection, we can see the rich reserves of information that we have been storing so long out of sight. Perhaps we have gathered with the intention to look into the unhealed past of World War II Germany. The scrying mirror of we-space consciousness shows us that we are also the Germans of that past; we are divinely interconnected.

Any energetic field formed and held by the gathering of multiple people is necessarily complex. To make it a conscious field—that is, to practice presence and we-space so that together we may bring to the surface what has been unconscious, requires clear intention, present witness, compassionate sensitivity, transpersonal insight, and gentle dexterity. In the CTIP, we are not only surfacing shared cultural traumas, we are holding an energetic through-line to the rest of humanity, as well as to the energies of our planet.

With attunement and presence, we can create collective coherence, and together become a grounding rod for the inflow of higher light. When enough coherence has been created, this light activates the space, striking a tuning fork for a divine harmonic whose vibration is a resonator for the unconscious waters beneath us. Our mutual intention for integration causes the light to ripple across the waters of the dark lake, creating sacred geometries from disintegration, order out of chaos. As we lean in and listen, our nervous systems begin to resonate, and a gateway into higher-dimensional relating opens between us. From that vantage, we can see the notes of our collective past playing out like a vivid and intricate symphony. Dramaturgical. Darkly burning. At times, painfully discordant. Yet, forever revelatory.

7

GUIDANCE FOR FACILITATORS, THERAPISTS, AND HEALERS

Compassion is not a relationship between the healer and the wounded. It's a relationship between equals. Only when we know our own darkness well can we be present with the darkness of others. Compassion becomes real when we recognize our shared humanity.

Pema Chödrön
The Places That Scare You

I have had the privilege of leading many CTIPs over the years and always the work has moved me. Some of these experiences have been particularly poignant and profound. In them I witnessed a level of collective pain that stayed with me well after everyone had gone home. After those groups, I needed to take additional time to digest the power of humanity's collective shadow.

In every part of the world, the dark lake contains different flavors, different artifacts, and varying degrees of intensity. Yet, it exists wherever humans exist. As facilitators of collective trauma integration, we must adopt the appropriate tools for the particular groups, cultures, and societies with whom and within which we work. Only the right key can unlock the right door. Knowing which tools to use and how best to employ them requires many competencies and much commitment. As with any higher quest, our commitment must be pure.

And real dangers exist. The impact of this work is exponential, so it must be done carefully and well. Our responsibility is great.

Leading others over that threshold, we permit air and light to flow through the staticky web of density and disorder, which causes so much stagnation in human consciousness and therefore suppression of our evolution. To throw up the shades from the windows is to allow the stream of emergence and potential to flow into the room.

Systems theory and its practice—from computer science, ecology, psychology, organizations, and beyond—emerged out of an evolutionary readiness to more deeply embrace the complexity of our universe. A human body is a system, just as a single heart cell within the body is a system. The heart cell is an open system, exchanging energy/information with the greater system in which it is encapsulated or nested. From a purely physical perspective, the cell walls of the heart cell are its system boundary, and the skin is the body's system boundary.

A system develops through an exchange of energy—that is, a *process*—between itself and its environment. The system receives inputs in the form of a resource from its environment and processes this resource to create an output. When the output offers a positive value to the system's environment (such as aided respiration to the human body by way of functioning heart cells) it is *energy*. But when a system's output to its environment is of a negative value (such as a waste byproduct), entropy is created. The environment becomes disordered.

Most organic systems are nested within other systems—it's "turtles all the way down." The individual fits within the family (ancestry) fits within the society fits within humanity. Across all time and all cultures, *right now*. Allowing ourselves to visualize this encapsulation is beneficial to our work as facilitators. But there is something else. Systems theory also explores *emergence*; it examines the relationships between the constituent parts of a thing and how those parts self-organized to form the whole. So, for example: What were the constituent parts of the deoxyribonucleic acid molecule, and how did they emerge as DNA? And further, how has DNA arranged and rearranged itself so elegantly across the vast array of emergent life-forms?

There is both elegance and complexity in the evolutionary process, and it is clear that self-organization is central to emergence. Group facilitation is precisely the same; it requires that we self-organize and shows us that this can neither be forced nor tightly controlled. Facilitation must be *adaptive* and *responsive*. As a conscious group, we actively become greater than the sum of our parts, and it is precisely that Greater Sum whose conscious emergence we seek.

We find ourselves at an exponential evolutionary juncture. The entangled matrices of human consciousness are riddled with entropy and waste. The field of the collective shadow dominates. From our vantage, this has created distortions in the fabric of time itself. We are split into alternate worlds, and our past is not past. As a result, our collective development may be halted. To progress as a species—to heal ourselves and our planet—all human systems will need to be cleansed and cohered. Many of us experience a feeling of pressure or a sensation of urgency around the need for humanity to engage in this work at this time, yet it comes with a message of clarity and hope. More will be called to discover systems-scale or higher-order approaches to healing. That is the grace of evolution's light at work.

EXAMINING OUR MOTIVATION TO HELP

I believe it's important to explore what our motivations are in wanting to help. What brings us to therapeutic work? Our family histories can be revealing. Certain entanglements collect energy, and often these are the places where water flows *up* the mountain. If I learned to be the "helper" in my family system, forever stepping into the supporting role in order to meet my own needs for acceptance, attention, and approval, it's especially important that I examine this early script when exploring my motivations to do healing work in general.

If I haven't fully cleared this past material, then my instinct to help or heal now isn't entirely a conscious act. I'm still driven by dark (unconscious/shadow) chi, to be seen and accepted and loved. There can be many kinds of unconscious attachments behind our desire to be of service to others, so it behooves us—and all we intend to help—to work to become aware of, and to heal, these hidden elements.

The commitment to lend our service to the care and development of the world is a beautiful and necessary thing and should be undertaken with awareness.

FACILITATION AS SERVICE

Trauma limits the flow of higher energy through the nervous system; ongoing trauma damages or delays the development of the nervous system. The spine is the main causeway for this energy and information, and when a person has been impacted by trauma, their personal field contains frozen or stifled energy. It can be perceived as a kind of static or a gray "bubble." Think of entering a large house in which a few of the windows have been opened to the spring breeze. Yet when you enter further into the house, you discover that other rooms have been closed off, their doors locked and their windows shuttered against the light. In those rooms, the air is stuffy and damp, and dust has gathered, and you have the sensation that something may have happened in them, but no one seems to remember what—or maybe no one wishes to. That shut-away energy no longer communicates with the rest of the house, just as the traumatized layer of the body field has been closed off from the rest of the system.

Because light or higher energy no longer flows into that portion of the individual's field, the frozen layer or "room" acts to block the receipt of vital evolutionary information. Every other room may be connected, but a person cannot *fully* progress without integrating this lost aspect. Many people in the world have not experienced trauma or have healed and integrated their experiences—and many have even begun to heal their ancestries. Yet, if a large portion of a city or country is without electricity, phone, or Internet service, the whole is affected. Communication, connectivity, and the pace of development will be dramatically slowed or even halted until all systems are brought back online. If this is sufficiently widespread and ongoing, innovation cannot emerge.

This is the state of our world. It isn't simply that developed nations have access to resources that less developed nations don't yet have, or that innovation purely follows material resource. Trauma blocks connectivity, freezes development, and inhibits emergence. These truths are interrelated.

Multiple unconscious trauma agreements inform our shared reality. Many people fall in love and enter into blissful intimate relationships only to become disenchanted by trauma agreements they unconsciously entered into. The same thing occurs in family systems and workplaces where people fall into patterns of discord, struggling for power, triggering one another, operating with victim/oppressor dynamics, and ultimately feeling the pain of separation. Yet, the repetition of these unconscious patterns is the steady call of the soul to feel into, acknowledge, embrace, and heal.

On a grander scale, our social or wicked problems arise as a call from the Collective Soul, proffering an invitation into mutual awakening. As facilitators of collective trauma integration, we are servants of that higher soul and messengers of its invitation. Every journey begins with the call, and for transformation to occur, the hero must inevitably accept.

ROLE OF THE FACILITATOR: DRAWING DOWN THE LIGHT

The most important capacity for the facilitator is the ability to stay present to the group's process, and this requires the ability to hold both a clear interior and exterior awareness. Full presence permits the facilitator to intuitively follow the flow of the group while maintaining a resonant container so that participants can feel trusting and connected.

It is vital that the facilitator is developed enough to adequately presence and hold the depth and intensity of the trauma integration process.

It is also essential that facilitators hold a connection with the dimension of higher consciousness or essence on behalf of the group. In this way, facilitators serve as a grounding or mediating influence, so that higher light, or the light of the future, can more easily enter the space. This luminous intelligence holds the pattern for the potential integration already existing within the group field and is therefore the most vital resource for the process.

For facilitators to be able to steadily and consistently access and channel light for the benefit of collective trauma integration work, they should come to their role with a deep capacity for transpersonal insight. They should be people who have done and continue to do their own work. They should be committed to integrating the destructive and constructive forces of their personal shadows; people committed to precise communication and healthy relation.

To be able to hold presence for the group process, a facilitator's individual identifications must take a back seat. If we become overidentified with any aspect of the process, we'll be unable to hold the higher perspective and cease channeling its light into the space. The process will stagnate, disintegrate, and potentially fail. But transpersonal insight allows us to hold a perspective of disidentification, so that as facilitators, we lower the risk of becoming absorbed by any element of the process itself, potentially failing to assist the group intention or causing inadvertent harm.

Intuition and inspiration are critical tools for the facilitator. Equal in importance are experiential knowledge; the qualities of openness, sensitivity, and responsiveness; and a willingness to proceed with the unknown, all of which allow us to stay present and attuned to the energies and needs of the group. A deepened sense of inner spaciousness permits the light of insight and information to enter our perceptive awareness and suddenly, we may sense or know things beyond our ordinary senses. We may feel inspired to speak on subjects that we hadn't planned to address prior to the event—a positive sign, suggesting we are connected to the flow.

As facilitators, we make ourselves available to channel higher vibrational information and conduct its intelligence into our past, and by clearing and releasing that past, this sublime evolutionary impulse is able to illuminate what we may become. Its light is that stream of insight, innovation, revelation, and mastery that has shone upon all those whom history has labeled visionary, genius, and "ahead of their time."

As we stand in the commitment to hold space for higher perspective, we ground and channel the light of the future into the room. As instruments of that light, we serve to shepherd the group to its transformational edge.

A RECOMMENDED STANDARD OF CARE

With this work, we find ourselves at the transformational edge, at a bold frontier of healing that encapsulates psychology, sociology, science, and spirituality. Much more will be discovered, and out of those discoveries, new best practices will emerge. What I present below are recommendations based on known best practices. They are intended to form a conscious structure through which new energies may begin to flow.

COMMITMENT

Facilitating group trauma integration requires a profound level of personal and professional commitment—to everyone participating in the room and to the heart of the process itself. In light of this, any person who seeks to facilitate the integration of collective trauma in a formal group process is called to vow their commitment to the following:

- Ongoing responsibility and care of one's psychological health and developmental progress

- Highest ethical standard of engagement with the work itself

- Utmost integrity in relation to the well-being of every soul who shows up to the process

In order to honor our commitments, we must rely on wise personal and we-space practices.

CLEANSING PRACTICES

After the intense energies of any CTIP, regardless of group size, it is essential for facilitators to take personal downtime, allowing the mind and body to digest the impact of what has been experienced. Whenever I schedule a CTIP event, I block out a period of time immediately following the event just for this purpose. This time should be used for rest and self-care.

Spend time in nature. Receive a massage or other form of bodywork. Move your muscles with yoga, dance, or whatever form of play delights you. Prepare delicious, nourishing meals and share them with loved ones.

Put simply: recharge your batteries.

It's also vital during this period to *return to your meditation practice*. Regular meditation is the most fundamental means by which we can clear the nervous system of any residual energies we may have taken on during a group trauma integration process. Stillness meditation, light meditation, and somatic meditation are all helpful practices.

INTERVISION PRACTICE

The term *intervision* is commonly used in the Netherlands, Germany, and elsewhere to refer to meetings between care workers or treatment team members who gather to discuss their work-related learnings with the goal of improving the quality of the care they provide. In this way, intervision is a client-centered approach to professional development.

Intervision is a time to come together with our peers and cofacilitators to consciously check in with others who do this work—for support, feedback, and growth. These meetings should occur regularly—in person wherever possible or electronically using video conferencing. We are working with immense energies, and it is vital that we are not isolated in that work.

In addition to formal intervision, facilitators benefit from connecting informally, meeting for coffee or web chats or planning dinners or casual retreats. Take time to share support and foster kinship and simply be together. Grow the bonds of community.

INTERVISION ROLES

Intervision is a peer practice; all members share responsibility for the group and its agenda. A volunteer chair member may be selected, and this role can be rotated. There are many ways to organize and self-manage; what is important is that the group meets the needs of its members.

When the peer group has gathered at the designated time and place, a relational practice may be engaged in to bring everyone into coherence. Depending on the size, the group can be divided into triads. Members are invited to check in and share. If a team member has been experiencing an activation brought on by their work as a facilitator, or any other concern, he or she may share as others in the group listen and attune, offering reflection and feedback as appropriate. This can activate further sharing so that group content may surface, which can then be processed and integrated by the whole.

Time should be given for mutual reflection and group learning (i.e., the meta-reflection process). Members can explore questions or thoughts that arose during the group process and reflect on their perspectives and potential learnings.

When a question arises after facilitating a group practice, it is important to tune inward. This initiates personal reflection and contemplation. We may recognize the answer to this question on our own, or we can bring it to intervision. Intervision may work very well to resolve the question, so that the additional guidance of a supervisor is not needed. However, when any part of the question is still uncertain, there is a third option for bringing fuller clarity, understanding, or resolution, which is to bring the question into supervision practice with one's designated facilitation leader, teacher, or mentor.

SUPERVISION PRACTICE

All facilitators of the CTIP benefit from the continued support of a teacher, mentor, or process leader. Just as psychologists and licensed therapists attend regular supervisory meetings with a more senior professional, facilitators of collective trauma integration benefit from the guidance and clarity that emerge from discussions with a trusted mentor.

During the supervision practice, the facilitator can address any unclear points or issues that may arise over the course of the group process. He or she can examine and own personal triggers—*very* important to the success of the work. In a clear and connected relationship, as all supervision at this level should be, the teacher or mentor has an opportunity to offer valuable insights or to assess whether a facilitator may need to take time out for self-care. Many benefits can be gained from supervision, all of which pay out to the individuals, communities, and, inevitably, to the cultures impacted by larger integration processes.

SUPERVISION ROLES

The individual acting in the role of supervisor serves as a mirror, reflecting back to the facilitator any blind spots or unseen trauma content that may be creating disconnection or emotional activation. The role of the supervisor is to help us to see more clearly, to point a lantern in the darkness so that we can aim in the direction of higher integration.

AFTERCARE

An essential part of good container building is aftercare. CTIP participants may need to meet periodically after the original group work has been conducted to further process any material that came up during the initial process or that may have been triggered afterward. I recommend that smaller groups meet regularly to work through such material for a three-to-six-month period following CTIPs, where aftercare may be beneficial or necessary.

Following these stages ensures that we seek our inner wisdom, that we utilize group intelligence, and that only the right questions are taken to supervision. We call this *the walking of the question*, and it helps to prevent overreliance on a single resource, which would bring imbalance. As facilitators advance, they require less time in supervision—and may even take on the mentor role for others. Intervision, however, is always important.

INNER RESOURCES FOR FACILITATORS

Any facilitator of collective trauma integration should have awakened to the subtle realms and healthfully integrated their own subtle perceptual sense. From this domain of awareness, we can recognize shadow in the energetic experience and can accurately discern the charges, waves, and residues of trauma in both the personal and collective fields.

Using this higher subtle awareness, the facilitator is able to sense the soul or transpersonal energy—the basic driving force of a human life—and discern the nature and condition of its flow.

THE POWER OF THE SOUL

The soul is the fundamental resource of the healing process. By facilitating alignment between the personal self, the higher self (the soul), and the light of the Divine, instant healing can occur. When the same synergistic alignment is facilitated between many souls at once, past and present, the healing it encodes is exponential. It is a powerful moment of mutual awakening and is both humbling and awe-inspiring. When it occurs, it feels as though the luminous heart of an already-healed future rejoices to receive us.

The forces within a collective trauma field are immense and powerful and therefore must be approached with skill and care. The vast underworld of our shared unconscious is the residence of nightmares and ghouls for a reason. It is no small feat to willingly attempt to enter there. To do so requires great personal lucidity and a strongly synchronized relational field. If we fail to enter that realm in either clarity or resonance, we will fail to stand in it (or possibly to exit it) with sanity. Neptune rules the dark waters, and it is said that to see in them clearly requires the dissolution of the false self. If we fail his test, Neptune shows us deception and illusion. But if we succeed, we find spiritual illumination.

THE POWER OF CONNECTION

Trauma results in retraction, numbing, and isolation and thus injures the innate capacity for relation. In this way, connection becomes the second most important resource for its healing. After a traumatic event, individuals are able to integrate their experiences and return to their lives much more quickly when they report feeling supported by their families and communities—that is, where relatedness and connection are present. In the literature referencing one-to-one mental health therapy, a great deal of attention is paid to the quality of the relationship between client and therapist. Where clients report feeling a sense of trust, comfort, and connection, outcomes are sufficiently better. These truths point to another: in a CTIP, the quality of presence and attunement and the degree of group coherence directly affect the outcome.

THE POWER OF SHARED CONSCIOUSNESS

As facilitators, it is our role and our responsibility to help strengthen these resources for the group. We must embody the coherence we ask of the group, guiding its process with compassion and clarity. For a room of people to cohere, a fulcrum must be reached at which the quality of connectedness across the whole becomes stronger than any fragmentation arising in individuals. (Indeed, the level of coherence of a system serves as the fundamental resource for integrating fragmentation in the system.) There can be an initial cohering and then a breaking away, and this pattern will repeat itself until the field stabilizes. The work is to gently encourage participants to feel into any fragmentation while inviting the group into deeper coherence.

Once energetic coherence is established in the group field, it can more easily be *re*-established should fragmentation occur. The intention is to create a container of shared consciousness through which we can safely process collective trauma energy. With adequate presence and attunement, any energies, emotions, or historical memories that surface are held *in relation*, and are likely to be processed well by all present. While we are always moving through a wider collective field, with CTIP work we are called together to establish *collective consciousness* so that we can perform *collective shadow work*.

Recall that energy requires adequate structure. Group resonance in the CTIP creates what can be understood as an extratemporal, multidimensional light matrix. Energetic coherence is we-space; it establishes an architecture, or structure. You can think of it as possessing geometric qualities and harmonic frequencies, but it need only be felt. At peak coherence, this field is recognized by all as a pure quality of presence, a heightened sense of togetherness. Its architecture is the precise vessel required to hold the flow of immense energies in a CTIP.

ADDRESSING POTENTIAL DANGERS

It simply cannot be said enough: Any facilitator of collective trauma integration must prioritize their own personal and transpersonal development, commit to a regular practice of contemplative awareness, and attend diligently to their personal health and well-being. This necessitates ongoing shadow work and a commitment to regular we-space practices (e.g., group presencing, intervision, etc.), as well as a willingness to surround oneself with others who are similarly committed. At heart, the work we do together is about much more than group trauma therapy—it is about mutual awakening.

To be wise and skillful shepherds of collective trauma integration, we as facilitators must be able to deeply attune to ourselves *and* to the group, simultaneously and throughout the process. We must enter the group space in clarity so that we can hold within us whatever arises—whether that is the fragmented energy present in just one person, or a mass wave of ancestral, regional, or historical content flowing into the room. We're called to witness and perceive these layers with acuity. The strength and power of the energy can be profound, and the challenge for group facilitators is to learn how to stand with both feet firmly planted so that these energies can flow through us without overtaking us.

Here's a rule of thumb: however it goes for the facilitator, it goes for the group. If some quality or content within the group trauma wave charges or activates the facilitator's personal shadow, he or she may become uncomfortable or even "triggered." Without adequate transpersonal awareness and continuous witnessing (on the part of the facilitator), this activation could strengthen the trauma wave for everyone in the room. Clarity can be lost, and the process may quickly become confused or chaotic. The facilitator's personal neuroses may surface, becoming mirrored and amplified by the group. Or an unresolved trauma may be activated and its symptoms may surface physically, perhaps in the form of a headache, abdominal pain, or other symptoms. Without sufficient capacity to attend to one's experience while simultaneously holding the group, attention flattens and the capacity for presence is constricted. Depending on the stage of the process and the strength of the activation, both the participants and the facilitator can be harmed.

In one-to-one trauma therapy, the clinician's level of transpersonal development, ethical focus, and amount of training and skill greatly impact the results. I believe the outcome of group trauma integration is equally dependent on the facilitator's development, ethical focus, and training, and as with one-to-one care, where any of these factors are missing, strengths become deficits and the potential for negative outcomes rises.

DANGERS RELATED TO FIELD COLLAPSE

If there is a failure to establish field coherence, the facilitator will be unable to initiate the group process. If group coherence is established, but the facilitator does not act to recohere the field after fragmentation or disintegration, there will be insufficient structure to contain the collective energies moving through the group, and participants will be unable to move through the process. In such an event, the dynamic is likely to stall out and may inevitably collapse. Remember that the first wave pushes to the surface the deep silt and sludge of collective denial and is often felt by the group as resistance, discomfort, tightness, restricted breathing, sleepiness or inattention, or other sensations. The nervous system has many ways of dissociating conscious awareness from the harsh realities of trauma. Without sufficient group coherence and the presence of a skilled facilitator(s), we stand little chance of being able to wade through the sludge in the surfacing bog of denial.

If the group processes this early wave of collective denial successfully, however, remaining or reestablishing coherence with the help of the facilitator, its resonance becomes more adaptive. A sense of magnetism and stability is often established, so that less effort is required on the part of the facilitator should fragmentations arise, or fragmentations may be subtler or less frequent. As the group continues further into the process, the energetic links or bonds between individuals and across the group become more tensile—even as the energies pouring through the room become stronger.

The further the group moves into the process, the more established is its coherence and the less likely its collapse. However, if the group field *were* to collapse at this stage, perhaps due to unskilled facilitation, a danger point will have been reached. Any trauma content surfacing within a collapsed field cannot be processed adequately by the group—there is too much energy and not enough structure. If collapse should occur at this stage, half of the room might disconnect, suddenly unable to feel or make sense of the energies present, while others could become activated and emotionally overwhelmed. In other words, numbing and hyperarousal symptoms could occur. This could be harmful to all present, which is why wise cofacilitation is so important.

NEED FOR TRANSPERSONAL PERSPECTIVE
AND HOLISTIC PERCEPTION

If the facilitator is unable to access or maintain a transpersonal perspective through the process, he or she will be unable to support wider group coherence. This is the case whenever a facilitator attempts to make sense of the trauma content being expressed purely from their mental or intellectual body. Even the most refined and skillful cognitive approach is not enough, because while intellectual understanding can be both broad and deep, relative to the multiple dimensional layers we work with, cognition is a single plane—necessary, but requiring assistance from other perspectives. By definition, shadow is that which is unknown to the conscious mind by way of logic and intellect, but it is not wholly unknowable. Like a ghostly apparition, we can discern its outlines or theorize its possible meaning, but to interact with its energies requires subtle attunement and holistic perception. The shadow contains our pain, our sins, and our nightmares, but it is also a realm of ancestors, prayers, and dreams. It is both the dimension of unresolved suffering and a portal to our unclaimed potential.

To be allowed to guide others successfully across its threshold and return requires at the very least embodiment, inner maturity (i.e., ego development), moral sensitivity, interpersonal understanding, transpersonal awareness, subtle energetic consciousness, and the capacities to witness and to attain unitive consciousness. Each of these developmental domains is necessary in facilitators of the group trauma process, because if even one of them is missing, the process fails. It may even become distorted.

Facilitators must hold many individuals within his or her awareness, with full presence and attention, while simultaneously connecting to the undercurrents of long-dissociated trauma. They must be able to sense when these energies are about to surface, or to skillfully initiate their flow and emergence into the group field at the right time. They must be able to accurately sense when the flow is becoming too intense and know intuitively how to calm that intensity. They must know when more content needs to be invited in, because the process is not yet complete, and they must be able to sense when it has culminated. They must be able to invite and hold space for higher light—that grace of future that has the power to transform the past. All of this demands more than cognitive understanding; it requires personal development, multidimensional awareness, and attunement with the higher principles at work.

PRESCREENING AND COFACILITATION

Higher light is the energy that supports the group nervous system and transforms the layers of fragmentation in trauma. Through field coherence, the nervous systems of all group participants become energetically linked. If some of the participants attending the process are themselves heavily traumatized, this may inadvertently activate strong dissociation toward the process within others in the room, while simultaneously reinforcing the symptoms or effects of the trauma. For these reasons, it is wise to incorporate a functional screening process prior to any CTIP event, in addition to ensuring there are always enough cofacilitators present during an event.

Therapeutic support staff should be well trained in the process and have a psychotherapeutic background. They should be able to recognize traumatized symptoms and responses. Their role will be to step quietly into the room whenever a single individual appears to need support and gently encourage him or her into a separate one-on-one space for direct care. Because some individuals may slip through even the most careful screening (e.g., those who do not consciously recall personal trauma histories, or others who are unaware of the way ancestral memory can be felt until the process begins), it is very important to have trained cofacilitators present. The CTIP is powerful and deeply affects the whole. Not all who attend will be affected in the same way, but everyone should feel fully supported.

To uphold the vision and intention of collective healing, trained and skillful facilitation and support staff are needed. We do this work in service of the collective, and it requires the highest ethics and integrity. It requires a commitment to self-care and aftercare, to ongoing intervision and supervision, and to an awakened community of fellow CTIP practitioners, all of us growing, working, advising, and knowledge-sharing together.

THE REWARDS

The collective trauma process isn't a clean, linear procedure with a direct, programmable outcome. To understand it, we can organize it into stages and waves, but it isn't a machine into which x input offers y outcome. The CTIP is a complex system; the components that enter into it (beginning long before we show up to the process) are variable and vast. It takes group intelligence, dedication, and synergy for the process to work. And the outcome of the process—whether it is conducted well or poorly—will be expressed exponentially, at the systems scale. It isn't just the participants who experience the effects but the families, communities, and cultures they interact with going forward. The CTIP is acupuncture for the collective body. The most humbling gift of the work is the recognition that afterward, there is a felt vibrational upgrade wherever it occurred. When CTIP healing is repeated in a particular city, region, or country, many feel that the energetic composition of the society begins to shift. Blocked evolutionary energies are released and innovation can surge. Over time, a problematic zone may become prosperous and thriving.

Perhaps this sounds outlandish, yet I and many others have observed these radical shifts again and again. By creating high relational coherence in groups and infusing these fields with inner and outer presence, we become tools of collective transformation. Many people create such fields to meditate on world peace. Others come together in different forms of religious or spiritual worship to pray for healing.

Others throughout the world form resonant fields, even without knowing it, in an effort to send healing energy to the Earth's vulnerable ecosystems. Aligned intention and focus are manifestly powerful. By awakening together in new fields of coherence, we begin to activate humanity's natural immune response, reviving the architecture through which our own divine intelligence can purify and repair the human system and help to detoxify our world.

Some people attend the CTIP out of a desire for deeper personal healing, which it can certainly activate, but collective trauma integration is the healing we attend to in service of one another, of humanity itself. It is the reparation we offer for the atrocities borne by our ancestors and for the suffering we all carry by virtue of living in a traumatized world. It is a light we can bring into our common darkness—not in rejection of the dark but in ownership and with reclamation.

8

PICTURE OF A
TRAUMATIZED WORLD

There are good reasons for suggesting that the modern age has ended. Many
things indicate that we are going through a transitional period, when it
seems that something is on the way out and something new is painfully
being born. It is as if something were crumbling, decaying and exhausting
itself, while something else, still indistinct, were rising from the rubble.

Vaclav Havel
New York Times

The collective field has been described as a *matrix*, a word that
originates from the Latin *māter*, for "mother," and *mātrix*, for
"womb." In archeology, the term *matrix* refers to the soil surrounding an excavation, and in sculpture and manufacturing, it refers
to a structure from which an object or art piece is molded into form.
Similarly, the unseen collective field is foundational and morphogenic;
it holds our assemblage patterns, our shared programming—drives for
creativity, meaning-making, and ancient and emerging archetypes—
and our codes for communication and connection. But the dark,
unconscious energy of historical and cultural trauma is overlaid or
superimposed on the matrix, and it too is formative, manifestational,
and demiurgic.

Our common shadow emerges as an invisible mass or inertia, pres-
surizing the field and bearing down upon us. By its nature, trauma

prevents integration and promotes *dis*-integration. Its symptoms surface in multivalent forms across human endeavor, feeding disconnection, dissociation, apathy, and malaise, and stimulating antisocial behavior in leaders, corporations, and institutions. Trauma constricts evolutionary development, delays progress, and inhibits innovation, manifesting a negative feedback loop of stagnation, systemic breakdown, and cultural collapse. Left unacknowledged and unresolved, the dark energy we carry hardens into the wicked problems of our time.

We find ourselves at a profound moment in history, standing together at an inscrutable edge. Whether that edge is the brink of destruction or the cusp of unprecedented change is up to us. One thing is clear: We can't convince ourselves into necessary transformation based purely on the facts. We must *feel* the deeper reality of our time in order to know the crucible it presents and thereby empower ourselves to change it, to make real a new future.

To truly feel is to embody, to become integrated and whole. Transfiguration arrives through presence.

PRESENCE, ABSENCE, AND CREATING A HOLDING SPACE FOR TRAUMA

OTTO SCHARMER, PHD

In many countries, contexts, and systems, we are dealing with three major divides—the ecological divide, the social divide, and the spiritual divide—that arise from the disconnect between self and nature, self and other, and self and self. So, if we look at trauma in light of an awareness-based systems change, it means looking at the symptoms of trauma from a viewpoint that takes all three types of root issues, including source, into account.

Then we can see that many issues throughout history, and that we have in our society today, are reenactments of trauma.

Violence usually happens when you reactivate the trauma. We cannot understand the Middle East without the Crusades. We cannot understand it without the Holocaust. They are deeper traumas, and they can be activated and result in violence. So, you can say that history is a repetition, a reenactment of trauma from the past. And there's a lot of evidence for that. But it may also be blinding us if we limit ourselves to only that perspective.

Because there's something new happening.

In the twentieth century, the totalitarianism of Hitler and Stalin and others was something we hadn't seen before. And in this century, something is happening that, again, cannot be understood with just a twentieth-century lens. I have been interested in how to shed more light on that from the perspective of today, the perspective of now. The current moment we are living in is a moment of disruption. And for all of us, this moment of disruption means the future is going to be different. We don't know exactly how—and we know even less about how to get there.

The presencing perspective on this situation suggests that, in order to deal with disruption, in order to move from here to there, we have to go on a journey. In part, this is an outer journey, which means going to the edges of the system. And in part, it is an inner journey that connects to the deeper layers of our own experience. Because, if we connect to the true, deep experience of the now, we realize that the future is already here. We realize that our current experience is not only based on the current "reality" or driven by the past, but that the future is already there in the deepest experience of the now.

But we often don't know how to respond to this moment of disruption and the situations we face as individuals or organizations, or as a global community. When we look empirically at how people are responding to disruption, as well as at the way disruption impacts organizational, societal, or global systems, we see, I believe, the same pattern in all countries, which basically includes two types of responses: *turning backward* or *leaning forward*. Turning backward is grounded in and operated by a freeze reaction. Freezing the mind, the heart, and the will—also known as ignorance, hate, and fear. We turn backward in order to "make great *again*." The most important word of that line is *again*, because it's an orientation to the past, a projected state that we seek to reestablish.

However, leaning forward into something that we don't already know—leaning into the emerging future—requires us to open the mind, open the heart, and open the will, which only works if we can access our capacity for curiosity, compassion, and courage. I call this second response the cycle of *presencing*, becoming present and connecting with your highest future possibility. The other response is one of *absencing*, because it results in being absent from our current situation. When we look at that in a little bit more detail, we see that having a closed mind means being stuck in one truth or in one ideology. Stuck in the past, basically. A closed heart means being stuck in one's skin—it's between us and them. And closed will is being stuck in one resolve, a kind of fear or fanaticism. With absencing, there is no evolution in our capacity as a whole being.

The interesting thing about absencing is that it's not about seeing but blinding. It's not about sensing but *de*-sensing. Getting stuck inside your skin as an individual but also in a collective skin. It's not about connecting to source and presencing but disconnecting from your highest future possibility. The gateways into absencing are denial, entrenching, and holding on.

We see a lot of this in our current society. President Trump by now has told more than 12,000 lies and false or misleading statements since he has been in office. How did that impact his popularity? Not at all. Not in any significant way. And that's kind of the post-truth politics world that we live in. And it's a collective condition in more and more countries. In all countries, in fact, but more or less activated.

We see societies falling apart. We can watch it here in the United States but also in many other countries. And one of the main factors contributing to this is the filter bubble—how social media has amplified our disconnectedness from diversity, from opening up to other views. The political strategy that is behind Trump's victory and behind the Brexit victory is an intentional data-driven strategy that is focused on lies. That's the ignorance part. It's focused on activating hate, anger, and fear. And there is the manipulation and suppression of voters. When we look at this as a social phenomenon, we see it show up in many different forms—in politics, the economy, and communication.

Blinding and de-sensing mean you are disconnecting horizontally. You're disconnecting from what's going on around you. And absencing is the vertical disconnect. You disconnect from your higher self, from your highest future possibility. When that happens, any social system that is dealing with these two disconnects will exhibit the same phenomenon, which is manipulating, blaming, abusing, and enacting violence and destruction.

Manipulation, blaming others, and the inability to reflect on yourself can be seen in the abuses of the Catholic Church and many other institutions across countries. And the result is enacting violence. I think in terms of three forms of violence. The first two are direct violence and structural violence. [Direct violence involves individual or group perpetrators and victims.] Structural violence is where you have victims but not a person(s) who can be seen as a perpetrator. For example, poverty, hunger, underdevelopment are all forms of structural violence that we see in many countries. And it is the economic structure that's behind them. So, the perpetrator is not an individual; it's our collective actions. And I think there is actually a third type of violence, which I call *attentional violence*. Attentional violence is to not see another person, another human being, in terms of who they really are, or for their highest future possibility. When who you truly are goes unseen by society, a form of violence is inflicted upon you, resulting in destruction of nature, other, and self—the three divides I mentioned earlier.

The phenomenon of presencing lies on the other side of manipulation, blaming, enacting violence, and destruction. It involves letting come, crystallizing, and giving birth to—prototyping and then embodying—the *new*. It's about bringing something into reality, a deeper, dormant potential, birthing that into reality, allowing something to grow within and then move into reality. Each of us is participating on either side of the equation, one way or another. And this framework and language allows us to not only look at the trauma that has been generated in the past but also to look at the deeper making of trauma and direct structural and attentional violence that is happening now, and that is unique to our century.

Today, there are really two narratives going on. There is the absencing story and all the problems around that. And then there is the deeper human awakening that is happening across the planet. And that is a very powerful narrative, the most important story not told. Why? Because the whole collective conversation is absorbed in the amplification of absencing, which happens through social media and traditional media. So, for example, according to a recent MIT study, when you share fake news, your tweet is 40 percent more likely to be reshared than accurate news. And for the big data companies like Facebook, absencing is better for business. Their advertising revenues are driven by user engagement, and user engagement is much higher when you activate hate, anger, or fear. Those are the most powerful drivers for user engagement, so they are the core business model.

The question is, How can we, as change enablers, engage with the phenomenon of ignorance, hate, and fear, with the phenomenon of collective absencing? That is the new condition that we operate on in this century. How do we engage it outside of ourselves and inside of ourselves on the level of the collective? I believe a main mechanism here has to do with making systems sense and see themselves. It has to do with creating a holding space, where through the use of data and through social technologies, we move into processes that allow us to not only see and sense and feel ourselves but to also see and sense and feel the system that we are enacting collectively in a more embodied way. In fact, in awareness-based systems change, that is the main focus. A lot of this work has to do with creating these holding spaces at a level at which we can hold the complexity, which is often very difficult when dealing with traumatic experiences from the past.

The holding space really begins with seeing the other person in terms of who he or she really is, through the deeper capacity of unconditional witnessing. And as we deepen this process toward the open heart, there is a holding of the other. You're not only seeing but also holding the current moment and that which wants to emerge. And there is the gesture of supporting, which means being 100 percent in the service of the evolution of the other—and of the collective. And that is grounded in the capacity of unconditional confidence that the other will step into his or her own highest possibility. It is also an unconditional confidence in the capacity of the collective, the unconditional confidence that we as a collective can reshape our economy, our democracy, and our learning and leadership systems in a significant and profound way. Which to some degree, we already are, more than most people think is possible.

After facilitating many CTIPs in different regions and countries, I've come to understand that the same energy of denial and resistance that emerges during the group integration process exists everywhere around us, all over the world. It can be sensed as a powerful pressure, pushing down on our communities and nations (except when that heaviness is suppressing our very ability to recognize that it exists!). Trauma energy touches every corner of our world, affecting our governments, institutions, and ways of life. In this chapter, we'll consider some of the larger-scale consequences of unhealed trauma and how it manifests in the world. At points, the content may feel bleak or even hopeless, so I urge you to stay present with whatever you feel as you read along. The tendency to despair or turn away is itself a symptom of unresolved trauma, and if you've made it this far, you understand the responsibility we share to care for it together. (In chapter 9, we will investigate the beautiful possibilities we might realize in our world through the continued integration of collective trauma.)

This is a good time to remember that the tendency to suppress trauma energy (the discomfort it brings up) is initially an intelligent response of the collective nervous system. It is a process that shields us from the overwhelming pain and suffering left behind by war, ethnic genocide, economic and racial injustice, and countless other inhumanities. The energy of intense suffering is pushed out of consciousness simply so that life can be allowed to go on. Denial permits us to survive the unsurvivable—for a while. Left too long, any unconscious defense mechanism becomes detrimental to life. When collective denial goes unaddressed, we see the proliferation of groups that deny that the Holocaust occurred, that a civil war was waged to defend the economic institution of race-based slavery in the United States, or that hundreds of thousands of Rohingya Muslims are subjected to state-sanctioned ethnic cleansing in the form of mass murder, sexual violence, and forced exile from the primarily Buddhist Myanmar.[1]

Suppression, resistance, and denial serve a crucial function in human survival . . . until they don't. When trauma remains too long denied, it begins to exact a steep price, a burden of debt that must eventually be paid, often by subsequent generations.

DISEMBODIMENT IN THE TRAUMA MATRIX

Dissociative reactions to trauma, such as flashbacks, amnesia, fugue states, depersonalization/derealization, sleepwalking, and dream states, speak directly to trauma's impact on embodiment. Reporting on a study concerning the benefits of embodied practice for trauma survivors, Alison Rhodes, PhD, writes,

Survivors have difficulty staying present in their lives. The conditioned fear response that is the legacy of living with trauma for a prolonged period leads them to react to new stimuli in ways that are at best irrelevant, and at worst seriously harmful; they tend to overreact to innocuous stimuli, underreact to danger, and shut down in the face of challenges.[2]

Survivors who participated in Rhodes's study "experienced their bodies as 'constricted,' 'unsafe,' or 'in pain,' or they experienced a complete detachment from their bodies and minds."[3] Over the course of the study, participants engaged in a regular yoga practice, incorporating conscious breathing and movement. At the end, participants overwhelmingly reported feeling safer, more trusting, and more connected to themselves and their bodies, and more at ease with other people in their lives.

When we are disembodied, our nervous systems are unable to fully innervate the physical body, dulling perception and restricting vitality or leading to unbalanced expressions of that force. We "possess" bodies without being fully present within them. Collective trauma creates collective disembodiment. As a consequence of living under the pressure of a traumatized field, groups fragment, dissociate, and disconnect from one another. We become less able to wholly or holistically inhabit the fullness of our potential as embodied beings. It's as though we've collectively agreed, albeit unconsciously, to be *on* the planet without being fully resident *in* it.

As embodiment strengthens, we begin to notice the intensity of *dis*-embodiment in the world. We begin to observe that some people feel partially off-center from their body's core. Others seem far away, as though the body is being operated remotely or may seem heavy or weighted, as though their voices emerge from beneath a cluttered or blanketed space held in the lower third of the body. Still others feel as though they reside somewhere above the region of the head, which can seem unattached to the rest of them, as though linked only by balloon string.

What we cannot see or feel may simply be unconscious and therefore unknown to us. We often discover these unknown parts only after symptoms arise or when another person with high perceptual sensitivity helps us to recognize them.

We've seen in previous chapters that grounding and embodiment are brought online through relation and safety. Groundedness is our natural state; feeling ungrounded requires effort by the body-mind. Disembodiment is disrelation. It prevents us from connecting well or fully—with ourselves, with other people, or with the Earth. Mass disembodiment separates us from nature, leaving many unable to feel either the truth or the urgency of our global climate crisis and thus incapable of addressing it.

I've written that unmet trauma damages the capacity for relation (and thus, creates disembodiment). When we cannot relate from the present, we *react*—meeting present circumstances from the unhealed past. Trauma fractures and splits away vital portions of the self, freezing split aspects outside of present time and arresting fundamental parts of the psyche in the past. These dislocated shards create energetic blocks in the meridian pathways, manifesting breakage in the nervous system, and encouraging future dissociation and suppression. The same negative feedback loop occurs in the collective body; we stand in fragmented parallels of time, rather than in synchrony, incoherence rather than resonance. We fail to see or sense one another accurately. Just as personal crises can never be solved from dislocation or disconnection (and will only be compounded by it), no cultural or planetary crisis can be adequately met while we are blocked, broken, and divided.

The term *responsibility* speaks to our *ability to respond*. We may expect personal responsibility from ourselves and others or demand social responsibility of our institutions, but when disembodiment is high, ability to respond is low. When we're numbly disassociated or reactively aroused, we appear zombie-like. Our limbs and faces are animated, but there's little light behind the eyes. We project upon and split others, failing to acknowledge our dispossessed shadow or disinherited light.

Any social crisis is a relational crisis—whether of the economic, immigrational, or climatic variety—and is therefore a crisis of embodiment. Many of our world's wicked problems are the inevitable consequence of unresolved collective trauma and the disembodiment and loss of relation these ills create. Systemic problems such as poverty, famine, crime, disease, and violence are considered intractable or even impossible to resolve. While nearly everyone acknowledges their existence, many remain unable to fully *feel into* them, which is the core of their irresolvability.

To feel the problems of our world is to know its suffering, but this requires compassionate "response-ability." If we fail to address the world's collective trauma with clarity and compassion, we imperil the survival of our children and our children's children—and countless other species. A year after atomic bombs were detonated over the Japanese cities of Hiroshima and Nagasaki, Albert Einstein pleaded with the public to recognize a key principle at the foundation of this truth:

> *Our world faces a crisis as yet unperceived by those possessing power to make great decisions for good or evil. The unleashed power of the atom has changed everything save our modes of thinking and we thus drift toward unparalleled catastrophe. We scientists who released this immense power have an overwhelming responsibility in this life-and-death struggle to harness the atom for the benefit of mankind and not for humanity's destruction. . . . [A] new type of thinking is essential if mankind is to survive and move toward higher levels.*[4]

On the one end is Cartesian dualism or the mind-body split, and on the other, the "ghost in the machine." The mind has either been revered as separate and therefore transcendent of matter or seen to arise entirely from it—consciousness as an accidental by-product of the brain. But what if mind and body, head and heart, spirit and matter, consciousness and form, and wave and particle are indivisible? What if we are integrated wholes—interrelated, interpenetrating, transformational, and cocreative? This is the foundation of embodiment and embodied practice, which sees burgeoning support across multiple disciplines: from linguistics, consciousness studies, philosophy, psychotherapy, psychoneuroimmunology and medicine, modern physics, spirituality, and more.

SYSTEMIC IMPACTS OF COLLECTIVE TRAUMA

Like truth, shadow always outs.

Suppressed energy doesn't go away, and even dark or disowned energy cannot be destroyed. It needs to move, to become, to transmute; it must find an expression. In this way, unconscious material rises again and again to the surface, seeking to be met, detoxed, and clarified. Until trauma has been acknowledged, felt, and released, it will be experienced from without in the form of repetition compulsion and projection and from within as tension and contraction, reduction of life flow, illness or disease.

INNOVATION AND SOCIETY

The modern era has seen startling advancements—breakthrough discoveries in science, medicine, and business, largely made possible by disruptive innovation across the technology sector. Improvements to standards of living in the form of sanitation, housing, labor reform, and health care have extended the human life span and ensured continued invention, innovation, and progress—from electricity, automobiles, airplanes, computers, satellites, spacecraft, and beyond, including AI, machine learning, robotics, autonomous cars, brain mapping, DNA mapping, and quantum computing. With every new discovery, we leap forward in our quest to understand.

And yet the legacy of Newtonian materialism and Cartesian dualism continues to inform our interpretations of self, other, and world. Scientific thinking is still dominated by the perspective that we live in a cold, atomistic, wholly accidental universe that can be analyzed, predicted, conquered, used, and exploited. This notion reigns supreme—in politics, capitalism, academia, medicine, psychology, and even religion. It is the worldview of individuation and individualism, reliant on the myth of separation.

Having split ourselves between mind and matter, we objectify the body, the "other," and the Earth. The mind is differentiated from the emotions and elevated above them, and both are held as distinct from the body. Little authority is given to intuition, instinct, emotion, compassion, communion, or creativity. Split and compartmentalized, we speak *about* instead of *from* life. We stand distant and remote from ourselves and one another, affixed to interpretation but cut away from feeling. We cling to our disembodiment through intellectualization, compartmentalization, and distraction, all of which help obscure our wounds.

But as long as we are split, divided, and separate, we remain unable to access our full subtle capacities. Unable to feel ourselves as belonging to one another or to the world. Unable to sense the numinous intelligence of our universe or to recognize ourselves as ultimately traveling along its evolutionary course. The illusion of separation allows us to fear and hate and exploit one another. To harm the body and damage the psyche. To reject nature and abuse the environment. To mistreat animals and children and ourselves. To repudiate the spirit and deny the soul.

We may become addicted to cooking shows, yet know very little about where our foods come from, what precisely has been added to them, or how far they've traveled to make it to our plates. We consume plants without knowing how they were grown, whether the soil was cared for, whether they were produced from genetically modified organisms, or what chemical pesticides may have been used to grow them. Biting into a store-bought apple, we rarely question whether its purchase inadvertently supported the widespread colony collapse of honey bees or if exposure to the same insecticides contributes to health risks for farmworkers and their families.

We may know the intimate details of celebrities' lives while being far less attentive to the deeper truths of our own. We accept it as normal that movie stars, athletes, and hedge-fund executives are paid multiple millions of dollars, while most teachers, social workers, paramedics, journalists, childcare workers, and artists struggle to earn a livable wage. We accept corruption as a fact of government and business, standing by as plutocrats, kleptocrats, oligarchs, and white-collar criminals rise to top positions of power in both. We recognize that professional sports, the cosmetics industry, social media marketers, and tabloid print and television rake in billions of dollars each year while throughout much of the world, schools go underfunded and essential education suffers. So we send our children to broken schools or accept it as a fact of life that other peoples' children must attend them. Schools where regimentation, control, and standardized test scores are valued over student fulfillment, so that curiosity and joy and *life* are zapped out of learning.

The longer we continue to disown our darkness, the greater the chance we will self-fulfill the prophecies we most fear. But as we reclaim the contents of our unconscious, we become better humans, more empowered to make a better world. Rather than encouraging harm and disconnection, the technologies we create from *that* vantage will further the benevolence of life itself.

HEALTH AND MEDICINE

Trauma doesn't just harm the mind; it injures the body. It leaves us less able to thrive. As the Adverse Childhood Experiences Study revealed, the number of key traumas a child experiences correlates to chronic and terminal disease in later life and even to early death.[5] The burden of inherited trauma in post-war societies is perhaps borne out in the dramatic rise of autoimmune disorders and the number or degree of mental health conditions we see diagnosed today.[6]

Unhealed trauma can manifest physically through cellular suppression, metabolic disequilibrium, hormonal imbalance, somatic pain, reduced mental clarity, emotional distress, and disease.[7] In the collective body, accumulating trauma manifests at scale—through environmental degradation, corporate exploitation, ethnic or religious oppression, political discord, social unrest, armed conflict, pandemic poverty, endemic disease, epidemic depression, rising rates of suicide (such as in Germany, Israel, and the United States), and in many other social ills.[8]

Because trauma is systemic, manifested all across society in nearly every sector, it therefore touches, and in some way informs, even our health-care institutions, and the mechanisms we employ to treat and prevent disease. Generally speaking, in developed nations that use some form of universal health care, access to medical care is guaranteed, costs deferred to the economy are lower, and public health outcomes are higher than elsewhere. Yet even in countries like the United Kingdom, hospitals and clinics may be underfunded, leaving systems overburdened and understaffed.[9] Patients are frequently forced to wait long periods for needed treatment or surgical care,[10] and medical services are rationed or reduced. Due to limitation and strain, physicians, nurses, and other core staff become overtaxed and vulnerable to anxiety, depression, and other concerns. In addition, vital innovation can become blocked, constrained, or poorly adopted. When our systems for health care are underfunded and underserved, it reflects the state of the global immune system. Not having enough energy is a collective trauma symptom. Not having enough resources for self-healing is something we may take as normal: *that's just how the world is.* But it isn't normal. It is a sign that vital aspects of our collective lives are less energized than they should be.

The United States, the only industrialized nation in the world without a system of universal health care, often prioritizes high cost and low regulations, which can result in unsound research, the proliferation of synthetic pharmaceuticals for profit, untested or poorly tested medical devices,[11] and unnecessary or invasive surgeries and procedures.[12] Medical ethics too often take a back seat to profits and acclaim, so that innovation is driven in part by the unconscious desire for supremacy, rather than alignment with the Hippocratic Oath and its vital dictum, "First, do no harm."

In a system run at the behest of for-profit corporations, people who cannot afford to pay are forced to go untreated. Other Americans remain trapped in economic uncertainty due to the rising costs of insurance, medications, doctor visits, and emergency or surgical care.

In this environment, the importance of the doctor-patient relationship and its impact on recovery and well-being is often undervalued or dismissed, and the role of sustainable lifestyles and natural foods in the same is either ignored or dangerously thwarted.

Regardless of the country or its system, many problems are common and widespread. Sectors may experience important advancements but, because health-care disciplines are highly specialized—and therefore heavily siloed—there is often too little crossover or interdisciplinary functionality. The left and right hands fail to communicate. In turn, patient health is negatively impacted, liability for hospitals and practitioners increases, and the occupational fulfillment of healers and scientists alike is limited. In one model, administrative staff are forced to prioritize productivity and efficiency, rigidly controlling every aspect of patient care, while in the other, administration becomes inflexibly mired in bureaucratic inefficiency. In either case, health-care workers experience pressure and stress, patients reap poor outcomes, and institutions become brittle and inelastic.

Unseen cultural trauma impedes our aims to adequately care for our sick or promote the health and well-being of our communities. Whether in the body or in society, shadow reduces data flow and inhibits the higher organizing principle. It lessens the capacity for communication not just of cells, but of communities, societies, and the systems that support them. Shadow, karma, trauma—the unhealed past—inhibits the evolutionary impulse and leaves us in a state of fragility rather than resilience.

Recent studies on the occupation of nursing in the United States, Hong Kong, and the United Kingdom report disproportionate levels of occupational stress, anxiety, and depression relative to the general public, as well as an increased risk of PTSD for intensive care nurses in the United States.[13] Working in a stressful environment in a dysfunctional institution, where professionals must contend daily with traumatized patients, triggers the activation of unconscious trauma within health-care workers themselves. First responders, emergency medical staff, trauma centers, and crisis-intervention workers are the firewall working to reduce or repair trauma as it surfaces across a society. They act as the immune system of their communities, the first white blood cells to race toward danger and surround it in order to limit its spread. With their effort and energy, they valiantly buffer the degree of trauma energy being transmitted through their communities. But they also absorb some of that shock.

Like hardened warriors sent into battle again and again, many in these occupations build up a tolerance to the suffering they witness. To be able to do this work day after day, health-care workers and first responders must suppress the impact of the trauma they witness or endure on the job. Paramedics, emergency-care nurses, firefighters, and police officers frequently become hardened to their experiences as a matter of survival. Their capacity for emotion and empathy is necessarily reduced. But again, dark chi must go somewhere, and too often the numbing response to the stress of this work can surface as poor health, anxiety, depression, or addiction. Stress increases, relationality diminishes, and over time, resilience is reduced.

Once we understand the impacts of trauma on the system of professionals who act as the firewall, the societal immune system, we recognize too that these professionals deserve special consideration and care. This includes access to therapy and trauma education. When organizations look out for their health-care workers, therapists, first responders, and police officers, these occupations become healthier and more actualized. The institutions that support them become more resilient and innovative, and the communities and societies they serve grow better able to thrive.

COMMERCE AND TRADE

From disembodiment and disrelation, corporations and governments exploit our world's natural and human resources. Workers are valued solely or primarily in terms of efficiency and profitability. Inhumane and unsafe conditions persist in the form of child labor, sweatshops, indentured servitude, abuse of migrants and minorities, "cheap meat" slaughterhouses, and beyond. Environmentally destructive systems continue to dominate—from oil and gas, strip mining, hydraulic fracking, agrochemical, palm oil, and an endless proliferation of plastics. The abuses are ignored and denied or simply accepted as the cost of doing business in free-market economies.

While animals, people, and habitats are treated inhumanely, toxic products are manufactured and sold, and unhealthful diets proliferate, because—in the shadow economy—illness and disease enhance market share. In every nation, underground economies generate a steady boost to the GDP via forced labor, sex trafficking, illicit goods, identity theft, racketeering, and countless other means. Illegal drugs create cartel kingpins and finance international wars, while legal drugs create multinational giants and finance government control. As a means to greater wealth and power, weapons of war are traded, trafficked, and legally sold. Conflict is a commodity, death is a service, and business is booming everywhere.

Even for the shining stars of corporate culture, for whom regulations exist and social responsibility matters, leading multinational companies struggle to address disparities related to fair treatment and equitable pay. In the age of #MeToo, executive scandals continue to surface and many among the best and the brightest are implicated. Poor management, inner turmoil, and dark financial or other practices get revealed. Win-at-all-cost strategies may generate rapid growth and even market domination, but the wins are temporary; collapse is inevitable.

These are the consequences of poor coherence, disrelation, and the mind-body/head-heart split borne of unintegrated shadow. When our systems are informed by the legacy of cultural traumas, the rapid advancement and innovation we see is unsustainable. Wherever profit is valued above human, animal, and ecological health, we are fated to misfortune.

WEALTH DISTRIBUTION

According to the World Inequality Database, the top 1 percent owns more than 70 percent of the total wealth in China, Europe, and the United States, while the bottom 50 percent owns less than 2 percent of the total wealth. "If established trends in wealth inequality were to continue, the top 0.1 percent alone would own more wealth than the global middle class by 2050."[14] This extreme disproportionality of resources is the product of our shadow, the long-standing legacy of colonialism, occupation, exploitation, expansion, and the broken relatedness these realities have wrought.

Poverty, crime, social inequality, and environmental degradation proliferate in the communities that have been most ravaged by collective trauma. These hot zones experience less flow, less living chi, so that the people living there have fewer resources for self-actualization. Shut down and dissociated, all available energy goes into the struggle to meet their most basic needs. The culture at large projects its shadow more intensely upon these places and their people, seeing them as ugly and repellant. Visitors experience discomfort and apprehension or avoid these places entirely, warned away by the energy of resistance: denial, tension, fear, or hatred. All the while, natives struggle to get out, frequently unable to do so.

But the vital life force that is suppressed and unused doesn't disappear. It is converted into dark energy and redirected elsewhere. In our world, much of this buried potential is diverted toward mass consumerism and the conspicuous acquisition of material goods. The lords of retail are masters of propaganda, indoctrinating a culture in powerful beliefs ("I am not enough") and filling people with perpetual desire ("To be worthy, I must acquire x, y, or z"). The outcome of this approach is mass accumulation, exponential waste, skyrocketing debt, and a pervasive feeling of scarcity.

Money is like oxygen. It can nourish a system with necessary energy, but wherever there is too much, it can become toxic. Too much energy in one direction depletes the flow of energy to other parts of the whole. In any fluid system where resources are unequally and unfairly distributed, zones of saturation become contaminated and corrupted, and zones of depravation are weakened or starved. When the circulatory system is damaged, disease proliferates and death follows.

ENVIRONMENT AND ECOLOGY

Split from ourselves and divided from one another, we ignore urgent alarms and continue to allow the active destruction of natural habitats. Rivers are dredged, diverted, levied, and contaminated. Oceans are polluted with wasted nets, islands of trash, and endless plastics, toxins, and agricultural runoff. Marine species are harmed by trawling, overfishing, sonar use, and other abuses, and fragile ecosystems are forever destroyed. Woodlands are clear-cut. Rainforests are demolished. Whole mountaintops are removed in service to coal giants who destroy communities and the environment and leave toxic waste behind in the form of sludge or "slurry ponds."

Only a few decades ago we believed we could toss out the rubbish and it would simply go away—or at least be far enough gone as to no longer concern us. Today, there is no more "far away"; our world has grown radically smaller with exponential advances in air travel, Internet communications, and population growth. Chemical contaminants—from lead paint to orchard pesticides, pharmaceutical drugs to cemetery formaldehyde—leach into the groundwater, finding their way to our streams and lakes and even our kitchen taps. Microplastics have colonized the world like a runaway virus, from the Mediterranean archipelagos and the South China Sea to Malaysian mangrove forests, Tennessee rivers, and Arctic sea ice. Astonishing levels of these microplastics have been found in drinking water and even in the air in places like India, Lebanon, Europe, the United Kingdom, and especially the United States. These chemicals are toxic but are found across the food chain, impacting the health of mammals, marine life, and even essential insects. They appear in the interstices of our own bodies.[15]

191

Species and habitat destruction, intense climate change, forced migration of humans and animals, the pollution of our bodies and our planet—these are the biblical plagues of our time. Genetic engineering versus organic agriculture. Monoculture versus permaculture. Industrial farming versus sustainable farming. We have turned our waters into blood, killing the fish and rendering it undrinkable. We've manufactured our own pestilence, sickened our livestock, and blighted our fields and our very bodies. To continue on this path is to guarantee the tenth biblical calamity: the death of our children and theirs, for what world will they have to inherit? In the biblical story, the ten plagues of Egypt impelled Pharaoh to free the Israelites after 400 years of bondage. It is an unfortunate truism of the human condition that positive and necessary change is most often preceded by crisis.

The writing has long been on the wall; scientists have issued warnings for decades. Yet we continue on, heedless of peril. In the apathy borne from denial, detachment, disowning, lethargy, complacency, and spiritual torpor, we participate in systems of collapse. Hovering over the precipice, we narcotize ourselves with food, alcohol, sex, social media, online shopping, video games, and series binge-watching. We numb out and disrelate: "Netflix and chill." When these anesthetics fail and our pain centers get activated, we erupt at our families, our neighbors, our leaders, and our screens, regressing toward tribalism and expressing outrage at one another's actions, ideas, or essential characteristics.

And when all that energy's spent? We retreat back to the comfort of indifference, ceaselessly swiping and scrolling. Acedia rules our lives once again.

Apathy is both a consequence of collective traumatization and a psychological defense against the suffering it creates. But like all defense strategies, if apathy (and its many manifestations) becomes habitual, it forms a rigid structure of consciousness that is no longer beneficial to survival but antagonistic to it. The very strategies we rely upon to protect us become dysfunctional and nonadaptive. As Jungian analyst, art therapist, and ecopsychologist Mary-Jayne Rust has written:

"We're completely fucked." . . . If many people are secretly thinking this, and I suspect they are, their motivation for taking action in the face of climate change will be zero. As therapists, we know that when we face our worst fears, and feel the effects, we stand a chance of moving through darkness into enormous creativity. . . . The "we're completely fucked" response is yet another layer of the defense system, which gives us license to give up thinking. . . . When the collective gets stuck like this we have a wipeout that becomes an apocalypse.[16]

By examining the impact of collective trauma with a critical eye, the intention is not to reaffirm the good/bad dichotomy or the mind-body disconnect, which would be further self-defeating. Collective shadow work invites us to see how we are showing up in the world, not with projected judgment or internalized shame but with compassion and clarity, an unflinching eye and an open heart.

Trauma is karma is entropy is waste. It is the oblivion of unconsciousness, the restriction of life force, the suppression of evolutionary light. It is endless repetition and snowballing calamity. It is to live and die in shadow, asleep in the dream of separation.

Before we sleepwalk over the edge, we must come awake.

DAYLIGHTING THE STREAM

Over the course of rapid expansion and development, countless headwaters are lost beneath new construction, buried under busy roadways, or diverted into culverts or storm or sewer drains. We find ourselves living in the Holocene extinction, or sixth mass extinction during the Anthropocene epoch, an age in which human activity is directly implicated in ecosystem devastation, endemic threats to biodiversity, radical species loss, and catastrophic climate change.

In Canada and the United States, urban developers and civil engineers have a poetic phrase for a particular kind of watershed restoration and remediation: "daylighting the stream." Daylighting returns buried watercourses to the surface and restores them back to life, encouraging biodiversity and revitalizing ecosystems. We might think of the practice as a form of reunion or reintegration.

Countless other fields and disciplines show signs of emergent renewal and even transformational leaps. These include organizational development and transformative leadership; narrative medicine, symbolic disease, and "mind-body coemergence"; the resurgence of gift and sharing economies; mutual awakening practices; and consciousness studies at the intersection of quantum physics. There's a lot to be hopeful about.

In his book, *The Heart of Understanding*, Buddhist monk and peace activist Thich Nhat Hanh writes,

> *Interbeing: If you are a poet, you will see clearly that there is a cloud floating in this sheet of paper. Without a cloud, there will be no rain; without rain, the trees cannot grow; and without trees, we cannot make paper. The cloud is essential for the paper to exist. If the cloud is not here, the sheet of paper cannot be here either. So, we can say that the cloud and the paper inter-are.*[17]

Applying the Zen master's lyrical vision, we see that we are inseparable from our furthest ancestors. Our bodies are indivisible of the sun, the rain, and the soil. We carry a sea of thriving microscopic life with whom we are interwoven and symbiotic. The carbon at our core was here at the dawn of the planet, so that we are not in fact the age printed on our passports; our roots coil back through every forebear, commencing long before the first human, the first mammal, the first bird or fish or sun-hungry plankton. We are made of electricity and magnetism and the mineral particulate of exploding stars.

With our cosmos, our planet, and one another, we *inter-are*.

The old story of separateness is a collective illusion, a shared dream. Perhaps this lies at the root of the simulation theory described by science fiction and hypothesized by scientists and philosophers, the deception being that we live in the present, when in truth, we live in a recurring dream of the unintegrated past. Only when we become lucid do we greet the limitless potential of *true* future, which is ever available and longing to be met. The bridge to that portal is never far, but it can only be discovered with clear eyes and embodied presence. It has the power to transform the cliff edge of annihilation into the threshold of becoming.

To heal trauma is to integrate the self—the shadow and the light. The rewards are deeper embodiment, repaired relation, and the capacity to presence our experiences from the now. In a renewed space of clarity and coherence, the spiraling river of evolution returns to flow. The dense vortex of personal and cultural shadows loosens, innovation emerges, and a new capacity for unity consciousness unfolds.

We are a resilient species living on a resilient planet. Even after terrible and repeated traumas, the brain and nervous system can be repaired; we can connect and cohere. It is the same for societies. After centuries of recapitulating karma, resulting in dissonance, disconnection, and division, we can open our eyes to the present and lean into a clear stream of conscious mutuality. We can discover ourselves as a new kind of being: distinctly individual, yet profoundly collective. As a conscious *we*, we may discover we are fully present, yet mysteriously nonlocal, operating inside of time, yet wholly available to a radical nonlinearity.

To heal our world is the journey of the collective hero/ine. The path requires that we enter our depths—the underworld, the dark lake, the unconscious matrix—as a rite of initiation. We are called to acknowledge all that we are and offer amends to one another and the Earth. To heal is to discover the truth of our interrelation and interdependence. We are called to daylight the stream of the collective unconscious, our unhealed cultural history, and return its hidden waters to the world.

To accept this call, we must lean together toward our furthest transformational edge, a conscious bifurcation point, and cocreate our phase transition into a better future; one that is wholly new, deeply real, and full to overflowing with evolutionary light. Indeed, that bright tomorrow is already here, waiting eagerly to greet us.

9

VISION OF AN
INTEGRATING WORLD

*[M]y being partakes of your being and that of all beings. This goes
beyond interdependency—our very existence is relational.*

Charles Eisenstein
The More Beautiful World Our Hearts Know Is Possible

*Ours is an age between worldviews, creative yet disoriented, a transitional
era when the old cultural vision no longer holds and the new has not yet
constellated. Yet, we are not without signs of what the new might look like.*

Richard Tarnas
Cosmos and Psyche

We have explored how the trauma process is an intelligent
evolutionary function of the human nervous system. The
psychological defenses engaged by trauma are protective
mechanisms, permitting us to live with reduced psychological strain
in the face of traumatizing events. But when we habituate to these
strategies over the long term, they become maladaptive—to people
and communities. We have hardwired these defenses over hundreds of
thousands of years, and they continue to be generationally transmitted
and reinforced. Indeed, our very cells sing the tales of our ancestors'
grief, whether or not we recognize the lyrics.

Humanity's vertical and horizontal trauma, the layers of which are almost geological in nature, have created the illusion of separation from which we operate. The dense silt of our unresolved past warps and distorts time, trapping us inside a dark matrix of perpetual *after-time*. This distortion confuses our perception of "past" and "future" and inhibits our free will. We project skewed depictions of others onto a creased and crumpled canvas, which filters and shrinks what we can perceive as real or blows it out of scale. Collective trauma energetically fragments and alienates, trapping us in a concussed field of static separation. We label "enemy" and "rival" and "evil" where there are only racial or national variations of ourselves.

In this traumatized field, our unconscious choices—even those we believe we make freely—are made for us by karmic destiny.

It is as though we're functioning automatically from the programmed script of some recursive algorithm that keeps us bound in coded simulations of prior events. Its various iterations are never-ending, but essential themes repeat. We rarely pause the program to question its design or functionality. Consensus reality is unlikely to be a technological simulation created by a dark cabal or diabolical alien agenda; *we* generated the trauma matrix.

By the close of the Industrial Revolution, rapid scientific, medical, and technological advancements had brought about a massive shift in public awareness on the subjects of safety, sanitation, and health. As a result, many practical changes were made to reflect them, even for the poor and working classes. Of course, understanding had to increase before tangible or lasting changes were made to working conditions or the infrastructure of rapidly growing metropolitan areas and outlying towns. The miasma theory of disease—a long-standing belief that illness was caused by "bad air"—had to give way to new scientific understanding that disease is transmitted by infectious agents.[1]

For humanity to use this new information, society had to transform. Communities needed to be cared for in new ways, public institutions (especially hospitals) needed to take appropriate action, and everyday citizens had to learn the importance of preventative action in order to care for their own and their families' health. Increasing public awareness took some doing, but in a relatively brief span, human life expectancy and infant mortality rates vastly improved and many other positive changes occurred.

As we enter a new age of complexity, society must again transform. Critical upgrades in awareness, based in both science and spirituality, are needed. To improve the health and well-being of all people and the planet we call home, we must raise public consciousness on the nature and impact of collective trauma. Dealing with only the external symptoms does nothing to address the cause. We must act as surgeons of consciousness and *go within*, directly attending to our karmic past as one, holding space for perpetrator as well as victim, for bystanders and descendants. For all of us.

Humans are not living "on" the Earth, separate and apart; we belong to it. Spirit and consciousness are innate properties of matter in all dimensions and at all scales of our cosmos, and the highest expression of each whole/part reveals its purpose. By aligning in coherence with Spirit, resistance ceases. The stagnant energies of unconscious and unethical decisions begin to shift and flow, and we begin to see and sense the residual energies of those who were harmed in prior atrocities. Wherever we go in the world, deeper relational awareness makes us present to our own and others' experiences, though we don't have to travel to feel the reality of our connection, even to those on the other side of the world. We no longer fail to see or feel the dire condition of our environment or the danger to living systems at all scales; we feel it in our own bodies, as belonging to ourselves.

The pain of the global village is a clarion call meant to awaken us to the truth that there is no more "out there"—everything exists *in here*. Initially, this is terrifying. Suddenly, we can sense the toxins, poisons, and nuclear and other wastes that flood from our marketplaces through the entire food chain, reaching into our communities, our homes, and our very bodies. Whether pesticides, microplastics, or heavy metals, *we* are responsible for having saturated our landscapes with waste. Recognizing this permits us the opportunity to choose healing and repair.

Uniting for the purpose of integrating collective trauma is environmental activism. Before we can reverse the anthropogenic mass extinction or resolve the growing climate crisis, we have to look at ourselves. No matter how many international resolutions are signed, past trauma that is left unresolved and uncared for will ensure that some of the signatories breach the agreement. And no matter how many corporations agree to adopt cleaner standards, karmic repetition will ensure that some will be dishonest and others will simply refuse. We must embrace real-world practices for remediation and environmental care, but to fully embody those changes in any lasting or systemic way, we will have to address the murky ecological terrain of the collective shadow.

AN INTEGRAL THEORY VIEW OF INDIVIDUAL AND COLLECTIVE TRAUMA

KEN WILBER

Human beings, of course, are part of an overall evolutionary unfolding. Going back billions of years to the big bang, there's a series of common patterns that evolutionary unfolding takes. It starts all the way back with subatomic particles, quarks, electrons, and protons, and it goes all the way up through human beings and how human beings grow, develop, unfold, and evolve. The stages of evolution tend to be, what Arthur Koestler called, *holons*. And a holon is simply a whole that's part of a larger whole.

Pretty much everything in the universe is a holon of one sort or another. We have whole subatomic particles, electrons, protons, neutrons. They come together as parts of a whole atom. Whole atoms come together as parts of whole molecules. Whole molecules come together as parts of whole organisms and so on. That goes all the way up through human beings, and human beings continue to evolve in terms of the biological and objective components. But they also begin an interior growth and development and evolutionary unfolding. These consist of various stages of development—stages of unfolding that have been studied pretty carefully by a large number of very bright, very gifted developmental psychologists.

These stages of development that human beings go through, starting at birth, are also holons. In other words, the whole of one stage becomes part of the whole of the next stage. That stays for a while, and then as development continues, the whole of that stage becomes part of the whole of the next stage and so on. It is a process of transcending and including and then transcending and including.

This is the same evolutionary process continuing forward. In complex biological and psychological organisms like human beings, because these stages are organic, because they're unfolding, and because they have moving parts, so to speak, they can break down. Things can go wrong with these stages of development. Whenever that happens, there's usually some sort of trauma involved.

As you get to each higher stage, it transcends, in some sense, the previous stage—it goes beyond it. It's more expansive. It's more inclusive. It includes some sort of new capacities. Some sort of new emergent realities come into being, and that's the transcend part. Molecules transcend atoms because molecules include atoms, but they also move beyond them. They have other characteristics that atoms don't and likewise, molecules are transcended and included in cells. So, cells include molecules. They literally enfold them, but then they also go beyond them. They do things that molecules by themselves can't.

Given the fact that there's this transcend-and-include, this going-beyond-but-enfolding or integrating, something can go wrong with either one of those aspects. The transcendence part can break down, and when that happens, you don't actually move beyond the previous stage like you're supposed to. You don't transcend it. You remain stuck in the previous stage through a type of attachment or a type of fixation to that stage. You're still holding on to that previous stage when you should have been able to let go of it. And if that happens, there's a secret attachment, a kind of addiction that occurs, in a sense. You are still seeking what that previous lower stage gave you and you're not ready to give that up.

On the other hand, sometimes you can transcend okay, but then not include. In this case, you're not remaining stuck at some aspect of the previous stage, but failing to include it. Rather than transcending and including, you're transcending and repressing or sealing out or dissociating. And instead of causing an addiction, it creates an allergy. You actively recoil from some aspect of the previous stage. You don't like it. You push it out of yourself. You try to deny it. Both scenarios are really problematic, and they directly address some of the problems that are associated with trauma.

When we look at evolutionary unfolding, we find that there are at least four fundamental perspectives that we can use to view these processes, and all of them are equally important. We call them the four quadrants, and they are as follows: subjective, objective, intersubjective, and interobjective. You can take almost any human discipline, whether it's history or medicine or psychotherapy or spirituality, and apply just one of those perspectives and say that it's the one and only correct way to look at something. For example, in the scientific worldview, the most common perspective is the exterior view of an individual holon. What's real is fundamental particles like electrons, protons, neutrons, quarks, and strings, and those are looked at in an objective third-person way.

So, if we looked at trauma just in terms of an exterior, third-person view (objective quadrant), then we would reduce everything to some sort of brain damage or biological material component damage. You can also look at just that exterior third-person view on a collective basis (interobjective quadrant), which includes all the institutional aspects of the cultures we're in, as well as the technological infrastructures. Things like monetary systems, transportation systems, birth rates, death rates—objective facts that we use to look at exterior realities. Of course, those exterior third-person plural systems (interobjective quadrant) are very important, because they're carriers and hidden holders of various types of collective trauma.

Then there's the collective dimension (intersubjective quadrant) that is looked at from within. It includes a cultural component—our social systems—and of course many, many traumas from our past history are embedded in our cultural systems. When we look at the interior individual subjective component (subjective quadrant)—how people actually *feel* their trauma—it's a psychotherapeutic approach. Almost every major discipline that has something to say about trauma will say it from one of these perspectives.

So, say you were sexually abused as a child. This, of course, can deeply traumatize your individual subjective psyche (subjective quadrant). It's also going to traumatize your exterior neurophysiological nervous system (objective quadrant), including its actual growth process, which is going to be disturbed. But then there's also the family culture that you were brought up in, which was disturbed enough to become a nexus for this kind of behavior (intersubjective quadrant). You will end up internalizing that, which will give you the tendency to repeat the trauma that happened to you because it was a pattern that you learned in the intersubjective quadrant. Then, of course, there are the exterior components of your culture (interobjective quadrant). What was your family structure? What was its income? Were your parents addicted to drugs or alcohol? You can see that all four perspectives have something extremely important to offer.

But there's another kind of trauma as well, which also has to do with development. Here, the cause of the trauma is not something that has already emerged in a person but results because of higher stages that have *not yet* appeared. Because of this, a person may unintentionally harm or oppress others, without even being aware of it. It's not that something went wrong for the oppressor necessarily, or that they had some early childhood shadow material that they were working out (although that can often be a cause). It's that their incapacity to take a bigger view inflicts trauma on those they interact with, particularly if they're in positions of power. Both slavery and the Holocaust are examples of this, and clearly, both are severely traumatizing events to the people that they were inflicted upon. So, a great deal of the trauma that has been perpetrated upon humankind by other humans happened because the oppressors had not yet developed or evolved to higher stages that were more inclusive and thus had a larger morality, a more inclusive morality.

This is one of the problems that we have to deal with when we're looking at the ongoing generational trauma in today's world. One of the slightly frightening pieces of data is that worldwide around 60 to 70 percent of the population is at an ethnocentric or lower stage of development. That means all of those individuals will be willing to do damage to other groups simply because they can't include them in their broader moral embrace.

Plotinus said that sin is not a "no," it's a "not yet." And there's a certain truth to that statement on the developmental side. The sin here is not that there was a no, that something bad happened and they repressed it, but that they have not yet developed to a stage that wouldn't want to "do" the Holocaust or slavery in the first place. Everybody is born at square one and has to go through all the stages of development.

And you can get stuck, fixated, or dissociated at any one of them. Things can go wrong that slow your growth and development, making it harder for you to reach higher stages of development that will allow your own moral sense to expand, to truly include all human beings and to not judge them on the basis of skin color or sex or gender or ethnicity or religious belief and so on.

And, yes, one of the main problems that slows that development is trauma, whether it's individually experienced or a more collective kind of trauma. When you've been traumatized, the energy that is meant to continue moving up as it transcends and includes and transcends and includes, just freezes. It no longer functions as it should because there is damage. And for the traumatized part, growth usually stops there. You may still kind of bump along in other areas, but whatever part of you has been broken, damaged, or hurt, is dysfunctional—and it's not going to grow. It's not going to move forward.

This creates shadow content, and almost no individual gets out of childhood without some sort of shadow material. And these shadow elements maintain essentially the same chronological age that they had when they were created, which is one of the reasons they are dysfunctional. You can have shadow elements from age three, and those elements are themselves three years old. They have the wants of a three-year-old, the impulsiveness of a three-year-old. They have a three-year-old's lack of capacity to reason. And you can have other shadows that are seven-year-old material. Others that are twelve years old. As you continue to go through adult development, you can generate shadow at any of those stages as well, and that material will remain at the age you were whenever that shadow was created.

That is one of the reasons that working with trauma is so important: to help humanity actually move forward into future issues so that we can help with the real problems that we're facing now. The tendency is almost always to say, "Okay, well, what do we have to do technologically or what do we have to do economically or what political systems do we need or what kind of food production?" Instead of looking at all these exterior material things, we need to look at the interiors of individuals who are actually responsible for doing those things. That's where working with trauma, to release trauma, can help consciousness to continue moving forward.

COLLECTIVE AWAKENING AND REPAIR

Cohering our collective S-T-R is a vital part of societal and planetary restoration. Synchronization balances our collective nervous system—the energetic roots of the collective body and psyche—so that we cease to function as separate laptops, disconnected and ineffectual, and instead function as a single supercomputer with more than 7.5 billion workstations. Humanity's strength is that we share an enormous power source, which has been fragmented and diverted as a result of unintegrated past trauma—our shared dissociation of the unconscious. It's simpler than we realize to repair.

Presence itself is the holy moment (divine time) and the sacred temple (divine space). Presence is the womb of the world, the birthplace of All That Is or will be. The power of shared presence releases our entanglements to the past. By returning to that sacred portico in mutual attendance, we awaken higher-order capacities and activate both revolution and innovation in our exterior world. We begin to download streams of higher clarity and intelligence and the will and courage that empower us to solve systemic problems. We take the living light of future on as collaborator and partner, firing new activations across the surface of the stuck and ordinary world.

Every human being is happy when growing in the direction of their highest potential, but it isn't just happiness we long for—it's purpose, a compelling desire to live for something beyond ourselves. We are called to create families, communities, and societies from a potential-orientation. Rather than living for the agenda of the week ahead as outlined in our daily planners or toward a rote "strategic five-year plan," potential-orientation invites us to lean toward the emergent and evolutionary, listening for the potential strengths, capacities, and outcomes that are possible if only we invite them forward. What is latent becomes transparent as living light flows vertically and horizontally through the collective body.

A Jewish philosophy holds that the "will to receive" is a basic condition of the ego, while the "will to bestow" emerges from a transcended condition, reflecting the state of creation itself, which is ceaselessly generous and creative. As we seek to align with the sacred nature of life, we begin to access higher dimensions and capabilities belonging to the Divine. Living becomes offertory; to exist in the world is to give plentifully, to bless and serve wholeheartedly, to share in the dynamic flow of supernal intelligence.

NEW VISION FOR EDUCATION AND LEARNING

Trauma injures a child's ability to respond appropriately to his or her environment and can delay or damage learning ability. Developmental trauma thwarts a child's capacity to self-regulate so that emotions and moods appear displaced and erratic or shut down and disconnected. Attention and inhibition may become suppressed, resulting in impulsivity, distractibility, and difficulty concentrating. Whether children inherit family trauma or are born into traumatized communities, they absorb those energies and reflect back the attendant personal and cultural symptoms.

Too often, teachers, administrators, and guidance counselors learn to see a traumatized young person as a "problem child," placing blame for behavioral or emotional dysfunction squarely on the child and possibly the parents. Systematized punishments or expulsions are employed to deal with these issues, but as long as societies lack understanding of the impact and consequences of individual and community trauma, we fail to meet the needs of our most vulnerable citizens. To change this, all educators and adults who work with learners must themselves be educated on the subject of trauma, so that they can be armed with thoughtful approaches for reaching students in need. To be effective in this task requires shared accountability and a collective approach across all sectors of society.

Our children are harmed by rigid and demanding systems that force them to conform like automatons, to look and behave no differently than every other copy. Authoritarian codes no longer function. (A person shouldn't be expected to become a soccer player if they were born for badminton or chess.) Such systems disallow the unique intelligence and beauty inherent in the soul of every child, which longs to be seen and received with love. We are called to foster spaces where relating, connecting, presencing—and therefore growth and learning—can thrive, and to create flexible, adaptive, and responsive educational structures that support human potential. Higher capacities permit us to feel into one another's distinct intelligences and learning styles in order to discover the gifts each of us was born to offer the world. As unique compositions in the collective orchestra, we each have an individual and a transpersonal purpose.

To be able to look into a student's eyes and truly sense how they're feeling and recognize their state of development and what we can do to serve their highest purpose requires coherence and presence. For this to happen in the educational world (or any other), teachers and educators must face and work through their own buried pains and unmet traumas. This requires courage. The purpose of the teacher is to facilitate a healthy knowledge stream to learners—to foster their becoming. The work is impeded by the blockage and fragmentation held in the intergenerational tree, creating dysfunction for the whole. To enliven the role of the teacher and the health of the system, communities must work to clear intergenerational trauma signatures so that less suffering is endured and more liberation is absorbed in each new generation. This is done through active presencing, group shadow work, group healing practices like the CTIP, and through a process I call Global Social Witnessing. As we work together to *be with* whatever is present, fully and actively, acknowledging and feeling even our discomfort, resistance, and pain with patience and grace, we find we have more space, more light, more freedom.

A new vision for education comes alive through inspiring leaders and educators who nurture creativity and stimulate motivation and engagement. It's further realized as young people grow into thriving and potent adults with open hearts and curious minds who want to participate in their societies. In it, inspired freethinkers are supported so that they learn to be both open and grounded. Self-healing, contemplative, and relational practices are taught, and learners become skilled very early in the power of presence. Schools become places where wisdom, not just information, is acquired and where courage, bravery, and compassion are empowered.

In that new world, our future leaders are people who no longer hunger for power but strive for integrity. Servant leadership is the norm rather than the exception. Instead of apathy and indifference, future generations freely engage, contribute, and participate—not because it's expected of them, but because they're able to feel the world within them. Rather than being incentivized by wealth or acquisition, future generations choose occupations based on each individual's unique purpose. They recognize where the gifts they have to offer align with the needs or desires of their communities, and that becomes their service to the world.

At its highest, education activates awareness, optimizes the gift of imagination, and ignites the power to download spirit into form. Evolutionary education supports listening and attuning to the future, so that even the collective intelligence of the very young can be fostered and fulfilled. The beauty of new art forms, innovative technologies, and visionary world building will be theirs, and our planet will become lit by the never-before-seen colors of millions of growing human souls.

NEW VISION FOR TECHNOLOGY AND SOCIETY

We live in a time of maximum information and access and maximum overwhelm and collapse. The structures of our nervous systems are inadequate for the reception of the massive terabytes of data flowing through the cognitive stream. Every day, we hear of new atrocities—school shootings, bombings of civilians, domestic and international terror attacks—and call this unending cycle of information "negative news." The world has been colored by chronic states of overwhelm, anxiety, and stress. To truly feel or digest the information we consume is too challenging, thus we're left ill-equipped to respond appropriately.

Through the practice of Global Social Witnessing, we develop the capacity to respond to our world with a clarity that's neither detached nor allergic. If all we can do initially is better recognize our reactions, we're making progress. As we learn to feel and hold information consciously, without numbness or hyperarousal, we grow better able to integrate the data that surrounds us.

The belief in an environmental doomsday or technological apocalypse (i.e., the planet is toast, so we'd better proceed off-world) unwittingly casts our species as a galactic virus. Underlying this prophecy is the presupposition that humanity is, at its base, not terribly different from a swarm of locusts in an imbalanced system and that our biological imperative is simply to propagate ourselves even beyond Earth's capacity to sustain us. Once all territorial resources have been consumed, exploited, or destroyed, we can just use our big brains to launch ourselves toward the stars. But this is a dangerous philosophy. It imagines us as separate from the Earth and does nothing to address our collective karma, which has become like a cosmic stockpile of lost luggage—perhaps large enough to require its own planet but unable to be transported without terrible risk. Regardless of how far we travel in this dimension, we can never escape ourselves. We can't carry our current level of karmic luggage off-world if we expect to survive, much less thrive. And we will never bridge the vast distances of boundless space by living out ceaseless repetitions of our history; the lag it creates is insurmountable. If we desire healthy societies on a sustainable planet with adequate resources where full, healthy, abundant lives are possible, we must first create it here. As they say, "It's an inside job."

The recursive algorithm of the old world is glitching in the break of the incoming epoch. These glitches appear as areas of restricted movement, slowing down or blocking the data flow of evolutionary intelligence through the human nervous system. The paradigm of the past few thousand years is aging into obsolescence; we can't make simple code adjustments to the algorithm, call it an update, and expect it to run. We have considerable RAM for the storage of karmic information, but not enough. Our processing power has become overburdened by the accumulation. To prepare for a new age, we require nothing short of a holistic upgrade. We must leave behind our old scripts and unconscious programs and step into a more regenerative and emergent way of operating. Our role in the time ahead is to come together consciously and do the work required to shift these blocks, so that energy and information flow easily and fully. As we evolve into our *new* neocortex, the mass global brain of Internet-connected synapses and devices, we restore the roots and branches of the great spiraling tree of humanity.

It isn't just technological innovation we need but a deeper understanding of epigenetic and transgenerational messages and codes and how to transform them. Our future depends on a willingness to work toward alignment with the intelligent impulse of life. Trauma consciousness is today's "flat Earth" perspective; holding on to it keeps us stuck in a snow globe. But by transcending trauma, we are liberated. Transforming separation into communion, we surpass the limitations in our current understanding of space and time. In that act of *enlightening*, science and spirit become two sides of the same coin. With a balance of both in hand, maybe we'll discover a propulsion force more powerful than solar sails or fusion rockets. Better still, we might learn the secret gift of how to luminesce, how to offer light back to the heart of our cosmos.

Higher capacities for distance healing, precognition, and enhanced experiences of connectedness and union will no longer simply be possible but accessible. The miracles attributed to ancient mystics and religious sages will become a part of the everyday. The bright worlds of fantasy and science fiction will no longer seem illusory but prophetic. Through integrity, faith, and the courage to love, our highest mystery will inevitably be revealed. Our ancient myths and fairy tales have always suggested as much, and deep in our hearts, we know it to be true. But this story requires more than the will and courage of a single hero or heroine. It calls out for the intelligent whole, the awakened collective, activated by many voices raised in unison.

We are called to rewrite the human story, acting as conscious coauthors with the emergent future through interrelation and presence. By practicing deep awareness through mindfulness, contemplation, and mutual integration (individual and collective), we can radically transform not just our personal lives but the life of the collective. The work requires attention, intention, and the discipline to practice, but when we show up, not only do we heal, we thrive! The past is less a story of what happened yesterday than it is the undigested pieces of yesterday, disrupting the flow of will and life force in the present. Similarly, the future isn't what will happen tomorrow; authentic future is *space*—a meeting place where higher consciousness can update and innovate in the present moment. By utilizing the heightened capacities of shared consciousness, we can cocreate a very different world than the one we perceive around us.

Remember: the future can change the past.

By raising public awareness on the critical subject of collective trauma and by wholeheartedly practicing collective trauma work together—such as we do with the CTIP—we ignite a movement in which communities, organizations, nongovernmental organizations (NGOs), and multidisciplinary initiatives all over the world can come together to effectively reduce collective trauma, layer by layer. Small or large, near or far, our efforts in the endeavor actively work to free up massive stores of potential energy, locked away in the collective unconscious at the time of trauma. In this way, collective trauma integration initiatives are like global acupuncture.

That newly released energy transforms us, liberating our creative potential by feeding radical new solutions and rapid innovation. Its continued liberation has the power to accelerate both individual and collective development, leading to a more just and democratic world. With the liberation of dark chi through integration, we are called to own, acknowledge, and atone for our actions. Imagine world leaders and heads of state humbly and sincerely apologizing for the sins of their nations: colonization, imperialism, racial and economic injustice, gender disparity, war crimes, ethnic cleansing, genocide. What would the world look like if, instead of systemic avoidance, blame, and denial, humans everywhere practiced standing in the truth, not in support of self-interest but because of a higher collective interest?

This vision of integration that focuses on the acknowledgment and ownership of error—of the terrible harm we have perpetuated—is not about what is politically correct; it is about what is mutually *good*.

As we learn to foster and enhance group coherence and collective intelligence, and as we commit to mutually process and heal our collective trauma through methods like the CTIP described in this book, I believe we will radically reshape and revitalize the collective. These steps will encourage the health and potential of all aspects of our world—our schools, hospitals, police, and emergency first responders; our governments and NGOs; our humanitarian, civil, racial-justice, and legal-aid organizations; our political and international affairs; all civic, corporate, and nonprofit sectors; all religious and spiritual organizations and institutions; and our local and planetary climate and environment.

What we learn will expand our openness, strengthen our resilience, and encourage our capacities to mediate conflict and find noble solutions for the growing challenges we face. Indeed, I believe these things and many more are not only possible but probable. They belong to our planetary and species unfolding, along the lit and spiraling stream of consciousness evolution. Creating such a future doesn't require that we arrive already knowing what to do. It needs only our curiosity and willingness to stay present to emergence.

If it is an ethical responsibility to attend to the suffering of traumatized persons, it is surely our communal duty to work together to formulate effective responses to humanity's shared traumas, both past and present. Only by addressing unresolved past suffering can we work effectively to prevent potential future suffering. A collective trauma requires a collective response. To restore human societies and our natural environment requires nothing less than collective spiritual activism: the sacred, shared intention to step into our places as inspired, empowered citizens of the world, willing to sing out together in the grand chorus of becoming.

THE COMING EVOLUTION

In certain surviving indigenous communities, symptoms that we in the West consider to be manifestations of mental illness are taken as a signpost of impending illumination rather than disease.[2] From this viewpoint, people exhibiting certain psychological symptoms are often seen as future healers, trying to be born. As such, a stricken individual is treated with care and guidance, though it's understood that they will have an arduous journey to make before their gifts can be revealed. Those gifts may emerge eventually as a capacity to heal the sick or to sense and communicate with the community's departed ancestors. These manifestations are perceived, not as isolated and individual occurrences, but as sacred conditions emerging from and belonging to the collective. For this reason, the community comes together to perform rituals and offer prayers and service. But if either the individual or the community fails this initiation, the higher capacities of the potential healer will never manifest, and he or she may become spiritually injured or lost. Not just their survival but the activation of their potential is considered the responsibility of the whole.[3]

Whether East or West, indigenous tribe or postmodern society, trauma and suffering are collective signposts. The task of acknowledging these indicators and attending and caring for the patterns to which they point is a communal responsibility.

When humanity believed the world was flat, almost no one questioned the dominant world order. Few could imagine a different scenario, and fewer still were intrepid enough to test prevailing wisdom by sailing far enough to either prove or disprove the existence of a great waterfall, plummeting to an abyss at the edge of the ocean. Those who dared to question or offer an alternative vision of the world were disbelieved, discounted, or persecuted until finally, enough people were willing and ready to receive the energy of a dawning age. One that would dismantle the structures of the old world by offering an audacious and exhilarating new one.

It is the same with dimensions of consciousness. When we accept convention as indisputable, remaining unwilling to challenge its margins or to accept the evidence of those who do, we're eventually left behind by the bold. The thunderbolt of action calls daring visionaries to new lands or new truths, while the outmoded structures built by the prior worldview begin to crumble and disintegrate. Ideologies, towers, and civilizations have a way of falling, but we don't have to be buried in the rubble.

The mass dissociation of memory, widespread suppression of emotions, and collective disembodiment people exhibit everywhere in the world feels normal to most. The global epidemic of disconnection is unfelt and therefore left unexamined. But as we begin to sing more light into the field—daylighting the stream of collective awareness—the sedimentary layers and static residual energies of our collective shadow will shift and release, restoring living light where there had previously been darkness. Our fragments will reconsolidate and the collective nervous system will rewire and connect in a field of assembly and correlation. Harmonic resonance will grow in the intersubjective spaces, and new and deeper faculties will be activated within and between us. Our focus will shift away from lack and separation toward presence and wholeness. We will recognize that the collective matrix is in fact vastly abundant and infinitely generative. Resources will be shared rather than hoarded, and higher states of health, happiness, and flow will be tapped and awakened.

Collective intelligence and shared courage are amplified by our individual notes, enabling us to restore the evolutionary potentials latent in our very DNA. With each new strength and sensitivity, we accelerate the liberation of trauma and innervate our collective nervous system. In mutual coherence, we create a dimensional gateway through which time is no longer linear or fragmented, but fluid, dynamic, and *conscious*. In the sinusoidal waves of a radical new future, the fragments of our divided world cohere into a more complete whole. Indeed, that beautiful new world is already and always available; it is our common country, our true home.

All of this and more belongs to the natural, living blueprint behind what we call "the human condition." Trauma exists as an interruption to our true condition, but connectedness, true intimacy, and total love belong to us by birthright. Our species blueprint, just like the planetary blueprint, radiates in multidimensional glory from our source. By following the blueprint back, we can reclaim our nature and heal our environment.

Eden is not a place from which we fell but an evolutionary future we bring into being—through differentiation and integration, individuation and communion. In that verdant, flourishing place, which is outside of time and simultaneously here and now, the sunlight of consciousness flows unimpeded, delivering bold insight, brilliant innovation, and radical vision. Having shed the heavy weight of the past and clarified its disabling distortions, we enter together through a portal toward humanity's wildest evolutionary possibility.

EPILOGUE

*God does not lie in our collective past, God lies in our collective
future; the Garden of Eden is tomorrow, not yesterday; the
Golden Age lies down the road, not up it.*

Ken Wilber
The Eye of Spirit

*The world we are experiencing today is a result of our collective
consciousness. And if we want a new world, each of us must start
taking responsibility for helping to create it.*

Rosemary Fillmore Rhea
New Thought for a New Millennium

Trauma is often unspeakable, even invisible. It is its nature to
provoke denial—in the survivor, who may dissociate from the
experience; in the oppressor, who may seek to avoid, distance,
or minimize culpability; and in the community, which remains silent
and unresponsive to suffering or encourages outright disbelief. Too
often, cultural traumas are made the subject of conspiracy theories in
which survivors are not only doubted, but vilified and attacked. These
things, too, are the inheritance of trauma.

Whether it reveals itself as denial, rejection, dissociation, or ignorance, the avoidance of trauma shows up as an inability to meet life,
which is the foremost symptom of *separation*. Circumventing awareness of trauma and its effects is the most essential form of spiritual
bypassing. Too often, we naïvely seek only "light and positivity," or we
spend hours or lifetimes using a meditation or other witness practice
to unconsciously distance ourselves from the pain and grit of our own

and others' suffering. Our intentions are good, but by avoiding the raw nakedness of what is real in an endless search for the ideal, we miss the deep spiritual intimacy that can only be experienced through a willingness to profoundly be *in* and *with* the painful dark. Of course, this is much too difficult to do alone. When we come together, willing to witness and receive one another's pain without judgment, without turning away, without minimizing or attempting to vanquish, we discover trust, connection, and healing release. We uncover our essential unity, held in the generous embrace of the Divine.

Shadow, like conflict, is a driver of evolution. It eventually pushes us to advance in complexity and clarity. The disassociated, contracted energy we hold in the dark lake seeks integration; dark chi longs to return to the light of consciousness, fulfilling its course along the great spiral of life. A willingness to go into the dark with a light is evolutionary work; it brings healing, clarity, and integration. If we're committed to the work, it opens us—not to more pain and darkness but to a more brilliant luminosity through which we can access higher capacities, deeper potentials, and a clearer, more creative state of being. These are the necessary ingredients for authentic future emergence.

After years of practicing in we-space with groups of many sizes, I've observed directly how states of coherence allow participants to begin speaking *from* the field, rather than about it. Together, humans are capable of entering into a more aligned sphere, a collective state of being and awareness. From that place, one member of a group (let's call her Adina) is able to speak from the energy and information of another (let's call him Gael). I call this transparent communication. Adina can do this by leaning into the quality of mutuality, by suspending her own images and interpretations of Gael and instead embracing or deeply attuning with the energy of Gael's origins or soul, that part of him that precedes apparent reality and its seeming condition of separation.

When we do this, we find that there is so much more space and so much more light available. Coherence brings us into the startling realization of mutual contemplation, shared witness—into the fullness and intimacy of the emerging We. Vibrating together in this state of collective awareness, a new level of human intelligence enters. By connecting from that stream of collective intelligence, Adina's words become a mediator for the greater consciousness the group becomes together, the *interbeing*. She no longer speaks from her separate and individual self, but from the whole.

When a group engages in this way, its members transcend the personal, subjective mind and its busy, often linear thoughts and are able to process a much higher degree of information more rapidly and holistically. We reach beyond our individual critical thinking or subtle sensing capacities and access our collective intelligence, which leads us toward what has been called "the simplicity on the other side of complexity." I refer to this quality as *field thinking*, a kind of systems processing that allows us to see not only ourselves and one another but our points of overlap and interconnection as an energetic whole. I believe this level of perception is an evolutionary emergence.

The Collective Intelligence Research Institute has coined the term *holopticism*, which appears to refer to field thinking and is defined as follows:

> From the Greek roots holos *(whole) and* optikè *(see), holopticism means the capacity for an individual to see the whole as a living entity in the collective in which he/she operates. Sports teams and jazz bands operate in a holoptical context because each player perceives the team as a whole and knows what to do.*
>
> *We should not confuse holopticism with transparency. Transparency means the capacity to see the actions of everyone. Holopticism applies only when a whole emerges as an autonomous, perceivable entity (the band, the team . . .). For instance, the crowd in a bus doesn't operate as collective unified whole (unless something special happens). One hundred players on a sports field won't make a coherent sports team either, although everyone can see everyone. In both examples, we have transparency, not holopticism.*
>
> *In a holoptical context, the individual knows what to do because he/she gets informed by the whole. Actions don't need to come from a blind chain*

of command. Individual and collective actions emerge at crossroads of rules and agreements, player's roles, individual personalities and styles, the current configuration on the field. Every individual action modifies the whole, which in return informs the player about what to do next, and so on. An unceasing feedback loop allows for the individual and the collective to communicate with one another.[1]

When we find ourselves in groups—whether religious, spiritual, organizational, corporate, or any other kind—and feel the energy rising with a profound quality of connection and shared intention, some degree of coherence and field thinking is occurring. We feel excited and energized by our shared aims and more closely connected with one another, despite our differences. Too often, we leave these groups and return to the ordinary reality of our separate lives, and the vitality and intelligence we felt with the group seems to disappear. Learning ways to stay connected to its living flow are important. All of this belongs to a fascinating and vital area of inquiry for future research.

Complexity is simplicity in the right container. In his 1982 book, *The Evolving Self,* developmental psychologist and Harvard educator Robert Kegan presented his subject-object theory, expanding on it in later works.[2] Kegan's theory is essentially this: At each progressive stage of development (what he terms "orders in consciousness"), the *subject* of the previous stage becomes the *object* of the next. Kegan's theory is one of ascending complexity. Put simply, *subject* refers to the "I am" self, which is both attached and nonobjective. The subject incorporates its own feelings, behaviors, personality traits, and/or assumptions about the world into the "I am" without differentiating these qualities from itself. As the subject develops in consciousness, he or she begins to differentiate, making subject into *object* ("I have"), now detached from self and therefore observable. Thus, at each succeeding stage of development, the subject grows able to reflect and consider—and therefore change—prior forms. As American philosopher Ken Wilber explains, humans develop or evolve in consciousness through a process of *transcending but including* previous stages.[3]

The Buddhist principle of nonattachment may be rooted here, teaching that when we're embedded in or overidentified with feelings, behaviors, or beliefs, we suffer. But as we grow in awareness and insight through witness consciousness, our suffering decreases.

Complex issues overwhelm a subject who has yet to differentiate and is therefore still entangled with the symptoms generated by the issues. At each higher stage, he is able to reflect on the symptoms with greater detachment and objectivity, holding them with greater presence, inner space, and connection. What was overwhelming in complexity in the prior stage becomes clear and apprehensible in the next. A liter of water (object) cannot be contained by a drinking glass (subject); the glass must "grow." Because issues like climate change and collective trauma are so large and complex, we need greater subject-object complexity (a more spacious cup) to apprehend and solve them.

We can actively advance our personal development in consciousness by presencing and attending to it. To achieve higher orders of *collective* consciousness requires the same; we must work individually and together to grow our cup. When we do, we find that greater change is possible and comes faster.

Trauma reduces the flow of energy in a system, creating a consciousness of scarcity. Integrating collective trauma brings more energy into the system, thereby permitting greater abundance. The source flow of our cosmos is endlessly streaming and infinitely abundant—and we are a living manifestation of that stream. Growing the cup of interior consciousness is the task; we need to develop ourselves so we are able to host and hold the complexity we meet in our exterior world. As Pierre Teilhard de Chardin, French idealist, philosopher, scientist, and Jesuit priest, wrote in 1955,

> we see not only thought as participating in evolution as an anomaly or as
> an epiphenomenon, but evolution as so reducible to and identifiable with
> a progress toward thought that the movement of our souls expresses and
> measures the very stages of progress of evolution itself. Man discovers that he is
> nothing else than evolution become conscious of itself.[4]

As energy flows into form along the individuation loop in the process of early development, vibratory light becomes solid, manifesting in 3D. Both weaving and following the map of a sacred self-replicating code, inspiration and energy become material structure. Light becomes brain and nervous system; skeleton, heart, and lungs; large vessels and tiny capillaries; muscles and fascia; lymph and nodes; hormones and glands; organs and tissues; skin and teeth; hair; even the intricacies of irises and fingerprints, unique to each in all the universe.

Yet, as ancient and perfected as this architectural process may be, a single traumatic experience has the power to create a fracture—a point of dislocation between the energetic field and its 3D expression in the material structure. Wherever it occurs, it creates constriction and disembodiment. In essence, trauma can be said to reduce, separate, fragment, or "flatten" an aspect of the body-mind complex into a 2D representation, which is thereby dissociated and disembodied. (Being cognitively aware that we carry these is not the same as being able to fully witness and feel them.)

In traumatic conflicts, such as war, people reduce, flatten, and separate from their perceived enemies. Fear, adrenaline, and the simple mechanics of shock create the experiences of dread, fury, or numbness, which allow them to fight, flee, hide, and otherwise survive, but these are not the embodied feelings of aware interconnection. Humans must make their perceived enemies into 2D cutouts in order to perpetuate war against them; this is perhaps an evolutionary strategy. When we perceive others fully in 3D, we feel them just as we feel ourselves—and who can reasonably explode himself? To turn away at the shore a small and unstable boat, crowded with frightened refugees, many of which are children, requires mass dissociation. To separate immigrant children from their asylum-seeking families and lock them in overcrowded cages requires mass disembodiment. To walk into a school or a nightclub carrying a semiautomatic weapon requires making every person inside into a 2D image, a flattened fiction.

Everywhere people go, they carry mental suitcases full of their own 2D fragments, their own ghosts. They understand on some level that they have them, and perhaps even why. But these dissociated aspects are unavailable to the body, and as such, remain unfelt and unrestored (i.e., unintegrated). Trauma reduces higher capacity, shutting off our energetic connection to the full multidimensional self. As we consciously develop, heal, and integrate, we slowly restore embodiment to the 3D self, accessing deeper resilience and higher capacities.

Trauma work can be a kind of spiritual search-and-rescue mission. It does not require that we endlessly revisit every tortured experience, crying, shouting, or talking it through. But we must locate our disembodied ghosts, buried somewhere in that frozen grave of the dissociated self. Our work is to liberate our 2D shards with the reclaiming energies of integration and love. To revive and restore them back into the body, through the central channel, reintegrating all of our parts into the whole of our essence.

Just as every individual is designed to develop and evolve, so is the collective—every race and culture and nation. When collective traumas slow or prevent our mutual growth, the collective body casts off its own ghosts. Parts of the collective body flatten other parts, reducing and separating—refusing to feel. But all aspects are necessary to the health of the whole. To begin resurrecting and restoring our collective shadows, we must move beyond 3D, incorporating space and time and flow. Mutual presence and group witness are the foundations of collective trauma work.

Whether individual or collective, our shadows cannot simply be buried and forgotten; they will haunt us until we return them to life. And if we never do, they will haunt our children and our children's children, passing each to the next in an endless repetition of karma and time.

In the end, the shadows on the cave wall were not a trick or an illusion. They were the frightened 2D forms of our own disowned ghosts, and those of our ancestors and our children's children. The task of the collective hero—which you are, and I am—is to reenter the cave together with a light. To stand in the shimmering power of shared presence and mutual witness. To reclaim our birthright as whole beings belonging to a whole planet within a whole and sacred cosmos.

Our ancestors are not gone; they live on with us and in us. This truth comes as a clarion call from future generations, who require that their ancestors be healed so that they may live in a better world—or that they may live at all. As we heal and integrate the traumas of our time, we assist in the integration and healing of theirs.

Like the Oracle in *The Matrix* said, "You have the sight now, Neo. You are looking at the world without time."[5] In the new dimension we enter together, time disappears, generations cohere, and nations become one. On that future field, may we discover two mystical truths: *We* are the ones we've been waiting for. And we have been in each other all along.

I pray that you and I and all others—our partners, children, families, colleagues, and friends—fill the world with the love of our fullest presence and deepest devotion. We need not worry with how we wish to be, or how we would prefer each other to be. We need not worry with any ideal version of ourselves, one another, or the world. My prayer of love is to meet you exactly as you are; to meet myself exactly the way I am; to meet the world precisely as it is—in the most specific detail, the truest, most naked form. That is my prayer.

APPENDIX
GUIDED PRACTICES

The following are the instructions for four guided meditation practices, taken from my workshops and retreats. They are offered here as a companion to the text and may be followed in whatever way best suits the reader. You might wish to read them aloud into a recorder in order to play them back during a meditation.

THE LIGHT MEDITATION

Across the spiritual traditions we find what seem like two contradictory descriptions of awakening. Some saints emerged from profound states and proclaimed, "Wow, I merged with the light! I became one with God." While others said, "I went into the heart of the deepest blackness, examining the thought, 'I.' And what I found there was the deepest spaciousness, the most magnetic presence. A unification with the Source."

At first, it seems as though these reports are referring to different things, perhaps to different levels of awakening. But there is beauty in understanding that these experiences—the numinous light and the blackness of space, of emptiness—are not two, but one.

There is a transformational effect when we come into alignment with the Divine Law, or with the *Light*. This light reveals itself as a transmission of consciousness flowing through all ancestors, all lifetimes, in an ongoing and unbroken stream. Finding alignment with Divine Law is about finding our rhythm with the flow of light and teaches us how we can transmit that light from one generation to the next, without attachment, karma, trauma, or violence.

In the *Tao Te Ching*, Lao Tzu asks, "Can you cleanse your inner vision until you see nothing but the light?"[1] Can you purify your inner sight until you see nothing but that which is sacred and alive and has wanted to be alive for countless generations?

The explosion of light in all directions is the very creation of the universe, and it is happening now. But because of our karma, our trauma, it appears to us as though it happened long ago, in the faraway past. Still, the God that is, was, and will be is in creation now.

The light meditation deepens our awareness of the inner sensation of light, but it is much more than an exercise in visual imagination. It is a meditation on—indeed, a *calling forth of*—Divine Light. It is an act of realignment and purification, which actively raises our frequency, much like a charged prayer, and infuses vital new information into our nervous systems.

GUIDED PRACTICE

If you're able, sit comfortably with an erect spine. Take a couple of deep breaths and let everything go.

Allow the breath to take you deeper into an awareness of your bodily sensations. Simply breathe and notice. Practice this inner journey into your physical body, attuning to different areas: the feet, ankles, calves, knees, thighs, hips, pelvis, abdomen, back, and shoulders. Notice which parts feel stressed or tensed or even less clear to you, perhaps a bit numb. As you inhale and exhale, observe those areas that feel more alive with energy and subtle sensation.

Continue breathing and take notice of any emotional content. What emotional impressions might be present alongside the physical sensations you detect?

Now, simply breathe and become aware of the dimension of inner space, the internal field that holds these impressions and sensations. Become aware of your thinking. Simply breathe and observe.

Notice how all of this exists in an inner dimension, which contains a sense of inner presence. This inner presence is *hosting* the experience of your bodily sensations, hosting your emotional awareness, hosting your thoughts. Notice how this inner presence or witness has a flavor of timelessness and is linked to a quality of spaciousness that surrounds your feeling and thinking processes. As you breathe, take notice of this spaciousness.

This inner dimension is the home of the mind.

Now, slowly bring your attention to the top of your head. Using your inner vision, concentrate on the top of your head and see if you can bring your awareness to and focus your senses on this part of your body.

Simply breathe and hold your attention there for a moment.

Gently inhale, breathing into a place at the top of the head, expanding upward and outward. Now, bring your awareness to just above you. Imagine that your body continues on above your head and that you can feel yourself in the space above. Simply breathe and explore this space.

As you continue exploring this area above your body, notice any faint sensations of light that begin to appear. Connect with these sensations as you continue traveling upward, expanding your sense of your body.

Whenever your mind offers you a thought, see if you can let it go and just continue to feel and sense as you expand your awareness upward, perhaps a few feet or so above your head, though still within your expanded sense of the body. You are simply expanding your awareness of your body's location, as if activating a new sensory organ in the brain. You can feel upward, look upward, sense upward, as if your spine had an extension, a pillar that went high above your head, up and up and up.

As you continue expanding your felt awareness, higher and higher upward, above what you had thought was the top of your physical body, you may begin to notice new, subtle impressions—perhaps a whitish or golden light. See if you can even *feel* this light.

(Don't be dismayed if you can't. What's more important for now is that you simply continue to concentrate your awareness on the space above the head. If you find it difficult, just stay gentle with the process. Take it as a playful experiment.)

As you notice any sensations of light or perhaps an inner visual illumination, connect to it. Feel into it. Whenever your thoughts intrude, let them go if you can and simply stay with this exploration. Continue elevating your felt awareness above your head, turning your inner vision upward. Keep exploring.

When you connect to the light, stay there—feel it. See if you can stabilize your awareness in this feeling of the light. Allow yourself to become receptive to it, letting it flow down into your body. This is the light of your soul. Set the intention to connect to this light, to the quality of intelligence that brought you into this life. Feel into this new illumination, letting it fill and surround you.

Stay with it as long as you can.

When you're ready, gently bring your awareness back into your physical body. Feel your body sitting in the afterglow of this light meditation. Simply sit and be open and listen. Listen for whatever wants to arise.

Then again, gently, take a few deeper breaths, feeling the sensation of your body sitting on the chair or the cushion, wherever you are.

And slowly come back.

Seeing into darkness is clarity.

Knowing how to yield is strength.

Use your own light

and return to the source of light.

This is called practicing eternity.[2]

THE PRESENCING MEDITATION

In *Theory U*, Dr. Otto Scharmer, founding chair of the Presencing Institute, writes, "Presencing is a blending of the words 'presence' and 'sensing.' It means to sense, tune in, and act from one's highest future potential—the future that depends on us to bring it into being."[3] When we presence, we tune in from the deepest part of ourselves.

Inner body competence is an available resource that allows you to see and sense and respond—to yourself and others—more clearly, as if you had eyes all over the body. It offers clearer discernment so there is less opportunity for confusion and misunderstanding. It also brings heightened sensitivity, greater clarity, and deeper presence.

Using this inner attunement practice, you begin to feel more grounded in the body. You can more readily navigate your inner landscape, surveying the whole body and all of your interior sensations, perceptions, and subtle impressions as if through a camera lens. You can more clearly observe areas of reduced communication and areas of open communication. And you can include the numb or disconnected areas of the body more, rather than rejecting them, simply by relaxing into these sensations.

GUIDED PRACTICE

If you're able, sit in a chair with an upright spine. Rest your pelvis comfortably on the seat of the chair with your feet shoulder-width apart on the floor.

As you begin, simply tune in to your breath. Feeling into your breath, bring your awareness to the sensations of your body. Allow every exhale to take you through an open doorway, deeper into the physical body.

As you continue tuning in more deeply, presence more and more of what your body is feeling right now, in different areas. Perhaps you notice that your awareness is taken up by the sensation of tension, a feeling of inner stress, or even pain in certain areas of the body.

In other areas, maybe you notice a feeling of aliveness, a subtle flow of movement with many small accompanying sensations.

As you continue breathing, feel the weight of your body touching the surface of the chair. Feel how the body's weight anchors it in the world. You're feeling the pressure of the weight at the surface. Gently breathe and sense into this pressure.

From this sensation, expand into different areas, like your upper legs, to see if you have access through your inner body attunement. See if you can get a sense of your thighs and explore the muscles, bones, tissue, skin, and blood flow.

Now, choose another area in your body and keep listening. Presence, listen, breathe, presence.

Notice any quality of grasping, the tendency to grasp objects that arise in our inner awareness: thoughts, images, emotions, bodily sensations, and external inputs like noises, smells, and visual impressions. Simply listen to the grasping.

We either grasp onto an internal thought or bodily sensation, or it is something that moves and flows. Each time a thought or sensation arises, witness that thought or sensation, noticing how you grasp it when it surfaces.

Continue breathing and notice that there is a quality of space, of inner space. When you listen, *you* are space. Listening is spacious. Witnessing is spacious. Watch your mind and simply observe whether it is grasping or listening.

See if you can allow your attention to become even finer, subtler. More open.

Continue breathing deeply and tune in again to your physical body. Feel the body, its weight, muscles, and skin. As you attune to the body, allow your attention to become gentler, softer, subtler—lighter. Continue breathing and feeling the body with this subtler sense. Listen for how much space you have inside.

Most of the time, our attention is occupied with the world outside, but now you have your attention inside. And you can sense how much space is available inside. Does it feel tight, tense, crowded? Or does this inner space feel more open and relaxed?

See if you can notice any areas in your body that have more space, that feel lighter and more open. Notice any places that are tighter or tenser, more stressed. Notice that in those places, there may be a feeling of greater density or congestion, of less space.

Now, gently return your attention to the flow of your breath. Notice how its movement through the body is like a pulse, a rhythm—a constant and repeating motion. See if you can observe any subtle details in the rhythm of the breath.

If you notice that your mind travels to other places, simply come back to the details of your breath. Notice the resting place, the brief stillness before the inhale shifts into the exhale, and the exhale shifts back into the inhale.

The more you zoom in on and presence these sensations, the finer and subtler they become and the more information appears, as if the resolution grows.

See if you can sense how the breath affects your head. Is there a connection between your breathing and the way your head feels? Look at how the breath affects your arms and hands and fingers. Your pelvis. Your legs and feet.

Perhaps now you may notice how the breath affects your whole body, all of its parts. While the chest and the belly expand and contract, the whole body is gently breathing. Maybe you can notice how your breath affects even the air around you.

As you explore the effect of your breathing, stay with the felt sense in your body. Listen to its experience. This listening creates a presence. As you are listening to the sensations in the body that the breath produces, you infuse that sensation with presence, awareness, a higher resolution.

Enjoy the rhythm of the breath. It is the simple, essential flow in your life, and you can return to it again and again, whenever you lose your rhythm in the hectic pace of the outside world.

Now, if you can, move your awareness to a part of your body that feels alive. Maybe it's your hands, your chest, or your face. Maybe you notice a small tingling or streaming sensation, where your body is most present and awake. Simply listen to those subtle movements. Presence their feeling of aliveness, flow, energy, and accessibility. The longer you look, the finer and subtler this aliveness becomes. Its wisdom is another resource available within you.

Every time a thought arises, gently release it and come back to this exploration of the movement in your body, to its resource of aliveness. Presence its rhythm and energy.

There is breath. There is space. There are sensations, perceptions, impressions, images, and thoughts. There is a quality of reduction, tension, or energy, and aliveness. And there is presence and awareness holding all of these.

Observe yourself as you presence your breathing. Witness yourself as you feel your bodily sensations or experience your thoughts and impressions. See that there is witnessing, presencing, stillness, and awareness. Notice that there is breath and space and trust.

Begin now to take a few deep breaths as you start to come back. Slowly open your eyes. Continue breathing and notice the objects in the external space around you. Maybe there is a computer or a phone or a window. As you breathe, notice the room. Listen for any noises in the background. Feel the temperature of the air.

As you're becoming aware of these external sensations and perceptions, see if you can continue presencing your inner sensations and perceptions. Try holding both together: your inner and outer awareness. Feel for the subtle details, the finer qualities. Notice that you can feel and sense and listen in both worlds with curiosity, intention, and presence.

As you go about your day, try making a regular practice of coming into presence with both your inner and outer fields of awareness.

THE CLEARING MEDITATION

At the end of the Fourth Wave of CTIP, which I refer to as the Group Clearing and Integration stage, massive amounts of energy, information, impressions, sensations, and emotions have been experienced. In order to ground, digest, clear, and integrate those experiences, it is important that we come back to center, able to feel clear, present, and embodied. For this, we choose a simple grounding or clearing meditation along with toning techniques, such as group humming, and may include the use of singing bowls.

Of course, simple grounding practices and clearing meditations like this can be used anytime, for any reason. They help bring us back to center, back into presence with our own hearts and into deeper attunement with our bodies.

GUIDED PRACTICE

Sit comfortably with an upright spine, if you're able, and begin with a few deep breaths.

As you breathe, drop into the body. Feel and listen: How at home in the body are you feeling as you practice? Simply observe as you rest in the simplicity of sitting.

Whatever degree of at-homeness and warmth and resting you can find as you listen—however little or much—is exactly where you are. And there's nothing better, nothing else you need to seek. There is no ideal, no "should." *A journey of a thousand miles starts beneath our feet.*

Continue breathing just as you are, listening to and presencing your inner state, illuminating the current state with awareness, just as it is.

One of your most intimate friends is the breath. It has been with you since the very first moment you arrived in this world. It has been with you through every experience, from the most pleasant to the most difficult. It walks with you wherever you go, through whatever you do, as it will until your last moment. And because the breath is always here, it can guide you into a deeper experience of yourself, exactly as you are right now. There is no better version you must hunt for. There is only this version, the most truthful, the most loyal to now.

This is simply how the breath flows.

As you follow the breath, let it take you deeper, showing you the flow of your experience as it is now. The breath is the movement of your life; it echoes your life's flow and unfolding as you swim in the river of your experiences. How you meet new people, how you meet daily tasks, how you hold intimacy and connection with yourself and others—all of these are revealed in the flow of the breath through the wider river of your soul.

Also flowing in this river is your intelligence, motivation, passions, interests, and potential. The light that carries your inspiration, creativity, and innovation is there. Your capacity toward awakening and illumination are present in the river, which streams the very light of your soul.

You can rest in this river and hold the intention to connect to its light, to your inspiration and creativity. Or you may wish to turn your inner vision upward, connecting to the light streaming above your head—gently, openly. Or you may simply sit like an open funnel, holding an intention to receive. Just invite the light of the soul to rain down upon you, as you open yourself and listen.

At the higher levels, the light has higher tones or frequencies—like the highest notes on a piano or the harmonic notes strummed on a guitar—that are far less dense than ordinary experience. When you feel upward above the head, you may sense a finer vibration, a higher octave of sound or color. This space is finer, subtler. When the world is noisy, inspiration is often only a whisper. This is why moments of silence, solitude, and stillness can be vital; they allow us to tune in to the finer, higher resonances.

When you're ready, gently return to the body, noticing the sensation of sitting and feeling your inner space. Just rest in the stillness a moment. Simply rest and listen. Bring your awareness to the heart and listen to the spaciousness inside you.

Then, gently, take a couple of deep breaths and open your eyes.

PRESENCING THE ANCESTORS MEDITATION

For groups that have a regular practice and have been able to achieve a high level of shared attunement and collective coherence, it is possible to mutually presence the energies, experiences, memories, insights, and information belonging to the ancestors of the given group's participants, or those of a particular place or time (such as the human ancestors who experienced the Holocaust or American slavery). This practice requires skillful facilitation and is done with the purpose of deepening our connection to and understanding of our ancestors—as well as for the potential of generational healing and liberation.

GUIDED PRACTICE

Sit comfortably in a quiet place and close your eyes.

As you breathe, take a few moments to just enjoy the simplicity of sitting. Allow each exhale to take you a little deeper into the body.

As you practice this way, you notice it gets easier and easier to connect to the body, to let the exhale take you into your body's awareness, deeper into awareness of your whole energy field. You can presence the entire body, observing its areas of aliveness and numbness. Attuning to its charges and rhythms. And to its places of restriction, tension, or disconnection.

Simply enjoy the different aspects of the body, feeling its many parts and how these are contained in a growing sense of the whole.

There is no pressure to feel. You may simply give yourself permission to not feel certain things, or give other people permission to not feel certain things. As you become more sensitive to the rhythm of your body, and to other peoples' bodies and experiences, you find the just-right speed of processing. You discover a simple path for dropping in with the breath and centering your chi, your life energy, grounding it in your lower belly or base, in order to quiet the mind.

As you become more present with the body, you become more available to your emotional environment. You experience more courage to feel with life, with whatever arises, more courage to enjoy the colorful experience of being human, and more courage to allow other people to be colorful humans.

No matter how life feels in the moment or what may trigger or activate your past, you are more available, more present to the experience. You find in this the spiritual courage to own the past, to embrace where you have come from. To integrate the streams of your parents and grandparents and ancestors—all that you are, genetically, historically, culturally, emotionally, and mentally—into the river of your soul. You find the courage to both embrace and outgrow this story, so that there is less and less friction with your past, and more inclusion. More space. More wholeness.

You begin to see how intimately your parents are part of you. The energy of who they are is inherently interwoven with the energy of who you are, and on and on it flows, forward and backward in time. Some of these energies you might be at peace with, others you might reject. Still others, you may be overly attached to. You are able to see clearly what is addiction and what is avoidance, which are both ways of saying unresolved fear.

Honor thy mother and father is a sacred commandment. By considering it in the context of embracing who you are and where you come from, you discover its true meaning.

You find a new willingness to be both comfortable and uncomfortable, to be here and available, no matter how life unfolds. This new availability and willingness arise alongside a profound and growing love, deepening the essential blueprint that holds the record of your birth condition and the entirety of your past up to now. This love is the key; its light opens the potential future latent in your blueprint.

The light of the soul wants to dive into the deepest corners of your past in order to illuminate, heal, and transcend it. To fill it with awareness, clarity, compassion, and love. As you are able, you can open the stream of the river enough to include one or two generations before: your grandparents and great-grandparents. When you make this invitation, allow your awareness to touch the vastness of the river of where you come from, the energetic stream of tendencies, evolutionary habits, qualities, and characteristics that are passed on. Notice those currents that are brighter; feel the many shining talents, skills, and distinct qualities of spirit present there. Feel also the parts that are darker, less illuminated, hidden in the shadow of the family unconscious.

Observe how your own energy field responds to this invitation and honor every step. Respect equally any feeling of resistance or urge to stop and any feeling of curiosity and interest. Everything has its place. If you go numb, be numb. If a lot of information comes up, be with it. Look and feel, open. Honor the process.

Again, if you widen the stream, pay attention to which parts you may be overly identified with or attached to. Note with clarity the aspects of your ancestral stream that you reject, that you just don't like, that you feel an urge to turn away from.

Enjoy your growing capacity to feel, see, and attune to whatever comes through. If something surfaces that interests you, tune in deeper, as if you were flying into that energy. Try to feel whatever surfaces more precisely, looking deeper at the information stored there. Stay open to any sensation that might enter. Notice its quality: maybe it feels distant and far away; maybe it feels very connected. Maybe it feels warm or open, loving. Maybe it contains a quality of coldness or emptiness. Be friendly with anything that enters—allow it to be what it is and meet it there. Simply offer it presence.

When you feel ready, move your awareness from this inner stream to the place just above your head. Connect with what's there. Maybe you sense an energetic tingling or a streaming sensation. Maybe there is a sound. As you look and feel in this area above the head, move your energy slowly up, higher. If you can, connect with the light in that place. If not, simply move your awareness higher and open yourself. Relax into the space above your head and just feel whatever is present.

When you notice a sensation of light, connect to it. Feel it. Stabilize yourself there.

If possible, go higher. Reach for a higher vibration of light and expand your awareness into that space. Make yourself wider and more available. As this higher vibration flows down through your central nervous system, or main channel, into the body, notice the change of frequency, how it affects the way you feel. Let it continue to flow through you, back through your roots, expanding the stream of light flowing through your ancestral line.

When you're connected to the light, feel into it and offer a short prayer or clear intention. Invite clarity. Perhaps there is something in your ancestry that needs your understanding or support. Invite healing clarification into your past: more conscious revelations, deeper integration. Send this prayer or intention upward into the light, even higher. And let it go.

Just sit in receptivity, feeling the afterglow of the light. In this space, there is more information, more insight. If anything important needs to be shown to you, you are resting in an open space, able to be shown. By spending time here, you open yourself to the true future, which pours through you, into the river of your past, touching your ancestors with clarifying and healing frequencies.

Simply rest and observe the spaciousness here. Let everything else drop away. Be with the deep unformed presence underlying this moment.

Whenever you're ready, come gently back. Take a few strong inhales and exhales and return to the place you're sitting.

POCKET PROJECT

I n 2016, my wife, Yehudit Sasportas, and I cofounded the Pocket Project, an international nonprofit organization whose mission is to *contribute to the healing of collective and intergenerational trauma, and to reduce its disruptive effects on our global culture*. Headquartered in Germany, we have a substantial advisory board of highly respected scholars and humanitarians.

At the time of this writing, the Pocket Project has held a one-year training program on the process of collective trauma work that included 150 people from thirty-nine countries. Some of those participants went through a further incubation period in order to establish local Pocket Groups in their own countries, helping to crystallize collective work in crisis zones around the world. The aim of each Pocket Group is to work directly in its own community, region, or country to assist in the overall healing of historical and cultural trauma. Our goal is to establish many local Pocket Groups around the world, like key nodes in a vital network. Every group will stay connected via synced global teleconferences, as well as through the Pocket Lab, an online knowledge database, which we plan to make accessible to all as a public service.

In the fall of 2019, the Pocket Project held its first online Collective Trauma Summit with leading global experts and more than 53,000 participants. In addition, the Pocket Project has established Competence Centers, where members focus on vital competencies (e.g., psychology, genetics, etc.) needed for the understanding and healing of trauma. At each Competence Center, the subject of mass trauma is analyzed directly through the lens of a given discipline.

Our aim is to bring together timeless mystical wisdom with the latest scientific and psychological research in order to do the following:

- Deepen our understanding of the often-hidden effects of collective and intergenerational trauma on individuals and society.

- Develop and teach the tools and competencies that enable collective trauma integration.

- Engage Pocket Groups to train and support individuals, leaders, and groups of people worldwide to work on the healing of collective trauma layers.

- Advise organizations, universities, institutions, and governments on how to deal with the aftereffects and cultural symptoms of collective traumatization.

- Develop first aid and emergency response networks for confronting recent and emerging traumas.

- Train individual and cultural competencies and foster resilience building against trauma in crisis areas.

- Create an online platform that provides the latest research and knowledge on collective and intergenerational trauma.

As an advisor and training center for collective trauma work, the Pocket Project aims to foster a global movement around the education and healing of trauma—both individual and communal, recent and historical. Thus, the work we do is necessarily multidisciplinary and cross-cultural. All people are inextricably interrelated; no matter how different from one another or how far apart, each belongs to the human system. Likewise, the Pocket Project views distinct cultural and historical traumas not as wholly separate and distinct events but as interconnected phenomena arising in the collective body. Integrating one helps liberate another, just as healing the present helps to heal the past.

At the Pocket Project, we serve "one client," which is the world. Together with fellow educators, researchers, and collaborators, it is our sincerest hope to assist humanity in making a clearer, brighter world.

Find the Pocket Project online at pocketproject.org.

NOTES

PROLOGUE

1. Cohen's phrasing invites us to consider how "sustaining memory" is perhaps not unlike sustaining injury. Arthur A. Cohen, *The Tremendum: A Theological Interpretation of the Holocaust* (New York: Crossroad, 1981), 2–3.

2. The notion of a "soul wound" may seem strange to most Westerners, but as Duran points out, the term *psychology* is "the study of the *psyche*," which in the original Greek translated as "spirit" or "soul." Eduardo Duran, *Healing the Soul Wound: Counseling with American Indians and Other Native Peoples* (New York: Teachers College, 2006), 49.

3. Duran, *Healing the Soul Wound*.

CHAPTER 1.
MYSTICAL PRINCIPLES OF HEALING

1. Joseph Campbell and Phil Cousineau, *The Hero's Journey: Joseph Campbell on His Life and Work* (New York: New World Library, 1990).

2. *Epigenetic* refers to heritable changes to DNA as a result of environmental influences, affecting how genes are expressed without altering the DNA sequence.

3. George Santayana, *Reason in Common Sense: The Life of Reason* (New York: Dover Press, 1980), 172.

4. Jan Grant and Jim Crawley, *Transference and Projection: Mirrors to the Self* (Berkshire, England: Open University Press, 2002), 38.

5. Matthew Leifer and Matthew Pusey, "Is a Time Symmetric Interpretation of Quantum Theory Possible without Retrocausality?" *Proceedings of the Royal Society A* 473, no. 2202 (2017), doi: 10.1098/rspa.2016.0607.

6. In Vedanta philosophy, *akasha* referred to ether, a subtle substance pervading all things in the cosmos. It has come to refer to an intelligent record or information field containing all history and memory.

CHAPTER 2.
THE MATERIAL SCIENCE OF TRAUMA

1. Sarah Graham, "Skulls of Oldest *Homo Sapiens* Recovered," *Scientific American* 12 (June 2003), scientificamerican.com /article/skulls-of-oldest-homo-sap/.

2. Bessel van der Kolk, "Is Your Client Traumatized? For the Answer, Look to the Body," *Psychotherapy Networker*, 1/2017, psychotherapynetworker.org/blog/details/311.

3. Bessel van der Kolk, *The Body Keeps the Score: Brain, Mind, and Body in the Healing of Trauma* (New York: Penguin Books, 2015), 78–87.

4. "Post-Traumatic Stress Disorder," National Institute of Mental Health, accessed February 2018, nimh.nih.gov/health /publications/post-traumatic-stress-disorder-ptsd.

5. Matthew J. Friedman, "PTSD History and Overview," US Department of Veterans Affairs, March 2016, accessed February 2018, ptsd.va.gov/professional/treat/essentials /history_ptsd.asp.

6. Judith Lewis Herman, *Trauma and Recovery: The Aftermath of Violence—from Domestic Abuse to Political Terror* (New York: Basic Books, 1992), 127.

7. Herman, *Trauma and Recovery*, 96.

8. "Complex Posttraumatic Stress Disorder," TraumaDissociation.com, accessed March 6, 2018, traumadissociation.com /complexptsd.

9. Bessel A. van der Kolk, "Developmental Trauma Disorder: Toward a Rational Diagnosis for Children with Complex

Trauma Histories," *Psychiatric Annals* 35, no. 5 (May 2005): 401–08, doi: 10.3928/00485713-20050501-06.

10. Alexandra Cook, Margaret Blaustein, Joseph Spinazzola, et al., "Complex Trauma in Children and Adolescents: White Paper from the National Child Traumatic Stress Network," Complex Trauma Task Force (PDF), National Child Traumatic Stress Network, accessed February 6, 2017, nursebuddha.files .wordpress.com/2011/12/complex-trauma-in-children.pdf.

11. K. Hughes et al., "The Effect of Multiple Adverse Childhood Experiences on Health: A Systematic Review and Meta-Analysis," *Lancet Public Health* 2, no. 8 (August 2017): e356–e366.

12. Christina D. Bethell, "Child Flourishing: Our Greatest Public Health Opportunity Needs a Policy Response," AcademyHealth, September 5, 2017, academyhealth.org/blog/2017-09/child -flourishing-our-greatest-public-health-opportunity-needs -policy-response.

13. Stephen W. Porges, *The Pocket Guide to the Polyvagal Theory: The Transformative Power of Feeling Safe* (New York: W. W. Norton, 2017).

14. Porges, *Polyvagal Theory*, 55.

15. Porges, *Polyvagal Theory*, 159–161.

16. Porges, *Polyvagal Theory*, 159–161.

17. Elissa Melaragno, "Trauma in the Body: Interview with Dr. Bessel van der Kolk," *Anchor Magazine*, no. 4 (November 2015), stillharbor.org/anchormagazine/2015/11/18 /trauma-in-the-body.

CHAPTER 3.
THE INNER SCIENCE OF TRAUMA

1. Elissa Melaragno, "Trauma in the Body: Interview with Dr. Bessel van der Kolk," *Anchor Magazine*, no. 4 (November 2015), stillharbor.org/anchormagazine/2015/11/18 /trauma-in-the-body.

2. Judith Lewis Herman, *Trauma and Recovery: The Aftermath of Violence—from Domestic Abuse to Political Terror* (New York: Basic Books, 1992), 1.

CHAPTER 4.
THE ARCHITECTURE OF COLLECTIVE TRAUMA

1. Largely taken from accounts reported by NAACP investigator Walter F. White, as reported in "The Work of a Mob," *The Crisis* 16 (September 1918) and from the account written by administrators of the Mary Turner Project, maryturner.org /mtp.htm.

2. "The Truth about Jim Crow," The American Civil Rights Union, 2014, accessed May 10, 2017, theacru.org /wp-content/uploads/The-Truth-About-Jim-Crow.pdf.

3. "Slavery vs. Peonage," *Slavery by Another Name*, PBS.org, 2017, accessed 2018, pbs.org/tpt/slavery-by-another-name/themes /peonage/.

4. "Slavery vs. Peonage," *Slavery by Another Name*.

5. A May 20, 1918, article on the lynchings in the *Atlanta Constitution* reported that Mary Turner had made "unwise remarks," putting the mob in "an indignant mood" as their members took exception to "her attitude." *Atlanta Constitution*, May 20, 1918, maryturner.org/images/VDT5-20.pdf.

6. "627: Suitable for Children," *This American Life*, October 6, 2017, thisamericanlife.org/627/transcript.

7. "627: Suitable for Children," *This American Life*.

8. Judith Lewis Herman, *Trauma and Recovery: The Aftermath of Violence—from Domestic Abuse to Political Terror* (New York: Basic Books, 1992), 7–8.

9. Martin W. DeVries, "Trauma in Cultural Perspective," in *Traumatic Stress: The Effects of Overwhelming Experience on Mind, Body, and Society*, eds. Bessel A. van der Kolk,

Alexander C. McFarlane, and Lars Weisaeth (New York: Guilford Press, 1991), 399.

10. Sue Coyle, "Intergenerational Trauma: Legacies of Loss," *Social Work Today* 14, no. 3 (May/June 2014): 18.

11. Bessel van der Kolk, "The Compulsion to Repeat the Trauma: Re-enactment, Revictimization, and Masochism," *Psychiatric Clinics of North America* 12, no. 2 (June 1989): 389–411.

12. van der Kolk, "Compulsion to Repeat."

13. Nathaniel Vincent Mohatt, et al., "Historical Trauma as Public Narrative: A Conceptual Review of How History Impacts Present-Day Health," *Social Science & Medicine* 106 (April 2014): 128–36.

14. Maria Yellow Horse Brave Heart, "The Historical Trauma Response Among Natives and Its Relationship with Substance Abuse: A Lakota Illustration,"*Journal of Psychoactive Drugs* 35, no. 1 (2003): 7–13.

15. Brave Heart, "Historical Trauma."

16. "Conversations About Historical Trauma, Part One," *Impact Newsletter*, National Child Traumatic Stress Network, May 2013, accessed May 2018, nctsn.org/resources /conversations-about-historical-trauma-part-one.

17. Brave Heart, "Historical Trauma," 7–13.

18. Mohatt et al., "Historical Trauma," 136.

19. Nihaya Daoud et al., "Internal Displacement and Health Among the Palestinian Minority in Israel," *Social Science & Medicine* 74, no. 8 (April 2012): 1163–71, doi: 10.1016/j .socscimed.2011.12.041.

20. Joy DeGruy, *Post Traumatic Slave Syndrome: America's Legacy of Enduring Injury and Healing* (New York: HarperCollins, 2017).

21. Herman, *Trauma and Recovery*, 2.

22. DeGruy, *Post Traumatic Slave Syndrome*.

23. Keri Leigh Merritt, *Masterless Men: Poor Whites and Slavery in the Antebellum South* (New York: Cambridge University Press, 2017).

24. DeGruy, *Post Traumatic Slave Syndrome.*

25. Gertrud Hardtmann, "Children of Nazis: A Psychodynamic Perspective," in *International Handbook of Multigenerational Legacies of Trauma*, ed. Yael Danieli (New York: Plenum, 1998).

26. Yael Danieli et al., "International Handbook of Multigenerational Legacies of Trauma," *PTSD Research Quarterly* 8, no. 1 (1997): 1–8.

27. Tori Rodriguez, "Descendants of Holocaust Survivors Have Altered Stress Hormones," *Scientific American* (March 1, 2015), accessed May 2018, scientificamerican.com/article/descendants -of-holocaust-survivors-have-altered-stress-hormones/.

28. "Inheriting Trauma: Holocaust Survivors Pass Trauma to Their Children's Genes," Neuroscience News, August 2015, neurosciencenews.com/epigenetics-trauma-transmission-2502/.

29. K. Gapp et al., "Implication of Sperm RNAs in Transgenerational Inheritance of the Effects of Early Trauma in Mice," *Nature Neuroscience* 17 (April 2014): 667–669, doi: dx.doi.org/10.1038/nn.3695.

30. Seth Mydans, "Police Beating Trial Opens with Replay of Videotape," *New York Times* (March 1992), retrieved April 20, 2010.

CHAPTER 5.
THE WISDOM OF COLLECTIVE TRAUMA

1. "Presencing: A Social Technology of Freedom," *Trigon Themen* (February 2002), ottoscharmer.com/sites/default /files/2002_ScharmerInterview_us.pdf.

2. John Mecklin, "It Is Now Two Minutes to Midnight," Bulletin of the Atomic Sciences, January 2018, thebulletin.org /2018-doomsday-clock-statement/.

3. Book of Revelation, 13:1.

CHAPTER 6.
A GROUP PROCESS FOR INTEGRATION

1. Daniel Siegel, *The Mindful Therapist: A Clinician's Guide to Mindsight and Neural Integration* (New York: W. W. Norton and Company, Inc., 2010), p. 31.

2. David Furlong, *Healing Your Ancestral Patterns: How to Access the Past to Heal the Present* (Malvern Worcestershire, England: Atlanta Books, 2014), p. 194.

CHAPTER 8.
PICTURE OF A TRAUMATIZED WORLD

1. "Who Are the Rohingya?" Al Jazeera, April 18, 2018, aljazeera.com/indepth/features/2017/08/rohingya -muslims-170831065142812.html.

2. Alison M. Rhodes, "Claiming Peaceful Embodiment Through Yoga in the Aftermath of Trauma," *Complementary Therapies in Clinical Practice* 21 (2015): 247–56.

3. Rhodes, "Claiming Peaceful Embodiment," 247.

4. Albert Einstein, "Atomic Education Urged by Einstein," *New York Times*, May 25, 1946, 13.

5. Shannon Monnat and Raeven Chandler, "Long Term Physical Health Consequences of Adverse Childhood Experiences," *PubMed* 56, no. 4 (September 2015): 723–52.

6. Grace Rattue, "Autoimmune Disease Rates Increasing," Medical News Today, June 22, 2012, medicalnewstoday.com /articles/246960#1.

7. Robert Wood Johnson Foundation, "Traumatic Experiences Widespread Among US Youth, New Data Show," October 19, 2017, rwjf.org/en/library/articles-and-news/2017/10 /traumatic-experiences-widespread-among-u-s--youth --new-data-show.html.

8. Marco Helbich et al., "Spatiotemporal Suicide Risk in Germany: A Longitudinal Study 2007–2011," *Scientific Reports* 7 (2017): 7673; Ido Efrati, "Suicides on the Rise in Israel after a Four-Year Improvement," Haaretz, November 28, 2018, haaretz.com/israel-news/.premium-suicides-on-the-rise-in -israel-after-a-four-year-improvement-1.6697321; Amy Ellis Nutt, "Suicide Rates Rise Sharply across the United States New Report Shows," *Washington Post*, June 7, 2018, washingtonpost .com/news/to-your-health/wp/2018/06/07/u-s-suicide -rates-rise-sharply-across-the-country-new-report-shows/.

9. Denis Campbell, "NHS Suffering Worst Ever Staff and Cash Crisis, Figures Show," *Guardian*, September 11, 2018, theguardian.com/society/2018/sep/11/nhs-suffering-worst -ever-staff-cash-crisis-figures-show.

10. Ceylan Yeginsu, "NHS Overwhelmed in Britain, Leaving Patients to Wait," *New York Times*, January 3, 2018, nytimes .com/2018/01/03/world/europe/uk-national-health-service .html.

11. "Dangerous Medical Implants and Devices," *Consumer Reports,* May 2012, consumerreports.org/cro/magazine/2012/04 /cr-investigates-dangerous-medical-devices.

12. "America Is a Healthcare Outlier in the Developed World," *Economist*, April 26, 2018, economist.com /special-report/2018/04/26/america-is-a-health -care-outlier-in-the-developed-world.

13. Alan Yu, "Nurses Say Stress Interferes with Caring for Their Patients," NPR, April 15, 2016, npr.org/sections /health-shots/2016/04/15/474200707/nurses-say -stress-interferes-with-caring-for-their-patients.

14. "World Inequality Report 2018," World Inequality Lab 2018, accessed November 2018, wir2018.wid.world/files/download /wir2018-full-report-english.pdf.

15. Andrea Thompson, "From Fish to Humans: A Microplastic Invasion May Be Taking a Toll," *Scientific American*, September 4, 2018, scientificamerican.com/article/from-fish -to-humans-a-microplastic-invasion-may-be-taking-a-toll/.

16. Joseph Dodds, *Psychoanalysis and Ecology at the Edge of Chaos: Complexity Theory, Deleuze, Guattari, and Psychoanalysis for a Climate in Crisis* (New York: Routledge, 2011), 69–70.

17. Thich Nhat Hanh, *The Heart of Understanding: Commentaries on the Prajnaparamita Heart Sutra* (Berkeley: Parallax Press, 2009).

CHAPTER 9.
VISION OF AN INTEGRATING WORLD

1. Stephen Halliday, "Death and Miasma in Victorian London: An Obstinate Belief," *British Medical Journal* 323 (December 2001): 1469–71.

2. Jonathan Davis, "The Shamanic View of Mental Health," Uplift, October 9, 2019, upliftconnect.com /shamanic-view-of-mental-health/.

3. Andrew Solomon, "Notes on an Exorcism," October 29, 2008, *The Moth*, youtu.be/-UBgBpFGODI.

EPILOGUE

1. "Holopticism: Definition," Collective Intelligence Research Institute, accessed March 2019, cir.institute/holopticism/.

2. Robert Kegan, *The Evolving Self: Problem and Process in Human Development* (Cambridge, MA: Harvard University Press, 1982).

3. Ken Wilber, *Integral Psychology: Consciousness, Spirit, Psychology, Therapy* (Boston: Shambhala Publications, 1998), 8.

4. Pierre Teilhard de Chardin, *The Phenomenon of Man* (New York: Harper Perennial, 1959), 221.

5. *The Matrix*, directed by the Wachowskis (Burbank, CA: Warner Brothers, 1999).

APPENDIX: GUIDED PRACTICES

1. Lao Tzu, Tao Te Ching, trans. S. Mitchell, chapter 10, thetaoteching.com/taoteching10.html.

2. Lao Tzu, Tao Te Ching, trans. S. Mitchell, chapter 52, thetaoteching.com/taoteching52.html.

3. C. Otto Scharmer, *Theory U: Leading from the Future as It Emerges* (San Francisco: Berrett-Koehler Publishers, 2009), 8.

INDEX

absence/absencing, 172–78

abuse. *See* child abuse

acceptance, 22

adaptive strategies, 76–77

addiction, 39

Adverse Childhood Experiences (ACEs)
Study, 20–23, 185

affect, developmental trauma and, 19

African Americans
adaptive strategies to enslavement,
76–78
family discipline among, 77
Jim Crow practices, 62
legacy of enslavement, 61–65, 75–78
lynchings and atrocities, 64–65, 84
National Great Blacks in Wax
Museum, 64–65
post-traumatic slave syndrome, 77–78
Rodney King beating, 82–84

aftercare, 160–61

aftertime, 57–58, 198

aggression, 78, 94
developmental trauma and, 19
PTSD and, 16

agreements
collective, 96–99
cultural, 58, 90, 93, 99, 116
trauma agreements, 155
unconscious, 97, 98, 100

akasha, 10, 244n6

al-Qaeda, 69

Amazon rainforest, 96

amnesia, 19

ancestors, 85, 105–6, 226
ancestral karma, 125, 148

ancestors (*continued*)
presencing the ancestors meditation,
237–40
reversed ancestral tree, 138
witnessing for the ancestors, 138–40

ancestral field, 92

ancestral hurt, xvi

Anda, Robert, 20

Angelou, Maya, 61

anger
being present with, 99
energy in, 102
historical trauma and, 74, 75, 78
suppression of, 101–2

apathy, 172, 192

Armenian Genocide, 68

art
Bezalel Academy of Arts and Design,
xx
healing through, xxi–xxii
new art forms, 210

artificial intelligence (AI), 116–17

atomic bombs. *See* nuclear weapons

attachment, 18, 36
secure vs. insecure, 39

attention, in children, 208

attentional violence, 176

attunement, 47–55, 139
in collective integration process, 144–46
group practices, 128
inner body, 23
power of, 143–44
strengthening, 47
supporting nuclear peace, 50–55
of therapist/facilitator, 143–46
vs. listening, 47

ABOUT THE CONTRIBUTORS

CHRISTINA BETHELL

Christina Bethell, PhD, is a professor at Johns Hopkins University in the Bloomberg School of Public Health, where she advances a new integrated science of thriving to promote early and lifelong health of children, youth, families, and communities. With roots in culturally competent, community-engaged approaches to assessing and improving health and well-being, she is the founding director of the national Child and Adolescent Health Measurement Initiative and the Mindfulness in Maternal and Child Health Consortium. Dr. Bethell led the design of a widely endorsed national agenda to address childhood trauma and promote healing and flourishing. She earned an MBA and an NPH from the University of California, Berkeley, and a PhD in public policy from the University of Chicago. She teaches mindfulness-based stress reduction and "healing through revealing" methods, and is an avid student of transparent communication, presence, and human evolution.

LAURA CALDERÓN DE LA BARCA

Laura Calderón de la Barca, PhD, is a psychotherapist, cultural analyst, author, and educator. She has lived, studied, and worked in Mexico, her home country, as well as Austria, Belgium, England, Australia, and Canada. Her work focuses on the personal and collective healing of individuals, couples, groups, and communities. She is a member of the Pocket Project's research steering committee.

PATRICK DOUGHERTY

Patrick Dougherty, MA, LP, is a psychologist, social activist, author, qi gong teacher, and a member of the Pocket Project. Patrick has spent more than forty years working as a therapist, focusing on individual and collective trauma. His work centers on developing efficacious group facilitation models around the issues of armed violence, war, and genocide, as well as racism and white privilege. Patrick is the author of *Qigong in Psychotherapy: You Can Do So Much by Doing So Little* and a memoir, *A Whole-Hearted Embrace: Finding Love at the Center of It All.*

SCILLA ELWORTHY

Scilla Elworthy, PhD, is a three-time Nobel Peace Prize nominee for her work with ORG to develop an effective dialogue between international nuclear weapons policy makers and their critics. She founded Peace Direct (2002) to fund, promote, and learn from local peacebuilders in conflict areas and cofounded Rising Women Rising World (2013) and FemmeQ (2016). Dr. Elworthy was an adviser to Peter Gabriel, Archbishop Desmond Tutu, and Sir Richard Branson in setting up The Elders, and in 2003 was awarded the Niwano Peace Prize. Her latest book is *The Business Plan for Peace: Building a World Without War.*

MARKUS HIRZIG

Markus Hirzig has worked professionally in physical therapy and osteopathy for thirty years. He has been involved in Thomas Hübl's work since 2002 and has been assisting group participants for several years. He supports the development of the Assisting Team members, facilitates mentoring groups in Thomas's Mystical Principles of Healing online courses, and has accompanied the Pocket Project training for trauma integration.

GABOR MATÉ

Dr. Gabor Maté is a retired physician who, after twenty years of family practice and palliative care experience, worked for over a decade in Vancouver's Downtown East Side with patients challenged by drug addiction and mental illness. The bestselling author of four books published in twenty-five languages, Gabor is an internationally renowned speaker highly sought after for his expertise on addiction, trauma, childhood development, and the relationship between stress and illness. For his groundbreaking medical work and writing he has been awarded the Order of Canada, his country's highest civilian distinction, and the Civic Merit Award from his hometown, Vancouver.

OTTO SCHARMER

Otto Scharmer, PhD, is a bestselling author, founder of the Presencing Institute, and senior lecturer at the MIT Sloan School of Management, where he chairs the MIT IDEAS program for sustainability and cross-sector innovation. Otto introduced the concept of "presencing"—learning from the emerging future—in his bestselling works. In 2015, Otto cofounded the MITx u.lab, a massive open online course for leading profound change, which has since activated a global ecosystem of societal and personal renewal, involving more than 125,000 users from 185 countries. In 2019, he cofounded the Societal Transformation Lab (u.lab-S), involving 350 place-based teams focusing on reinventing education, governance, and our economies in the context of their ecosystem. In 2018, the Deputy Secretary-General of the United Nations (UN) appointed him to the UN Learning Advisory Council for the 2030 Agenda. And for 2019, he was ranked by Global Gurus at number three among the world's top thirty education professionals.

GREGOR STEINMAURER

Gregor Steinmaurer is a systemic family therapist, trauma therapist (Somatic Experiencing®), counselor, coach, and facilitator. He lives in Austria, where he maintains a private practice, in addition to leading international workshops and trainings with his wife, Komala de Amorim. Gregor is a Pocket Project team member and a valued part of Thomas Hübl's core Assistant Team.

KEN WILBER

Ken Wilber is one of the most important philosophers in the world today and the most widely translated academic writer in America, with twenty-five books translated into some thirty foreign languages. He is the originator of the world's first truly comprehensive or integrative philosophy, aptly named "integral theory." Ken founded the Integral Institute, the first organization fully dedicated to the advancement and application of the Integral Approach in relation to contemporary global issues. He also cofounded Integral Life, a social-media hub dedicated to sharing the integral vision with the worldwide community, as well as documenting and catalyzing the progress of the integral movement.

ABOUT THE AUTHOR

Thomas Hübl is a contemporary mystic, spiritual teacher, and renowned facilitator whose work integrates the core insights of the great wisdom traditions with the discoveries of contemporary science.

Thomas's teachings offer a unique approach for living as a mystic in the modern "marketplace" of human activity. He developed a method of fostering deep individual transformation within the supportive context of group presence and witness—balancing individual integration with collective learning. His work combines somatic awareness practices, advanced meditative practices, a sophisticated analysis of cultural architecture, and transformational processes, which address the human shadow and personal and collective traumas. His teachings aim to guide practitioners toward a deeper level of self-awareness—from an ego-centered worldview to a life of authentic expression, service, and alignment.

Since 2004, Thomas has worked with tens of thousands of people all over the world, leading international workshops, multiyear training programs, and large-scale events and festivals. A sought-after advisor to social entrepreneurs, business leaders, organizations, therapists, coaches, consultants, and spiritual aspirants, he is a regularly featured speaker at conferences and workshops worldwide. In 2020, Thomas was awarded an honorary doctorate by Ubiquity University. He founded the Academy of Inner Science, the School of Collective Trauma Integration, and the Pocket Project.

Thomas is a native of Austria and now resides in Tel Aviv, Israel, and Oldenburg, Germany, with his wife, award-winning Israeli artist and teacher Yehudit Sasportas, and their daughter, Eliya.

ABOUT THE COAUTHOR

Julie Jordan Avritt is a professional ghostwriter, author collaborator, content advisor, and integral thinker working with global changemakers, cultural upstarts, and renegades on a mission to inspire humanity in a time of great transition. Her clients have had bestsellers on the *New York Times's* and *Washington Post's* bestseller lists and have been placed in highly ranked publications.

She lives in Asheville, North Carolina, with her daughter, Journey, and two feline companions, Truman Catpote and Esther, Destroyer of Worlds.

ABOUT THE ARTIST

Yehudit Sasportas is a prominent and prolific Israeli artist internationally recognized for her political relevance. She has presented more than ten international museum solo exhibitions during the last decade, in venues such as The Kunsthalle Basel; The Berkley Museum of Art, San Francisco; The Kunstverein Braunschweig; DA2 Domus Atrium, Salamanca; and The Israel Museum, Jerusalem. In 2007, Sasportas represented Israel in the Venice Biennial. A senior professor at the Bezalel Academy for Art and Design in Jerusalem, Sasportas works in Tel Aviv and Berlin and is a lecturer in the International Academy of Consciousness and Evolution in Germany and the US.

ABOUT THE COVER IMAGE

Sasportas's work is focused on site-specific installations, intense sensory experiences that incorporate sculpture, drawing, video, and sound. These installations adapt and respond to the architecture of various museum spaces, forming artworks that present a new way of reading both architecture itself and the wider cultural context in which it was created.

Cad-Ot no. 1, the image on the cover of this book, is a core chapter from the Liquid Desert Project, a unique project that deals with the archaeology of the unseen. Sasportas has been engaged for years in mapping of the personal and collective subconscious space. This project embodies a purified, profound phase in Sasportas's work in which the work space functions as a cinematic site and is built as a complex and unique architectural structure.

The art work was created in a sculptural process called Recording Time, in which different fragments of original graphite drawings were photographed in long-exposure photography as one assemblage.

ABOUT SOUNDS TRUE

Sounds True is a multimedia publisher whose mission is to inspire and support personal transformation and spiritual awakening. Founded in 1985 and located in Boulder, Colorado, we work with many of the leading spiritual teachers, thinkers, healers, and visionary artists of our time. We strive with every title to preserve the essential "living wisdom" of the author or artist. It is our goal to create products that not only provide information to a reader or listener but also embody the quality of a wisdom transmission.

For those seeking genuine transformation, Sounds True is your trusted partner. At SoundsTrue.com you will find a wealth of free resources to support your journey, including exclusive weekly audio interviews, free downloads, interactive learning tools, and other special savings on all our titles.

To learn more, please visit SoundsTrue.com/freegifts or call us toll-free at 800.333.9185.